# Expanding Opportunity
# in Higher Education

SUNY Series
FRONTIERS IN EDUCATION
*Philip G. Altbach, Editor*

The Frontiers in Education Series draws upon a range of disciplines and approaches in the analysis of contemporary educational issues and concerns. Books in the series help to reinterpret established fields of scholarship in education by encouraging the latest synthesis and research. A special focus highlights educational policy issues from a multidisciplinary perspective. The series is published in cooperation with the School of Education, Boston College. A complete listing of books in this series can be found at the end of this volume.

*Capitalizing Knowledge: New Intersections of Industry and Academia*
        —Henry Etzkowitz, Andrew Webster, and Peter Healey (eds.)

*The Academic Kitchen: A Social History of Gender Stratification at the University of California, Berkeley*
        —Maresi Nerad

*Grass Roots and Glass Ceilings: African American Administrators in Predominantly White Colleges and Universities*
        —William B. Harvey (ed.)

*Community Colleges as Cultural Texts: Qualitative Explorations of Organizational and Student Culture*
        —Kathleen M. Shaw, James R. Valadez, and Robert A. Rhoads (eds.)

*Educational Knowledge: Changing Relationships between the State, Civil Society, and the Educational Community*
        —Thomas S. Popkewitz (ed.)

*Transnational Competence: Rethinking the U.S.-Japan Educational Relationship*
        —John N. Hawkins and William K. Cummings (eds.)

*Women Administrators in Higher Education: Historical and Contemporary Perspectives*
        —Jana Nidiffer and Carolyn Terry Bashaw (eds.)

*Faculty Work in Schools of Education: Rethinking Roles and Rewards for the Twenty-first Century*
        —William G. Tierney (ed.)

*The Quest for Equity in Higher Education: Towards New Paradigms in an Evolving Affirmative Action Era*
        —Beverly Lindsay and Manuel J. Justiz (eds.)

*The Racial Crisis in American Higher Education (Revised Edition): Continuing Challenges for the Twenty-first Century*
        —William A. Smith, Philip G. Altbach, and Kofi Lomotey (eds.)

*Increasing Access to College: Extending Possibilities for All Students*
        —William G. Tierney and Linda Serra Hagedorn (eds.)

*Burning Down the House: Politics, Governance, and Affirmative Action at the University of California*
        —Brian Pusser

*Mixed Race Students in College: The Ecology of Race, Identity, and Community on Campus*
        —Kristen A. Renn

# Expanding Opportunity in Higher Education

## Leveraging Promise

*Edited by*

Patricia Gándara
Gary Orfield
Catherine Horn

*State University of New York Press*

Published by
State University of New York Press, Albany

© 2006 State University of New York

For information, address State University of New York Press,
194 Washington Avenue, Suite 305, Albany, NY 12210-2384

Production by Susan Geraghty
Marketing by Michael Campochiaro


**Library of Congress Cataloging-in-Publication Data**

Expanding opportunity in higher education : leveraging promise / edited by Patricia Gandara, Gary Orfield, Catherine L. Horn.
    p. cm. — (SUNY series, frontiers in education)
  Includes bibliographical references and index.
  ISBN-13: 978-0-7914-6863-0 (hardcover : alk. paper)
  ISBN-10: 0-7914-6863-1 (hardcover : alk. paper)
  ISBN-13: 978-0-7914-6864-7 (pbk. : alk. paper)
  ISBN-10: 0-7914-6864-X (pbk. : alk. paper)
    1. Discrimination in higher education—California. 2. Universities and colleges—California—Admission. 3. African Americans—Education (Higher)—California. 4. Hispanic Americans—Education (Higher)—California. I. Gandara, Patricia C. II. Orfield, Gary. III. Horn, Catherine L. IV. Series.

LC212.422.C2E97 2006
379.2'6—dc22

10   9   8   7   6   5   4   3   2   1

# Contents

# Acknowledgments

We want to thank Jorge Ruiz de Velasco and Mike Smith at the Hewlett Foundation, Marty Campbell at the Irvine Foundation, and Jorge Balán at the Ford Foundation for their generous support of the conference that resulted in this book. Foundations make work like this possible, and we are grateful for our friends in the foundation world who have supported our work over the years. We also want to thank Vice President Winston Doby at the University of California, who supported our efforts in multiple ways and has always been there when we needed him. We greatly appreciate the help of the Civil Rights Project staff, especially Patricia Marin, Marilyn Byrne, and co-director Christopher Edley. At UC Davis, Anysia Mayer, Lina Benandez-Mendez, and Julie Maxwell-Jolly devoted countless hours to the organization of the conference and preparation of materials for this volume. To them we are especially grateful. Also, we would like to thank the policy makers who took the time to actively engage with us in this work in an unprecedented way.

Finally, this book would not have come into being without the support of former executive editor Priscilla Ross, and our editor, Lisa Chesnel, and the expert editing of Dana Foote. Thank you to all.

PATRICIA GÁNDARA
GARY ORFIELD

## Chapter One

# Introduction:
# Creating a 21st-century Vision of
# Access and Equity in Higher Education

The United States is facing a severe crisis of opportunity for higher education compounded by inadequate financing, failure to address the educational needs of an exploding population of students of color, excessive reliance on flawed testing systems, inadequate investment in increasing space for a growing population, and major reversals of civil rights policies that have changed the face of selective colleges. As often happens, these problems have become critical in the most vivid form in the nation's largest state, California, the state that prided itself on the strongest system of public universities in the country: a three-tier system that became the model for many states and was supposed to guarantee access for all.

This book reports on the massive challenges facing California and the responses of both academics looking at the state's educational system as a whole and those within the policy system who are trying to keep it going in difficult times. The book reveals a system that simply is not up to the challenges it faces and presents a range of large and small ways in which it can become more responsive and more equitable. This volume began with an extraordinary exchange between researchers and policy makers in Sacramento in the fall of 2003, and the resulting chapters and analyses raise issues that will be of interest to those concerned with higher education policy and with racial, ethnic, and socioeconomic equity across the nation.

During the last several decades a disquieting change has been occurring with respect to the United States' educational standing in the world. Once the unquestioned leader in availability and quality of public education, with the highest per capita level of education, the United States has fallen behind several other nations. Although among 55–65 year olds, it still ranks number one in college completion, among 25–34 year olds it has fallen behind Canada, several Northern European and Asian countries (OECD, 2006). The growing percentage of students from groups with high drop out rates threatens to make this pattern even worse. For example, in a new analysis of the Census Bureau's current population survey data, Swanson (2004) argues that the four-year graduation rate for Blacks and Latinos in the US is no more than about 50 percent. Moreover, while about 29 percent of Whites in the 25- to 29-year-old age cohort achieve at least a bachelor's degree, only 16 percent of Blacks and 11 percent of Latinos—who now comprise almost one-third of that population cohort—achieve this level of education. What has happened to U.S. higher education policy over the last half century that resulted in such extraordinary success and now such loss of status?

On the heels of World War II, the Congress saw the need to reintegrate hundreds of thousands of young men and women back into a changed economy and to reward them for service to the nation. Public Law 346, also known as the GI Bill, was passed by Congress in 1944 and opened the doors of higher education to many individuals who would otherwise not have been able to attend college. The GI Bill helped open what had been a very narrow path to college for lower income ex-servicemen, including African Americans and Latinos, and the nation footed the bill for tuition[1] as well as for the major capital investments that were required to radically increase capacity in institutions of higher education. It is widely acknowledged (Henry, 1975; Olson, 1974) that the huge investments in higher education created an educated citizenry that far outpaced other industrialized nations and fueled what would become during the 1950s an economy without rival; the United States became the unquestioned leader in research and technology. As a result, the American economy flourished in areas as diverse as agriculture and computer chip technology. Post–World War II education policies created what came to be known as the American Era.

Even in the face of such cultural and economic successes, the second half of the 20th century was not without serious social challenges. The civil rights movement, the women's movement, and a new consciousness about the inequalities that existed in Western society blossomed in this period. In 1961, in response to the growing civil rights movement, President Kennedy created the Committee on Equal Employment Opportunity and issued Executive Order 10925, which referenced the term "affirmative action" to describe measures designed to achieve "nondiscrimination" (Eisaguirre, 1999). In 1964 the Civil Rights Act was passed, and Title VII of the Act affirmed the illegality of discrimination in hiring on the basis of race. Subsequent legislation and judicial opinions strengthened the role of affirmative action in redressing the wrongs of the past and helping to ensure greater fairness in the present with respect to hiring and access to higher education. Although affirmative action has never enjoyed either universal support or implementation, its greatest achievement may have been in fostering the debate about the nation's responsibility to redress a history of discrimination against some groups of Americans. While its effects have been muted by continuing controversy, it has also been the impetus for some gains for women and minorities. In fact, the gains for women have been highly significant; the gains for ethnic minorities somewhat less impressive, but nonetheless real. While women have continued to gain ground vis-à-vis men in higher education and today form the majority of all college students, ethnic minority progress stalled at the end of the 1970s and did not begin to rebound until the late 1980s. The subsequent decade saw substantial growth in college-going, but once again in the 2000s we are faced with backsliding and an impending crisis in access to *equitable* higher education options.

In 1976 the United States reached a postwar peak in access to higher education for ethnic minority students. While about one-third of all students were going on to college after high school graduation, 22 percent of African American males and 23 percent of African American females in the 18- to 24-year-old cohort were enrolled in college. Similarly an all-time high of 21.4 percent of 18- to 24-year-old Latino males were enrolled in college in 1976, while a peak of 19.5 percent of Latina females had been reached the year prior, in 1975. These rapid gains were certainly related to affirmative action policies during the late 1960s and early 1970s. However, a waning of commitment to affirmative action toward the end of the 1970s and the Reagan-era aid cuts took their toll on college-going among Black and Latino students. The 1976 high in enrollments for students of color was not reached again for African American males and females until 1987 and 1986 respectively. Since that time there has been a slow but steady increase in college participation for African Americans, however most of the gains in college-going have been for women. In 1986 African American women overtook their male counterparts in college enrollment and by 2000, 63 percent of 18- to 24-year-old Black college-goers were female. Likewise, in 2000, 57 percent of Latino undergraduates were female. By comparison, in 1976 women accounted for 47 percent of the undergraduate enrollments among White 18 to 24 year olds, but by 2000 they were 55 percent of all White undergraduates in that age cohort. Thus, women of all ethnicities have been the major beneficiaries of affirmative action policies, but White women have fared better than their sisters of color as a percent of total college-goers.

While all ethnic groups have seen some gains in college going over the last two or three decades, the gap in college participation for high school graduates ages 18 to 24 has widened among Whites, African Americans, and Hispanics. In 1999–2000, the college participation rate of 18- to 24-year-old White high school graduates was 46 percent, compared to 40 percent of African Americans and 34 percent of Hispanics (ACE, 2003). Of course, the colleges and universities that White and Asian students attended were generally different from those attended by Black and Latino students. Latinos, in particular, are much more likely than any other group to attend two-year colleges, where the probabilities of transferring and completing a four-year degree are variously cited as between about 3 and 8 percent for Black and Latino students (Gándara & Chávez, 2003).

In spite of the continuing gaps in access to college between White students and students of color, the mid-1990s saw an anti-affirmative action movement sweep the country. Proponents of the various initiatives and legal decisions that flowed from this movement contended that affirmative action was giving an "unfair" edge in college admissions to ethnic minorities, that the playing field had been leveled, and that since "anyone who wanted to work hard could go to college" there was no further need for affirmative action. The argument then follows that if low-income and ethnic minority students did not apply or go on to college it was because they either hadn't worked hard enough to gain admission legitimately or they had insufficient interest in higher education to pursue it. In either case they did not "deserve" a break just because of the color of their skin.

Linking the issue of affirmative action to his previous success in pushing through an anti-immigrant initiative, California Governor Pete Wilson was quoted as saying, "It is wrong to reward illegal immigrants for violating our borders. . . . It is wrong to engage in reverse discrimination, giving preferences . . . not on the basis of merit but because of race and gender" (cited in Chávez, 1998, p. 52). Thus, Wilson was casting affirmative action not only as an unfair advantage for students of color—whose mean family income was *half* that of Whites and Asians applying to college, who came disproportionately from impoverished schools, and who as a result routinely had lower test scores—but part of a larger set of injustices against "the people who work hard to pay those taxes and . . . deserve a guarantee that their children will get an equal opportunity to compete for admission to this university" (cited in Chávez, 1998, p. 63). Oddly, the students that would be turned away with the demise of affirmative action would be just that, sons and daughters of people who worked hard and paid taxes but rarely had the opportunity to compete for admission to the university because their schools did not prepare them for this opportunity. But, Governor Wilson was talking to quite a different constituency.

The reality of the impact of affirmative action on admission to the University of California, of course, is substantially different from the rhetoric. While affirmative action was a concept designed to redress both formal and informal policies that had denied access to jobs and education for people of color and women, during its relatively brief 30+ years' existence, some gains were made, but these were far fewer than many people had hoped for or than its opponents contended. Enrollments for students of color in the University of California, if anything, were slower to show progress than those nationwide and were profoundly affected by the demise of affirmative action in that state. In 1995, just prior to the passage of Proposition 209 banning affirmative action in the state, African Americans comprised 4.3 percent of the freshmen entering the University of California while they were 7.5 percent of the graduating seniors from California's public high schools. In that same year Chicano (Mexican-origin) students were just 11.1 percent of the University's freshman admits, while they comprised about 26 percent of the high school graduating seniors. *Before* the demise of affirmative action, Blacks and Chicanos combined were admitted and enrolled in the University of California at a rate less than half of their representation in the high school graduate population. A number of observers were writing at the time that the under-representation of students of color had reached crisis proportions. *After* the implementation of Proposition 209,[2] there was an immediate plummeting of enrollment of these groups—from 4.3 percent to 2.9 percent for Blacks and from 11.1 percent to 8.8 percent for Chicanos in 1998. By 2003 (the most recent year for which confirmed enrollment data are available), freshman enrollments for Blacks had still not returned to pre-Proposition 209 levels, with a representation of only 3.2 percent of the freshman class, and Chicanos had barely returned to those earlier levels with 11.2 percent of the freshman enrollment. In the interim, however, the pool of Chicano/Latino high school graduates had grown by about 3 percentage points, resulting in a net decline in representation at the University of California. What in 1995 appeared to be a crisis in access, in 2003–2004 had become considerably worse.

Admissions policies are only one impediment to access to higher education. In California, another major impediment is the lack of investment in building capacity within its higher education institutions. In the ten year period between 2003 and 2013, the California Postsecondary Education Commission (CPEC) estimated that an additional 741,000 students, representing an increase of 34 percent, would seek enrollment in a system already bulging at the seams (CPEC, 2004). Estimates are that by 2010 the community colleges alone will have a shortfall of 315,000 seats to meet projected enrollments, and by 2013 the University of California will need to add 50,000 more spaces. To simply cover the operations costs of these increases will cost an additional $3.1 billion without any outlay for capital expenditures. Only one UC campus has been added to the system in the last 40 years, Merced, which opened in fall of 2005 with fewer than 1,000 students—hardly sufficient to absorb the burgeoning demand.

In the absence of massive new expansion of the system, policy makers have focused on achieving greater efficiencies—reducing the average time to graduation, sending more students abroad to study, sharing campuses across systems, relying to a greater extent on private colleges, and expanding the use of distance technologies—to help meet the demand. But these strategies alone will not relieve the pressure on the system or on the most selective campuses. Increasing competition for access to the University of California will mean that more and more students will have to be diverted to less selective—and less expensive—alternatives. With an average high school GPA of 3.8 and SAT scores in the 1200 range already (and over 4.0 and 1300 at the flagship campuses of Berkeley and UCLA), students admitted to the University of California will have to be increasingly competitive, well beyond the range of the great majority of *high achieving* Black, Latino, and Native American high school graduates. Lack of capacity will play a significant role in increasing pressure to divert students of color away from the most selective institutions and into the poorly funded two-year college sector where their chances of actually completing a degree are reduced significantly.

Another critical part of the crisis in access to higher education is the chronic under-representation of faculty of color. A growing literature finds a relationship between faculty diversity and perceived campus climate for students of color. Black and Latino students point to increased opportunities for mentorship with faculty of color, important role models in academe, and a greater understanding of their social and educational circumstances. Yet, in spite of an expanding pipeline, there has been little to no progress in hiring and retaining Black and Latino faculty within the university. In 1989, African Americans were 2.1 percent of the university ladder-rank faculty and in 2004 they were 2.5 percent of the faculty. Chicano/Latinos (a large portion of whom are Latino and *not* Chicano, unlike the great majority of Hispanics in the state) were 3.6 percent of the faculty in 1989 and only 4.9 percent in 2004, in spite of about a 10 percentage point increase in this population group over that 15-year period. Little serious attention has been applied to this problem by the university, although the university in large part is responsible for developing the pool of potential faculty that it contends it cannot find.

It is not simply empty rhetoric to worry out loud about the future of the state of California—and other states as they more closely parallel the demographics of that state—with respect to its economic viability. A number of studies have called attention to this looming economic crisis, as well as to the benefits associated with addressing it proactively. A recent RAND study, based on several simulations of government investments in education along with costs of social services, concluded that whether the goal was to bring Blacks and Latinos to parity with Whites and Asians in high school completion, college-going, or college degrees, meeting any of those goals always results in a net public financial benefit (Vernez, Krop, & Rydell, 1999).

The estimated public benefits of increasing the education of Blacks and Latinos exceed the estimated costs of providing this education, regardless of the specific educational goal considered, in both California and the rest of the nation. For instance, the public benefit-cost ratio of 1.9 for the "full equalization" (same educational outcomes for all ethnic groups) implies that "every $1 spent on equalizing education would save, over the long term, about $1.90 in 1997 dollars in California. The . . . ratio is even more favorable for the rest of the nation, where every $1 spent . . . would save $2.60" (Vernez et al., 1999, p. 73).

Moreover, the RAND investigators compute that "the costs of closing the educational attainment gap may be recouped within a decade or so—and thus well within the lifetime of most of those called upon to make the investment—provides a strong argument that indeed the investment is in the taxpayers' self-interest as well" (Vernez et al., 1999, p. 79). On the other hand, in California, where nearly half the student population is Latino, "failure to close the education gap . . . will result in a large share of future (and larger) cohorts being unprepared to compete in a labor market that increasingly requires at least some postsecondary education" (Vernez et al., 1999, p. 78). In fact, without such investments, we are creating a future that few people would knowingly want to bequeath to their children.

Acknowledging this crisis, in October of 2003, the University of California, Davis and The Civil Rights Project at Harvard University joined forces to host a conference on the crisis in higher education access in California and the nation. Intending to take a more positive stance, the conference was entitled "Expanding Opportunity in Higher Education," and the focus was on solutions as much as on documenting the existing problems. The immediate focus on California is particularly appropriate given the size of the state—it educates one of every nine students in the country—and its checkered political record with respect to civil rights and educational inequities. A dozen papers were commissioned from the foremost scholars in the country and the most key policy makers in the state were invited to comment on the state of higher education access from their perspectives. What resulted was an unprecedented conversation between policy makers—heads of legislative committees and legislative watch dogs, heads of higher education institutions and agencies—and scholars who have dedicated their careers to understanding the dynamics of education access. The conference yielded two major sets of papers: one that recounted the depth of the challenges that California and the nation face, which was published in the May 2005 issue of the journal

*Educational Policy*, and the second set, focusing on responses to these challenges, which appears in this volume.

We were warned by several of the conference speakers that we must treat the problem of access to higher education as a systemic issue affecting the entire pathway from preschool to college. Winston Doby, vice president of the University of California, warned that the solutions lay in statewide policy and not in adjustments to admissions policies in single institutions. Doby, citing Glenn Loury, noted that "selection rituals are political acts with moral overtones." We think this is a particularly apt description of the system by which some are selected for elite institutions and others not. As we attempt to understand the selection system in place it is critical to remember that "merit" is a social construction that reflects a political process. Who is merit worthy is decided by officials, and those who make the decisions are, for the most part, from the same group who benefited most by the existing system. It is difficult to find the motivation to change something that doesn't appear to be broken from one's own perspective. But, Doby's invoking of the moral dimension suggests that statewide policy cannot be made solely from the perspective of the traditional beneficiaries of those policies. In order to meet the test of fairness—the moral dimension—all perspectives must be considered, and we need to care as much about the perspective of those who have traditionally failed to gain access as those for whom admission to university is viewed as a birthright. It occurs to us that included in this moral dimension is the problem of social policy in a country that purports to value its children but provides no real support for them or their families. For millions of low-income children who attend the nation's lowest performing schools, there is no social or educational safety net. It is hard to get to college when you go to school hungry and without adequate housing or medical care every day. This, too, must be a consideration as we weigh the policies that will shape the fates of our youth. Neither in the conference that generated it, nor in this volume, could we undertake to study all the social ills that lead to such disparate outcomes for young people. But we must, at the least, consider that the problem is systemic in the most profound sense, and so we begin part 1 of this book with a set of chapters that examines the contribution of K-12 institutions to the deep inequities that exist in the opportunity sorting machine that is the higher education system in the United States.

This first section begins with a chapter by Oakes, Mendoza, and Silver, entitled "California Opportunity Indicators: Informing and Monitoring California's Progress Toward Equitable College Access," in which the authors, all principal researchers with the University of California's All Campus Consortium on Research for Diversity (UC ACCORD), lay out their system of indicators to monitor the opportunity structure in different high schools in California. Consistent with the view that the college admission process takes place in a highly politicized space, the UC ACCORD team provides a profile of the indicators for all the schools in each senate and assembly district in the state. Legislators are always interested, and sometimes shocked, at how the schools in their districts perform with respect to preparing students for college. The Indicators Report is a prime example of scholarship that pays attention to the social and political context in which it is conducted, using data to raise the visibility of a problem in legislators' own backyards. This is a model that could be easily adapted in other states and even enhanced in states with better data collection systems than California's.

Fitzgerald follows with chapter 3, which looks at the impact of financial aid on college access, entitled "Lowering Barriers to College Access: Opportunities for More Effective Coordination of State and Federal Student Aid Policies." Recent shifts from need-based to merit-based financial aid and billions of dollars in shortfalls in Pell grant funds have exacerbated an already acute situation for low-income students and large tuition increases have compounded these problems. As Fitzgerald points out, money matters, and many low-income students who are well-prepared for college do not go because of inadequate financial aid. California, through its Cal Grant entitlement program, has one of the most generous financial aid programs in the country, yet the complexity of the process, lack of timely information for families to plan for college, and uncoordinated efforts at the state and national level mean that many students who could benefit from these funds do not know how to access them. The authors contend that better coordination of federal and state policies, tying financial aid to intervention programs in the schools, and more effective utilization of resources can mitigate access barriers and increase enrollment opportunities for low- and moderate-income students in California and across the nation.

A thorny issue in the politics of admission in California higher education has been the awarding of an extra grade point for Advanced Placement courses taken and passed. In other words, a student who receives a B in AP English is given grade points equivalent to an A. The policy was adopted as another way to distinguish among highly qualified students in a highly competitive admissions process. Chapter 4, entitled "The Role of Advanced Placement and Honors Courses in College Admissions," by Geiser and Santelices, looks at the predictive power of simply taking and passing AP courses for grades in college. The authors find no significant relationship between AP course-taking and college GPA and therefore argue that providing extra grade points for taking the courses (but not necessarily passing or even taking the AP test) is not justified as a factor in admissions. And, since they are a source of inequity because schools that serve low-income students are less likely to offer these courses, such a policy would help to equalize opportunity for low-income students. The authors note that students who take AP courses also receive university course credit and holistic reviews of applications consider the degree to which students have challenged themselves with demanding coursework, so incentives remain for students to take these courses where they are offered even in the absence of extra grade point credit.

Charles Ratliff rounds out the first section of the volume with a perspective from inside the California Legislature on how the state—and other states—might address the inequities that result in such uneven chances for young people from different socio-economic backgrounds to gain access to higher education. Ratliff argues that there are no silver bullets that will equalize opportunity for all of California's students, but that educators can tackle many of the technical aspects of the education system that prevent it from functioning as well as it might. Working in the day-to-day environment of the legislature, Ratliff offers solutions that are politically "doable" and that hopefully move the system closer to the larger goal of equity. Included in his suggestions are using market forces to better distribute highly qualified teachers across both low-income and middle-class schools, reducing restrictions on the way that public education funds are spent, providing better trained administrators that can more successfully address the diversity in their schools, and giving the states' students the opportunity to become fluent in more than one language. These are the very real problems that are debated daily on the floors of the legislature, and while seemingly commonsensical, they have defied easy solutions. To the extent that their resolution would result in much better prepared students, it would appear that these strategies can advance equity in access to higher education; whether it is enough to create fundamental change in access is an empirical question.

One theme that runs through most of the chapters in part 1 of the volume is the necessity to start preparing young people earlier for postsecondary options. The various authors note that low-income and ethnic minority parents have inadequate information with which to plan financially for their children's education and insufficient knowledge of the coursework and other requirements for college admission. Many critics of the existing system argue that postsecondary options need to be presented to students while they are still in elementary school, so that they have developed a disposition to higher education and are better prepared to take the classes they will need for college admission when they begin secondary school. Given that the typical California high school has about one counselor for every 850 students, and elementary schools are not likely to have any, there are far too few school personnel assigned to help students examine their postsecondary options or begin to prepare for them. The dearth of counseling available for low-income and students of color, who often have no other sources of information, must be addressed. Currently, one of the primary ways in which students receive this kind of information and support is through honors and AP courses. However, as Geiser and Santelices (this volume) point out, the likelihood of the students who most need this support receiving it in those contexts is very small. Another way is through special college preparation programs, but these have never reached large numbers of eligible students and they too have been defunded to a large extent in California as a result of recent budget crises.

Part 2 of this volume focuses on potential interventions at the postsecondary level. We open with a chapter by Estela Bensimon and her colleagues, entitled "Measuring the State of Equity in Public Higher Education," in which they present an educational equity indicators system for higher education. Similar to the Oakes and colleagues' High School Indicators project, Bensimon et al. attempt to provide a framework for institutions of higher education to evaluate their own effectiveness with respect to diversifying their campuses *and* ensuring positive outcomes for their students of color. A critical component of this work is the focus not just on attracting students to the campus but on the experience they have there and the record of the institution with respect to retaining and graduating them. A forthcoming publication authored by Deborah Santiago provides a cogent critique of many Hispanic serving institutions that proudly wave the banner of diversity based on their enrollments, but pay little attention to graduation rates of the Latino students they attract, or to their educational experience at the campus. Bensimon's work, like that of Oakes and her colleagues, has far reaching applicability in California and beyond.

In chapter 7, entitled "Reaping the Benefits of *Grutter*: College Admissions and Racial/Ethnic Diversity," Catherine Horn and Patricia Marin remind us of the evidence for the critical importance of diversity in higher education and the opportunity that the recent Supreme Court decisions allowing affirmative action in higher education represent for continuing the battle for diversity. They also present the evidence on race-neutral admissions strategies that have been used to replace affirmative action in situations where it has been banned, such as in California, but that may also augment affirmative action. They provide a cautiously optimistic view that such things as percent plans and alternative admissions strategies can be important complements to affirmative action, but reiterate that nothing else comes close to providing the same yield as affirmative action. They urge states that can still implement affirmative action strategies to do so vigorously. At the October 2003 conference the chair of the Assembly Higher Education Committee, Carol Liu, was asked if overturning Proposition 209 and the ban on affirmative action was a possibility from the point of view of the California legislature. Her reply: "Anything is possible in California!" It strikes us that if such a thing were to come to pass, it would need to rely heavily on the kind of evidence presented in the chapter by Horn and Marin.

Stephen Handel and his colleagues follow in the next chapter (8), entitled "The Effectiveness of the Transfer Path for Educationally Disadvantaged Students: California as a Case Study in the Development of a Dual Admissions Program." The chapter provides a discussion of the rise and fall of the highly touted but ill-fated Dual Admissions Program (DAP). A core diversity strategy of the former President of the University of California, Richard

Atkinson, the DAP was intended to increase diversity by ensuring students from low-income schools who were close to achieving eligibility for the university that they would have a reserved place at a UC campus upon completing their first two years of general education requirements. The critical innovation of the DAP, in addition to the written guarantee, was the attention that students were to receive from UC counselors and the very personal recruitment strategy that included a series of personal communications with these students. Unfortunately, cuts to the higher education budget and a new strategy introduced by the governor to move fully eligible students into the community colleges with the same guarantee undermined the DAP program and placed it on indefinite hold. However, Handel, Heisel, and Hoblitzell write about the lessons learned in building and implementing the program, including the need for better incentives to attract students to such a program. As observers of this program, we have also wondered at the lack of attention to providing a supportive peer group for these DAP students at the community college. The research shows that most first-in-the-family college students need to have peers who share their backgrounds and support their aspirations. Creating a cohort of students within the community college who share the same classes and many of the same college experiences on the way to transferring to the four-year university would almost certainly help to ensure the success of such a program.

Chapter 9, entitled "A Strengthened Community College Role in Teacher Preparation: Improving Outcomes for California's Minority Students," by Nancy Shulock and Colleen Moore, considers an expanded role for the community colleges in providing a more diverse teaching pool for the K-12 schools and simultaneously providing incentives for diverse students to stay in the higher education pipeline. These authors tackle two deep problems in higher education: the critical shortage of teacher candidates who come from the same communities as the students most at risk in our public schools—low-income and ethnic minority students—and the difficulty that community colleges experience in retaining and transferring students of color to four-year colleges. The teacher candidate problem is part of a vicious cycle in education. Most students of color who go to college in California first attend community colleges. Yet, community colleges have a weak record of transferring students of color to four-year universities where they can earn the bachelor's degree, a prerequisite to becoming a teacher. And, many have noted that the absence of faculty of color, important role models, reduces the likelihood that young minority students would see teaching as a viable career for themselves.

In fact, the community college student population is potentially the richest source of diverse teacher candidates, if the colleges were more successful in transferring these students to four-year colleges. Thus, Shulock and Moore propose that by starting the pathway to teacher education in the community colleges, it is possible to identify and support potential teacher candidates of color, create a clear pathway to the teaching credential, and help to provide more teachers who look like the students they teach. The early pathway model has particular value in states like California that rely heavily on their public two-year colleges for postsecondary education, but could be widely adapted to stimulate the pool of teachers of color and increase the holding power of postsecondary institutions.

In chapter 10, entitled "The Educational Pipeline and the Future Professoriate: Who Will Teach California's and the Nation's Latino and African American College Students?," Jorge Chapa presents data on the state of faculty diversity, a nagging and too often overlooked problem in academe. He argues that the faculty diversity problem has two aspects: the need to provide opportunities for more diverse faculty and the need to place college faculty in classrooms with diverse students who understand and can support these students' educational aspirations. Chapa concedes that the solution to the latter problem may not be the same as the solution to the former. In other words, while attempting to diversify the faculty, he argues that institutions must also be paying attention to the pedagogical skills of the White faculty who will for some time be the majority of college teachers. Creating culturally sensitive faculty who will be successful teachers of Black and Latino students must, according to Chapa, be one of the goals of faculty hiring and reward systems, and he offers examples of how this might happen.

UC President Dynes, in his opening statement at the beginning of the October 2003 conference, noted another important reason to pay keen attention to the issue of faculty diversity. He used the example of scientific discovery and noted how bringing diverse perspectives to the investigation of problems was most likely to result in real scientific breakthroughs. The quality of the research produced by the university, he contended, would be strengthened by diversifying the people in it. The U.S. Supreme Court concluded that there was compelling evidence for this proposition in its 2003 *Grutter* decision upholding the legality of affirmative action. Yet, as Chapa points out, significant progress in creating more diverse faculty in highly selective institutions remains a difficult challenge. The pipeline to the research doctorate for Blacks and Latinos dwindles to a trickle in the latter stages, and individuals who are first in their family to go to college do not often think of the academic life as an appropriate or even desirable choice. Much of the problem lies in the culture of the university and the paradoxically conservative self-replicating nature of the professoriate. It is a fact that faculty produce faculty. Especially in the case of professors of color, it is common to hear that they decided to pursue an academic career because one professor in college told them they were PhD material, helped them get into graduate school, or invited them into their laboratory or onto a research project. Unfortunately, this is less likely to occur with students of color than with middle-class White students who more closely resemble the existing faculty. This social reproduction must be interrupted, and faculty must be educated in their role as creators of a more diverse new generation of college professors.

In chapter 11, entitled "Access in California Higher Education: The Promise and the Performance," Bruce Hamlett, former college professor and current chief of staff for Assembly Higher Education in the California legislature, summarizes the state of higher education in California and reflects on the lessons shared in the foregoing chapters. He finds that a well-intended financial aid system in California has been under-funded and does not meet the needs of California's low-income students, that the state's heavy reliance on its under-funded community college system cannot deliver on the promise of a college education for all the state's students. He argues that policy needs to be rethought with respect to what the community colleges can realistically do given their constrained resources, and he seriously questions the wisdom of the 20th-century policy—a cornerstone of the California 1960 Master Plan for Higher Education—of channeling two-thirds of the state's students into community colleges where they are unlikely to attain the education necessary to compete in a 21st century economy. He also notes that legislation that would create a guaranteed transfer process for some students could only work if it addressed the weaknesses identified in the earlier DAP policy.

Hamlett also finds that a sound accountability system for higher education is lacking and that some of the indicators that Bensimon and her colleagues suggest ought to be included as accountability benchmarks to help ensure better graduation outcomes for the state's colleges and universities. Finally, Hamlett admonishes that "we know that higher education is the engine that drives the state's economy. We also know that existing state policies are not supportive of an expansive, effective higher education system. If the policies are not soon revised, the state's economy will not be competitive internationally." And so, Hamlett ends where we began, with a system in crisis, under-funded and unprepared for the escalating numbers of students—increasingly from communities of color who have not fared well in this system and with admissions policies that exacerbate an increasing social divide between Whites and Asians on the one hand and Blacks and Latinos on the other.

The serious conversations that occurred among academics and policy makers during the Sacramento conference and through these chapters show that although both groups saw a crisis of considerable dimensions, it was seen differently according to where the speaker was in the educational and political structure. Importantly, however, policy makers repeatedly asked for the help of academics in thinking through ways to address the crisis, and academics were eager to find ways to craft real policy from the findings of their studies. While the policy makers necessarily focused more on the day-to-day political battles that must be won to move any progressive idea forward, the academics often called for more comprehensive changes. In reality, however, the sweeping changes that all acknowledged needed to occur would ultimately have to meet the test of political viability in an era of constrained resources, and from big ideas smaller pieces of legislation would have to be fashioned until and unless there are major changes in public opinion and politics.

We hope that the thoughtful analyses presented in these chapters, paired with solid strategies for equalizing access to *quality* higher education can result in significant change before it is too late. But there is little time to spare. Californians already face shrinking educational opportunity as the state fails to keep up with its exploding population and the increasingly urgent need for college education. The new majority of non-White youth in California has little chance to share the great opportunities available at the top of the state's educational pyramid. The golden days of California's growth and prosperity are not likely to persist long without investing in an education system to meet the needs of a new century and a vastly different population. Once hailed as a document of resounding vision, California's Master Plan for Higher Education was undeniably the driving force behind the enormous expansion of the state's economy. But, that time is past and a new vision is required. We hope that the chapters that follow will contribute to creating that new vision and that it might be a lighthouse for the nation.

## NOTES

1. The GI Bill provided for up to 48 months of "full school costs, including tuition, fees, books, and supplies . . . paid directly by the Veteran's Administration, up to a maximum of $500 per school year, plus a monthly subsistence allowance between $50 and $75" (Henry, 1975, p. 57).

2. While Proposition 209 was passed in November 1996, it did not go into effect until 1997, and therefore the first freshman class to be selected for admission did not enroll until Fall of 1998.

## REFERENCES

American Council on Education. (2003). *Minorities in higher education*. Washington, DC: Author.

California Postsecondary Education Commission. (2004). *Student access, institutional capacity, and public higher education enrollment demand, 2003–2013*. Sacramento, CA: Author.

California Postsecondary Education Commission. (2005). *An update of the commission's community college enrollment demand projections by region*. Sacramento, CA: Author.

Chávez, L. (1998). *The color bind: California's battle to end affirmative action.* Berkeley, CA: University of California Press.

Eisaguirre, L. (1999). *Affirmative action.* Santa Barbara, CA: ABC-CLIO.

Gándara, P., & Chávez, L. (2003). Putting the cart before the horse: Latinos and higher education. In D. López & A. Jiménez (Eds.), *Latinos and Public Policy in California, An Agenda for Opportunity* (pp. 87–120). Berkeley, CA: California Policy Research Center, University of California.

Henry, D. (1975). *Challenges past, challenges present: An analysis of American higher education since 1930.* San Francisco, CA: Jossey-Bass.

Organization for Economic Cooperation and Development. (2004). *Learning for tomorrow's world: First results from PISA 2003.* Retrieved on December 6, 2004, from http://www.OECD.org

Olson, K. (1974). *The GI bill, the veterans, and the colleges.* Lexington, KY: University of Kentucky Press.

Swanson, C. (2004). Sketching a portrait of public high school graduation: Who graduates? Who doesn't? In G. Orfield (Ed.), *Dropouts in America: Confronting the Graduation Rate Crisis* (pp. 13–40). Cambridge, MA: Harvard Education Press.

Vernez, G., Krop, R., & Rydell, C. P. (1999). *Closing the education gap: Benefits and costs.* Santa Monica, CA: RAND Corporation.

Part 1

*The Role of K-12 Education
in Access and Opportunity
in Higher Education*

JEANNIE OAKES
JULIE A. MENDOZA
DAVID SILVER

Chapter Two

# California Opportunity Indicators: Informing and Monitoring California's Progress Toward Equitable College Access

## BACKGROUND

We begin with a reminder of what is well known. There are stark statewide disparities among California's racial and ethnic groups in high school completion and college participation—a finding that is not unique to this region but exists across the nation. Figure 2.1 documents these disparities for a cohort of students who graduated from California public high schools in spring 2002. It shows the proportion that each racial and ethnic group makes up of the state's 9th-grade enrollment compared to the proportion they comprise of high school graduates and first-time college freshmen four years later. Notice as Latinos and African Americans move through the educational system, their share of the enrollment declines dramatically as a proportion of the freshman class at the California Community Colleges (CCC), the California

State University (CSU), and the University of California. Particularly striking is the extreme under-representation of both groups in the selective University of California (UC). For example, in 1998, Latinos represented 40 percent of the state's 9th-grade enrollment. Four years later, they comprised 32 percent of the state's high school graduates, 28 percent of freshmen enrolled in California community college, 22 percent of CSU freshmen, and only 13 percent of UC freshmen. Figure 2.1 not only documents dramatic disparities in high school completion and college participation among California's diverse student population, it underscores the need for the state to carefully monitor barriers known to impact college participation.[1]

As bad as they are, the 2002 disparities represent a substantial recovery from the significant drop in the rates of admissions of African American and Latino students to the University of California following the Regents' 1995 resolution ending affirmative action at the university and the 1996 passage of Proposition 209, a ballot initiative prohibiting the consideration of race, ethnicity, and gender in admissions and hiring in California. The ban on affirmative action prompted the University of California and California State University systems to become far more aggressive in their efforts to use "outreach" programs to create a more diverse pool of high school graduates who are eligible and competitive for the university in a race-neutral admissions environment.

In 1997, a blue ribbon UC Outreach Task Force proposed a four-pronged approach for reaching students at these schools: (a) student-centered academic

FIGURE 2.1

California Student Diversity: 1998–1999 Ninth Graders Compared to 2001–2002 High School Graduates and to Fall 2002 First-time Freshmen

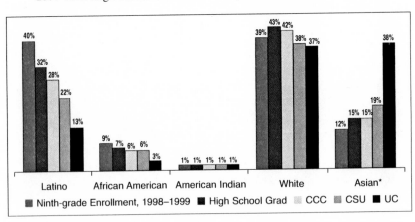

*Includes Pacific Islanders and Filipinos (chart created by Celina Torres, MPP, Tomás Rivera Policy Institute)

development; (b) school-centered systemic reform; (c) recruitment and yield activities; and (d) research and evaluation. In 1998, the Task Force plan was funded rather generously by the legislature, with the proviso that within five years the university double the number of African American, Latino, and American Indian students that were graduating from high school eligible for admission to the university and increase by 50 percent the number that were "competitively eligible"—for admission to the system's two most selective campuses—Los Angeles and Berkeley. Unfortunately, the expanded Outreach programs and their partner educators in K-12 schools had little information to guide them as they devised policies and programs that would make college access more equitable. Existing data about K-12 schooling—test scores, API (Academic Performance Index) rankings—and rates of CSU and UC eligibility conveyed information about educational outcomes, including inequities in college preparation. However, they provided almost no clues about inequalities in learning resources and opportunities within schools or about the types of interventions that would be most effective in removing barriers known to contribute to differences in student achievement and college-going. Neither did they provide answers to other important policy-relevant questions: Are the college-going disparities a statewide phenomenon? Are they worse in particular regions or in particular types of schools? Where along students' schooling trajectories do the disparities appear? What policy-alterable conditions underlie the disparities? When and where might intervention be most effective?

Without empirical data to answer such questions, policy makers and the public lacked meaningful ways to monitor the system's progress toward meeting the legislature's ambitious goals. Specifically, there was no way to know how effective the new interventions were or if college preparation was becoming more equitable. Consequently, policy makers and the public were consigned to wait patiently for the long-term outcome. This wait-and-see approach did not mesh well with California's contemporary fiscal reality and the pressures to make appropriations and budget cuts based on cost-benefit analyses. The State's highly charged political environment around diversity and admissions was only exacerbated by the lack of empirical data to justify the benefits or cost-effectiveness of the UC's new outreach policies and programs.

Not only were reliable, research-based answers to these questions needed, but the answers should be easily understood, widely reported, and updated over time. That way they could become part of public deliberation, policy making, and educators' decision making. UC ACCORD sought to fill this information gap by using the considerable academic research on K-12 schooling and college preparation to develop a set of "opportunity indicators." These indicators, UC ACCORD believes, could be useful both for informing efforts to make college access more equitable and for monitoring the impact of those efforts.[2]

## HOW MIGHT OPPORTUNITY INDICATORS HELP?

UC ACCORD's California Opportunity Indicators project uses existing and new data to construct and report indicators about the status of college access in the state and the distribution of K-12 schooling conditions that are critical to making college accessible.[3] ACCORD seeks to use the indicators as a mechanism for translating equity-focused research into a format that is useful to policy makers, educators, and the public. The goal is to provide credible, provocative, and useful information on college preparation, college access, and college success among the state's diverse students; explain the conditions under which the struggle for college access occurs; and monitor and inform the state's progress toward greater equity.

ACCORD envisioned a set of college opportunity indicators serving similar purposes to the indicators that are used to monitor the economy, the criminal justice system, or other social systems. In each of these important domains, we use statistical indicators to describe and monitor complex conditions that we would probably judge imprecisely or miss altogether in day-to-day observations. We use indicators as yardsticks to measure progress toward some goal or standard, against some past benchmark, or by comparison with data from some other institution or country. Indicators characterize the nature of a complex and hard to measure system by regularly measuring some of its key components (Oakes, 1986; Shavelson, McDonnell, & Oakes, 1989). They represent not just the measured components themselves, but also underlying properties that are not directly or perfectly measurable. For example, we recognize that the quality of the teaching force is central to a well-functioning school system and to college preparation, but we also know that there is no direct way to measure it. So, we measure aspects of teaching, such as years of academic training in the discipline taught, or possession (or lack of) a credential in the subject matter, or years of experience—or some combination of these—as indicators of teacher quality, even though we realize that these aspects of teaching do not completely measure the underlying properties of teacher quality. The most useful indicators tell a great deal about the entire system by reporting the condition of a few particularly significant features of the system. For example, the number of seniors enrolled in a school is an important fact, but it does little to inform judgments about how well the education system is functioning. In contrast, data on the proportion of seniors in a school that complete the college-prep curriculum required for admission to four-year colleges provide considerable insight about a school's college-going culture.

ACCORD's goal is to develop a set of opportunity indicators that will report the current status and monitor changes in California's underrepresented[4] students' opportunities and outcomes; permit a glimpse of future levels of achievement and rates of college preparation; provide insight about barriers to achievement and rates of college preparation; and inform policy discussions aimed at increasing underrepresented students' achievement and college participation. Accordingly, ACCORD is developing and reporting status indicators and leading indicators. "Status indicators" will report educational outcomes that are needed to understand rates of school success and college access. These outcomes include such measures as the size of the achievement gaps among various groups of students and the relative representation of students from various groups among UC eligible students. "Leading indicators" monitor whether the state is furthering its capacity to reduce disparities in learning resources and opportunities. As described more fully later in this chapter, ACCORD has conducted and drawn upon existing research to develop leading indicators. These indicators point to a set of conditions that students in educationally disadvantaged communities require for learning and successful college preparation. For the most part, middle- and upper-middle class youngsters from college-going families routinely enjoy these conditions in their schools and communities.

## THE COLLEGE OPPORTUNITY RATIO—
## CONSTRUCTING NEW INDICATORS FROM EXISTING DATA

Over the past two years, ACCORD has designed, developed, and presented a new status indicator—the College Opportunity Ratio (COR). COR is an indicator of a highly complex phenomenon: schools' success at preparing college-hopeful ninth graders to become college-ready graduates. COR is calculated using cross-sectional data collected by California's Department of Education. The data are combined into a three-number ratio. The first number in the ratio represents ninth grade enrollment,[5] the second number represents the number of graduates four years later,[6] and the third number represents the number of graduates who completed the minimum college preparatory curriculum[7] required for admission to both the University of California and the California State University systems.[8]

For example, if a high school had 300 ninth graders in Fall 1998, 200 graduates in Spring 2002, and 100 graduates that completed the A-G requirements with a C or better, the COR for this school would be represented as: 100:67:33. A reader would know that for every 100 ninth graders, the school had 67 graduates four years later, and 33 graduates who had completed the A-G requirements. Although COR is not a truly longitudinal indicator, it offers more useful information than any other publicly reported statistic now available about graduation rates and college preparation in the state.[9] In addition, it helps us see the need for the state to report graduation and college preparation rates as a percentage or ratio of all those students for whom the state's schools have been responsible.

In addition to calculating and reporting the COR for each high school in the state, aggregate CORs can be calculated for school districts, counties, legislative districts, and the state as a whole. Additionally, the COR can be calculated for all students, and for subgroups of students by race, ethnicity, and gender at each of these levels. For example, figure 2.2 shows the average COR across 854 California comprehensive public high schools in 2002 was: 100:69:27.[10] In other words, for every 100 ninth graders enrolled during the 1998–1999 academic year, California high schools graduated 69 students, on average, four years later, and 27 college-ready graduates. We compared the statewide average CORs for the class of 2000 with the class of 2002 and found virtually no difference between these cohorts.

In contrast, our analysis of disparities among California's 58 counties in preparing ninth graders to become college-ready graduates showed considerable regional variation. For example, the ratio of ninth graders to college-prepared high school graduates averaged 100 to 31 or greater in the San Francisco Bay area counties of Marin, San Francisco, Santa Clara, and Alameda. In contrast, the ratio of ninth graders to college-prepared high school graduates across most of the Central Valley counties averaged 100 to less than 20. This analysis makes clear there are considerable differences by county and suggests that region may be one important variable to consider when exploring disparities in college preparation and access for all of California's students.

The most significant variation, however, appears when the COR is disaggregated by racial and ethnic groups across the state, by individual high schools,

FIGURE 2.2
Statewide COR for the Classes of 2000 and 2002

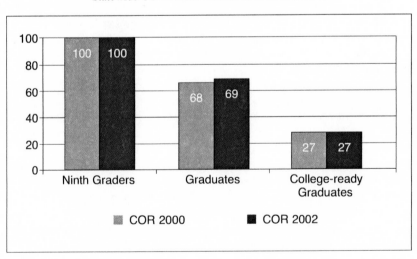

and by racial and ethnic groups within high schools. Figure 2.3 illustrates the disparities between the average statewide COR for White and Asian American students and for students from racial and ethnic groups that are underrepresented in the University of California system (Latino, African American, and American Indian). Notice the difference in Spring 2002 graduates. For every 100 White and Asian American ninth graders in 1998, 74 graduated four years later, compared to 64 Latino, African American, and American Indian students. Thirty-four White and Asian American ninth graders graduated college-ready, compared to only 18 Latino, African American, and American Indian students.

We also found considerable variation among schools in preparing ninth graders to become college-ready graduates. This variation is found among schools' overall CORs and in their CORs disaggregated by race and ethnicity. Figure 2.4 (in appendix) illustrates this variation in one legislative district in Southern California. Senate District 21 includes Pasadena, Glendale, Burbank, and a portion of the city of Los Angeles. It is a legislative district with tremendous racial and economic diversity and in some ways serves as a microcosm of the state. As the figure illustrates, in addition to analyzing the CORs by race and ethnicity for each high school in the state, ACCORD designed colorful Geographic Information System (GIS) maps to display the CORs for every high school in each legislative district against the context of median household income of the high school's community.

Figure 2.4 (see appendix) displays the CORs for 19 high schools in Senate District 21 for two groups: students who are underrepresented in the UC system and those who are not. It depicts the COR for each high school mapped against the context of the base map, which is median household

FIGURE 2.3
Statewide COR for the Class of 2002 by Student Race and Ethnicity

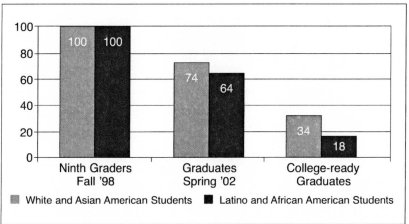

income. The top portion of the figure displays the CORs for groups of students with low rates of UC participation (African American, Latino, and American Indians), and the bottom portion displays the CORs for White and Asian American students in the same schools. Each school has a bar chart on both maps and the chart shows how well the school is doing with the group of students featured on the map. The first bar of each chart represents 100 ninth graders at the school in 1998 for each group of interest. We varied the heights of these bars among schools in an effort to show the relative differences among schools in the overall size of their student populations from the various groups.[11] The second bar represents the number of 2002 graduates for every 100 ninth graders in 1998, and the third bar represents the number of college-ready graduates for each 100 ninth graders. This map clearly illustrates how well the schools in Senate District 21 are doing in preparing students for college.

In Senate District 21, as elsewhere in the state, we see enormous variation in COR ratios between schools and within schools. In general, we found that schools in higher wealth communities in this district and across the state prepare more ninth graders for college. Importantly, however, this map clearly shows that the wealth of a community *does not always* predict how well schools prepare students for college.

The overall pattern is that White and Asian American students emerge from schools in Senate District 21 better prepared for college than their Black and Latino peers. We also see dramatic differences in the effectiveness of these 19 high schools in preparing ninth graders for college.

Figure 2.5 (see appendix) zooms in on the western region of Senate District 21 and displays the CORs for underrepresented students in two high schools: Grant and North Hollywood. These schools are located in communities with similar median household income and the schools have similar school characteristics such as the percentage of students in the school participating in the free/reduced lunch program; the percentage of Latino and African American students; the number of teachers with emergency credentials; and the number of English learners. Both schools graduate roughly the same number of ninth graders, 44 and 43, respectively. Yet, the difference between the schools in the number of graduates who are college-ready is great. For every 100 ninth graders enrolled in Grant, 23 students graduate college-ready compared to only 7 at North Hollywood High. This map suggests that the wealth of a community *does not always* predict the educational outcomes for schools. It provides compelling evidence that school context matters, and that educational policy makers need to monitor each school's progress toward reducing disparities in academic success and college-going as well as monitoring the state's progress as a whole.

Organizing and presenting equity indicators by legislative district illustrates how the reporting of existing educational data can be made more compelling and more useful than simply reporting statistics in traditional formats. COR GIS maps help stakeholders and legislators visualize information in new ways that reveal relationships, patterns, and trends not visible with other traditional data reporting methods. GIS maps also provide new insights to policy makers and their constituents about how well the education system is functioning in their own communities and help to generate thoughtful discussions of how policy alternatives might remedy inequalities that have become salient locally.

In 2003, ACCORD researchers hand-delivered COR GIS maps to every member of the California Legislature. We also held a legislative briefing in the State Capitol to unveil this new equity indicator. During visits with legislators and their staff we were able to tailor our message to each elected official in ways that helped the policy maker reconsider important educational issues, redefine the problem, and help them discard old assumptions or myths about student achievement and college access. For instance, many elected officials believed that the disparities in college opportunities among racial/ethnic groups existed because Latino and African American students are concentrated in high poverty schools with inadequate resources such as limited college-preparatory course offerings, out-of-date textbooks, and poorly trained teachers. The fact that we documented extraordinary differences in CORs among racial/ethnic groups enrolled in the *same* high school provides a noteworthy signal that other factors may contribute to this disturbing finding.

## WHAT ELSE DO WE NEED TO KNOW? LEADING INDICATORS

The College Opportunity Ratio tells us a great deal about how well schools are preparing students. It certainly tells us far more than the grossly underestimated dropout rates that schools now report or the "graduation rates" that schools will have to report under the No Child Left Behind (NCLB) Act. However, outcome indicators like the COR, alone, cannot explain *why* particular students, schools, and communities achieve at low levels and fail to realize their hopes for college. The narrow focus on outcomes tends to make the gap in learning resources and opportunities in California schools invisible. Outcome indicators on their own also risk misrepresenting schooling inadequacies as the failure of individual students and their families.

A great deal happens between the time a child enters school and when he or she becomes a college-hopeful ninth grader—and between the ninth grade and high school graduation. The school conditions and opportunities between these points in time help determine whether that student graduates from high school with the minimum eligibility to enter a four-year college or university, and that determines whether a prepared student applies and is admitted to a four-year college. While having adequate opportunities to learn is important for all students, it is particularly important for subgroups of students who historically have been underrepresented in four-year colleges and, by extension, whose families are less likely to have higher education experience from which to draw guidance. Importantly, these conditions and opportunities result from educational policies and professional decisions—decisions that we can change. Interrupting the patterns of inequitable college access requires that we better understand the consequences for young people across California's diverse communities of educational policies and educators' decisions.

Consequently, UC ACCORD is also developing "leading" indicators that measure conditions in K-12 schools that affect the quality of education students receive and their access to college preparation and admission. After an extensive review of the literature on school achievement and college preparation, we identified the following seven critical conditions for student achievement and college access:

- Safe and adequate school facilities
- College-going school culture
- Rigorous academic curriculum
- Qualified teachers
- Intensive academic and social supports
- Opportunities to develop a multicultural college-going identity
- Family-neighborhood-school connections around college-going

We define and explain the importance of each of these conditions below. Examples of studies that support the importance of each condition are reported in the notes at the end of the chapter.[12]

*Safe and Adequate School Facilities*

*What is it?* Students must attend schools that are free from overcrowding, violence, unsafe and unsanitary conditions, and other features of school climates that diminish achievement and access to college.

*Why does it matter?* Schools must be free from overcrowding and deteriorating facilities so that students and teachers can devote their attention and energy to learning and teaching. Faculty quit at alarming rates at schools where laboratory, athletic, and teaching facilities are in decay or under-resourced. Unsafe, deteriorated, and overcrowded schools threaten students' social values of integrity, discipline, and civic-mindedness and allow little enthusiasm for lifelong learning (Fine, 1991). Overcrowding reduces students' ability to pay attention and increases school violence (Astor, Meyer, & Behre, 1999). In such schools students achieve less, and rates of teacher and student absenteeism are higher than at schools that do not have these problems

(Corcoran, Walker, & White, 1988; Rivera-Batiz & Marti, 1995). Sometimes overcrowding is addressed by putting students on year-round, multi-track schedules. These students can suffer interrupted and lost instructional time and limited access to advanced courses and specialized programs; when breaks are ill-timed, this can lead to limited access to extracurricular activities and enrichment programs and poorer academic performance (Mitchell, 2002).

## College-going School Culture

*What is it?* In a college-going school culture, teachers, administrators, parents, and students expect students to have all the experiences they need for high achievement and college preparation. Adults encourage students to exert the necessary effort and persistence throughout their entire educational career, and adults work diligently to eliminate school-sanctioned alternatives to hard work and high expectations. These high expectations are coupled with specific interventions and information that emphasize to students that college preparation is a normal part of their childhood and youth. Students believe that college is for *them* and is not only reserved for the exceptional few who triumph over adversity to rise above all others.

*Why does it matter?* Students' learning is strongly tied to the expectations of those around them and the quality of their opportunities to learn. Minority students, in particular, perform poorly when their teachers do not believe in their abilities (Ferguson, 1988). Consequently, in a school with a strong college-going culture educators believe that all of their students can learn at very high levels. The school culture that expects all students to spend time and effort on academic subjects and that emphasizes effort will pay off fosters high levels of academic achievement (Lee & Smith, 2001; Phillips, 1997). Of course, high expectations alone are not enough. However, when high expectations are present, teachers seem more able and willing to provide rigorous academic instruction and press for high standards. In turn, students respond to high expectations with greater effort, persistence, and achievement (Lee & Smith, 2001; Newmann et al. & Associates, 1996). Caring adult advocates who provide specific information and assistance for college-going help students achieve that goal (McDonough, 1997). They facilitate close, supportive relationships and keep tabs on their students' progress (Oakes, Quartz, Ryan, & Lipton, 2000). Similarly, school-created peer groups can help students believe that college-going and the hard work it takes seem "normal" (Mehan et al., 1997). Students in such groups support one another's aspirations, share information, and counter the many forces in low-income communities that work against high achievement.

## Rigorous Academic Curriculum

*What is it?* Students are prepared for, and have access to, algebra in middle school and college preparatory and AP courses in high school.

*Why does it matter?* Students' course-taking is key to their attending a four-year college, and the sequence of these courses—leading to advanced work in high school—must start in middle school and early high school (Oakes, Muir, & Joseph, in press). Students learn more in advanced courses with a rigorous curriculum. Further, advanced courses are prerequisites for admission to competitive four-year universities. The impact is particularly powerful for African American and Latino students. Often, students who thought they were "succeeding" in high school by getting good grades are devastated to find out that their courses have not prepared them with the skills, knowledge, or advanced credit to enter a four-year college.

The more academic courses students take, the more positive their schooling outcomes. Advanced courses (particularly in science and mathematics) have positive effects on students' achievement, in students' preparedness for college, and in their success in college-level work (Adelman, 1999). Eighth graders who take algebra perform considerably better on the National Assessment of Educational Progress (NAEP) mathematics exam, and the more math they take the better they do (Education Trust, 1988). Moreover, the intensity and quality of students' high school courses is the most powerful factor in increasing students' chances for completing a four-year college degree, and that impact is far greater for African American and Latino students than any other pre-college opportunity (Adelman, 1999). Preparing for challenging high school classes demands rigorous middle school curricula—one undifferentiated by ability groups or tracks. Most students learn more in high-level classes (ability groups or tracks) than do students *with comparable prior achievement* who take lower level classes (Oakes, 1996; Oakes, 2000). This should give pause to those who may believe that if students do not take advanced classes it is because they are lazy or are not smart enough.

### Qualified Teachers

*What is it?* Knowledgeable, experienced, and fully certified teachers provide instruction that engages students in work of high intellectual quality. Importantly, in diverse communities, high-quality teaching makes highly valued knowledge accessible to students from diverse backgrounds.

*Why does it matter?* One of the most powerful factors in students' academic success is their access to well-prepared teachers. Teacher quality, including teacher certification status, degree in field, and participation in high-quality professional development all have a significant impact on student outcomes (Betts, Rueben, & Danenberg, 2000; Darling-Hammond & Youngs, 2002; Ferguson, 1988). Improving the quality of teaching in the classroom has the greatest impact on students who are most educationally at risk. In some instances, the effects of well-prepared teachers on student achievement are stronger than the influences of student background factors, such as poverty, language background, and minority status (Fetler, 1997; Sanders & Rivers, 1996). Well-qualified teachers provide a wide range of teaching strategies: they ask questions that make students think and answer fully; they address students' learning needs and curriculum goals; they make subject matter accessible to diverse groups of students (Wenglinsky, 2002); and they make rigorous learning satisfying and fun. Poorly qualified teachers spend more time on drill and practice (Carter & Doyle, 1987; Doyle, 1986). Moreover, well-prepared teachers of students of color and language minority students use strategies that bridge students' home culture and language with the knowledge and skills that matter at school. They demonstrate a valuing of all cultures in the academic curriculum (Ladson-Billings, 1994; Valenzuela, 1999).

## Intensive Academic and Social Supports

*What is it?* Teachers and counselors play a pivotal role in informing and preparing high school students for college. Yet, all students require supports and assistance that take place outside the classroom or school. To navigate the pathway to college successfully, students need support networks of adults and peers who help access tutors, material resources, counseling services, summer academic programs, SAT prep, coaching about college admissions and financial aid, and a myriad of other timely assistance.

*Why does it matter?* Pointed efforts to provide students with the resources and information crucial for college preparation are particularly important for low-income minority students who may not have the "social capital" or "college knowledge" necessary to negotiate the academic pipeline (Stanton-Salazar, 1997). Interventions that bring additional assistance to low-income minority students boost their achievement in elementary school, their success in college preparatory middle and high school classes, and their likelihood of admission to and success in college. This help is more effective when it provides additional instruction on the material in students' regular classes than when it consists of a separate remedial curriculum. Teachers and counselors are the primary sources of "college knowledge" for Latino families, and they serve as "cultural brokers" for students seeking information and strategies for college access and academic success (Cooper, Jackson, Azmitia, Lopez, & Dunbar, 1995; Tomás Rivera Center, 2001; Vasquez, Stanton-Salazar, & Mehan, 2000). As the College Board makes clear to schools offering Advanced Placement (AP) courses to disadvantaged minority students, "schools with successful AP programs realize that not only should students be challenged with rigorous curricula and motivation for learning, but the support network should also be present that makes it possible for them to succeed and difficult to fail" (1993, p. 9). Moreover, the social networks students develop when they work one-on-one or in after-school settings with college students and well-informed adults can provide a form of access that students lack elsewhere in their families and communities (Kahne & Bailey, 1999; McDonough, 1997). When students in academic support programs become friends, they are more likely to succeed (Oakes, Rogers, Lipton, & Morell, 2001; Gándara & Bial, 2001).

## Opportunities to Develop a Multicultural College-going Identity

*What is it?* Students see college-going as integral to their identities. They have the confidence and skills to negotiate college without sacrificing their own identity and connections with their home communities. They recognize that college is a pathway to careers that are valued in their families, peer groups, and local communities.

*Why does it matter?* Race and culture play an important role in shaping students' college-going identities, and this role is related to the historical under-representation of many minorities in colleges. Partly as a result of past and present cultural and racial attitudes in the broader society, students of color may believe that college "is not for me." Alternatively, they may believe, often with some cause, that they cannot hold both the cultural identity and language they have and value, as well as the identity of a high-achieving student. Adults must work to shape a school culture that does not force students to choose between the culture, language, and values of their home and community and the majority culture and values that are broadly, if unnecessarily, associated with high academic achievement.

In contrast to commonly held views that low-income students devalue education, studies suggest that they more likely turn away because of a real or perceived lack of opportunities (Steinberg, 1996). A recent RAND study of low-income high school graduates who were eligible to attend the University of California but chose not to found that the students were most deterred by their beliefs that the university is "not for people like me," and that that they were not prepared for the university's high demands (Krop, Brewer, Gates, Gill, Reichardt, Sundt, & Throgmorton, 1998). These perceptions arise, in part, as students internalize negative labels assigned to their racial and cultural groups. African American and Latino students are most susceptible to what Claude Steele terms "a stereotype threat." That is, students who perceive that their race plays a role in their performance perform more poorly on measures of academic achievement (Steele, 1997).

Creating community- and school-based programs help establish environments where college attendance can be seen as the norm, not the exception, for students of color. Students benefit when outreach and student support programs are located in the worlds that they inhabit (Cooper, 1999; Davidson & Phelan, 1999). And when these students can look up to older youth and adults as models for college and college-based careers, they develop identities that also define these choices as valued ways to give back to their families and communities.

*Family-Neighborhood-School Connections Around College-going*

*What is it?* Connections between families and schools build on parents' strengths and consider them a valuable education resource for students. Educators and community groups work together to ensure that all families have access to essential knowledge of college preparation, admission, and financial aid. Moreover, parents and the community are actively involved in creating all of the other critical conditions described previously.

*Why does it matter?* Ongoing, respectful, and substantive communication between schools and families is as important to school success in low-income neighborhoods as it is in affluent ones (Auerbach, 2002; Cooper & Gándara, 2001). Going beyond the annual parent-teacher conference, successful urban schools engage parents in seminars, workshops, and other outreach efforts to help parents gain knowledge about a wide range of education issues. These may include national standards and assessment; tracking and access of under-represented students to postsecondary education; sharing of information sources within the school, on the Internet and elsewhere, to name just a few. The emphasis of this "scaffolding" is not just to transmit necessary facts and procedures, but to give parents the tools to become effective advocates for their children. This emphasis, already adopted by affluent parents, is necessary to help low-income parents understand and negotiate the pathway to the post-secondary education system (McDonough, 1997). Community organizations such as local churches and boys' and girls' clubs can help communicate to parents the importance of providing their children with a challenging curriculum, as well as supporting parents who want to see positive changes implemented. Coordinating community and social services and university-school partnerships can support families and provide essential scaffolding for school success (Noguera, 2001).

The seven critical conditions just outlined are the basis for a comprehensive, research-based framework for understanding the barriers to equity in college-going and for monitoring the state's progress toward removing those barriers. The college chances of every student—wealthy or poor, regardless of race or ethnicity—will be affected by whether he or she has access to these seven critical school conditions. It is important to note that none of these conditions is within the control of the student. Each condition is alterable through improved policy and practice and suggests important targets for intervention. Thus, having indicators of these seven critical conditions can provide us guidance for intervention and allow us to track important trends in students' college access.

Few of these critical conditions are currently measured by the state's public data systems. As a result, educational stakeholders and legislators have no way of knowing whether or not the conditions are present in California schools or the extent to which their absence underlies disparities in educational outcomes like those evidenced by the COR. However, to accompany the COR maps, ACCORD also released data tables that would allow comparisons among a high schools' CORs and the following indicators of school conditions.

## College-Going School Culture

*SAT participation.* Because of the SAT's central role as a gatekeeper for four-year college entry, it can be considered an indicator of a college-going school culture. When school personnel and academic structures orient students toward college, the SAT participation rate should be high. The rate reported here is calculated as the number of twelfth graders sitting for the exam in 1999–2000 as a percentage of the ninth grade cohort four years earlier. College Board and California Basic Educational Data System (CBEDS) data are used to construct this indicator.

*PSAT participation.* Like SAT participation, PSAT participation is an indicator of a college-going school culture. The rate reported here is also calculated as a percentage of ninth graders four years earlier, but represents the number of students in the class of 2000 who sat for the PSAT before taking the SAT as seniors. CBEDS and College Board data are used to construct this indicator.

## Rigorous Academic Curriculum

*The Advanced Math Rate.* An indicator of rigorous academic curriculum, the Advanced Math Rate is specifically the rate (from CBEDS) at which students in each district were enrolled in advanced math courses in 1999–2000 in grades 9–12. Mathematics course-taking is among the strongest correlates of college-going.

## Qualified Teachers

*Uncertified Teacher Rate.* A teacher quality indicator is the likelihood that a student will encounter an uncertified teacher in any given class. If 10 percent of the teachers at a school are uncertified, the Uncertified Teacher Rate is 10 percent for all students at that school. Because it assumes that within a school all students are equally likely to be assigned to certified teachers, it is actually a conservative estimate for underrepresented groups of students. CBEDS data are used for this indicator.

*Certification Disparity Index.* This indicator reveals whether underrepresented students in a legislative district, on average, attend schools that employ higher or lower percentages of uncertified teachers than schools attended by White and Asian American students. This index is the percentage by which the Uncertified Teacher Rate for underrepresented students differs from that of others. In all but a handful of legislative districts (where the index is a negative number), underrepresented students are more likely than others to be taught by uncertified teachers. With a Certification Disparity Index of 25, underrepresented students would be 25 percent more likely than others to have an uncertified teacher. Returning to Senate District 21, table 2.1 shows how the districts' schools measured in 2000 on the other set of indicators:

Because these conditions are predictive of college attendance, the degree to which they are available to all students in California schools will tell us a great deal about educational equity. Any effort to provide fair and equal access to the state's institutions of higher education must rely in part on a system of tracking these critical school resources and assessing their equitable distribution.

## PILOTING LEADING INDICATORS

The development of a full set of opportunity indicators is hampered by a lack of statewide data that permit us to place outcome indicators in the context of more than a fraction of the critical conditions and opportunities that affect these outcomes. As a result, we have no way of understanding whether or not they are present in California schools or the extent to which their absence underlies the outcomes reported in the COR. The state also lacks longitudinal data on students that would allow us to measure students' progress through critical conditions and assess the impact of interventions and program improvements that students' experience.

To specify how such indicators could be constructed if data were available, ACCORD administered a survey to a random sample of 3,000 18 year olds who had just graduated from California public high schools. We designed the survey items to elicit information both about the conditions and about the young people themselves. Each of the respondents was asked a series of question about each of the critical conditions for college-going. We used the survey to construct composite indicators (using cluster and factor analysis) that allow us to report the extent to which conditions the literature tells us are related to college-going are present in the experiences of California high school students and explore whether or not the presence or absence of these conditions can help explain differential college preparation and admission to

TABLE 2.1
Senate District 21 Indicators of Critical School Conditions

| Senate District | Adv Math Takers % | SAT Takers % | PSAT Takers % | Uncertified Teachers Rate % | Certification Disparity Index |
|---|---|---|---|---|---|
| 21 | 5.1 | 16 | 11 | 25 | 23 |

four-year colleges. The result should be a set of pilot indicators that could be adopted by the state to inform and monitor its efforts to make college access more equitable.

## THREE INDICATORS OF A
## COLLEGE-GOING SCHOOL CULTURE

In what follows, we use one of the conditions, "College-going School Culture," as an example to show how student survey data can produce meaningful and useful indicators of school characteristics that are linked to rates of college admission. A school with a strong College-going Culture is one in which college is viewed by students and school adults as an expected step in the normative educational pathway. Adults encourage students to strive and persist, and high expectations are coupled with vital help and information about college. Theorists have long suggested that students in such climates are likely to realize the high goals for educational attainment that are typical of most adolescents.

In order to measure this particularly complex construct, we asked students an extensive battery of questions. Factor analysis revealed that the items fell into three particularly important categories: Information/Assistance; High Expectations; or Steering Away from Four-year College.[13] Below we provide a sampling of the items that make up each of these composite indicators of a College-going School Culture.

*Information/Assistance*

- How many times did you talk to an adult at your school about how to choose the right college?
- How many times did you use the college-planning center at your high school?
- Did your school offer counseling regarding courses that would prepare you for a four-year college?
- Did your school offer assistance with filling out college applications?

*High Expectations*

- Did your teachers have high expectations of you?
- How much did your teachers encourage you to go to college?
- Which students were encouraged to take the SAT or the ACT?
- Did anyone at your high school encourage you to go to a four-year college?

*Steering Away from Four-year College*

- Did anyone at your high school encourage you to go to a community college?

- How much did your teacher encourage you to go to a trade or vocational school after high school?
- How much did your teacher encourage you to get a job after high school?

The items that load most highly on each of these dimensions appear in table 2.2, with factor loadings.

Our analysis reveals that various groups of students differ considerably in their access to these College-going School Culture factors and in the relative impact of these factors on college-going. In addition, the coexistence of these factors has a compound impact on students.

## DOES A COLLEGE-GOING SCHOOL CULTURE ACTUALLY AFFECT ADMISSIONS?

A natural question, before going any further, is to ask if a College-going School Culture actually matters. It is often assumed to be important, but we cannot expect policy that aims to bolster it without first being able to measure it convincingly and prove that it matters—and how much, where, and for whom. Our analyses began by addressing the following questions: Does college-going school culture predict college admission? Does it predict for both represented and underrepresented students? The question of whether, and how much, each of the factors matters—and the degree to which they contribute to the college-going equation independent of the other conditions in the schools is central to our work.

The survey data show that each of the dimensions—Steering, Expectations, and Information/Assistance—are highly predictive of admission to UC and CSU. On all three dimensions, students on the high end of the scale (those who receive good and plentiful information and assistance, those who experience high expectations at school, and those who were not steered away from college) have admission rates three or four times greater than those who do not (figure 2.6). For those in the lowest quartile of each factor, the admission rates hover between 10 percent and 13 percent, whereas those at the other end of the spectrum enjoy admission rates of over 40 percent (and in the case of Steering, 50 percent).[14]

As important as it appears to be that students experience any one of the dimensions of a College-going School Culture, the effect is compounded for students whose schools provide high levels across multiple dimensions. Figure 2.7 shows the average admissions rate for students scoring high on none of the dimensions of College-going Culture is 6.9 percent, but outcomes improve dramatically for those who experience a rich College-going Culture across multiple domains. In the most extreme example, those with high levels on all three factors had an average admissions rate of nearly 80 percent.

TABLE 2.2
College-going Culture Factor Structure

| Survey Item | 1 | 2 | 3 |
|---|---|---|---|
| Q.9. How many times did you talk to an adult at your school about how to chose the right college? | 0.66 | | |
| Q.9. How many times did you talk to an adult at your school about how to get into college? | 0.64 | | |
| Q.43. How many times did you use the college-planning center at your high school? | 0.58 | | |
| Q.42. Did your school offer counseling regarding courses that would prepare you for a four-year college? | 0.58 | | |
| Q.9. How many times did you talk to an adult at your school about the classes or teachers you should take? | 0.56 | | |
| Q.42. Did your school offer assistance with filling out college applications? | 0.54 | | |
| Q.29. Did your counselor encourage you to take college prep? | 0.45 | | |
| Q.23. Did you learn from a counselor about college? | 0.45 | | |
| Q.8. Did a counselor or teacher explain to you the classes required to attend a four-year California public university? | 0.44 | | |
| Q.48. Did your high school offer workshops on college admissions test preparation? | 0.30 | | |
| Q.38. Did your teacher have high expectations of you? | | 0.59 | |
| Q.38. How much did your teacher encourage you to go to college? | | 0.54 | |
| Q.5. Which students were encouraged to take the SAT or the ACT? | | 0.49 | |
| Q.37. How often would you say you had substitute teachers in your English, science, and math classes? | | 0.48 | |
| Q.25. Do classes a student takes influence their chances of getting into college? | | 0.41 | |
| Q.11. Did anyone at your high school encourage you to go to a four-year college? | | 0.34 | |
| Q.10. Did anyone at your high school encourage you to go to a community college? | | | 0.62 |
| Q.38. How much did your teacher encourage you to go to a trade or vocational school after high school? | | | 0.59 |

*(continued on next page)*

TABLE 2.2 *(continued)*

| Survey Item | 1 | 2 | 3 |
|---|---|---|---|
| Q.38. How much did your teacher encourage you to get a job after high school? | | | 0.55 |
| Q.42. Did your school offer resources regarding information about community colleges? | | 0.35 | 0.45 |

*Extraction Method:* Principal Component Analysis.

*Rotation Method:* Varimax with Kaiser Normalization. Rotation converged in seven iterations.

*FACTOR 1 can be described as an "Information/Assistance" factor; FACTOR 2 can be described as a "High Expectations" factor; FACTOR 3 can be described as a "Steering" factor.

FIGURE 2.6
Dimensions of College-going Relate to Colleged Admission

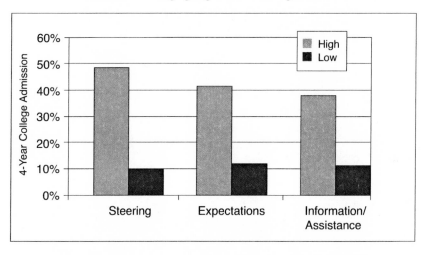

Figure 2.8 shows that, although these College-going Culture factors are important for all groups of students, the relative importance of the dimensions varies considerably across groups. The bars represent the percentage of the variance in college-going explained by each dimension for each group. The figure shows that, across the board, Steering is quite influential. Expectations are also strongly predictive among African American students. For Latino students, the Information/Assistance factor is particularly important—a finding that can be understood in part by the greater needs along this dimension for a group with lower average levels of college attendance by parents, lower lev-

FIGURE 2.7
College Admission Rates for Students Experiencing
0, 1, 2, and 3 Dimensions of College-going Culture

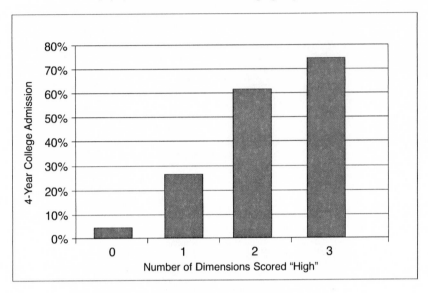

FIGURE 2.8
College-going Culture Factors Do Not Affect All Groups in the Same Ways

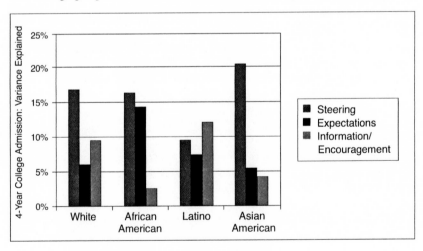

els of English language fluency, and less familiarity with the education system among a disproportionate number of recent immigrants.

Figure 2.8 describes the relationship between College-going Culture
and college admission for different groups of students. It does not show the
prevalence of the factors for each group. With respect to this question, the data
show that Steering is more severe, and Expectations are significantly lower
for Latino and African American students. This is an important finding
because each of these factors contributes to the ethnic differences in college-
going rates in our sample.

Steering away from four-year colleges is most commonly experienced
by Latino students (by a wide margin), but it is actually more predictive of
college-going for other groups. The strongest predictor of college-going for
Latinos is having good information and assistance. (Interestingly, availability
of information/assistance is not reported at lower absolute rates for Latinos
than for White students. It *is* reported at rates substantially below those of
Asian American students). Perhaps the importance of Information/Assistance
for Latino students can be explained in part by the high proportion of relatively new immigrants, second-language speakers, and the comparatively low
levels of college information available to Latino parents, who are less likely
to have attended college themselves. For students whose parents are unfamil-
iar with the higher education system, one would expect Information and
Assistance to be of paramount importance.

In sum, our analyses show that California students who experience
strong college-going supports in their high schools have UC and CSU admission rates that dwarf those of other students. Over 60 percent of students with
strong supports are admitted to UC or CSU, in contrast to fewer than 7 percent of those who report low levels of support. As expected, the strongest predictor of college admissions is the degree to which students take necessary
courses and exams. While both result, in part, from College-going Culture,
they are also influenced by a wide array of other conditions that affect preparation and academic choices. Importantly, our analyses show that these College-going Culture factors predict college admission—over and above the
obvious things such as taking the right courses.

Figure 2.9 shows the extent to which the effects on four-year college
admissions of Rigorous Curriculum and College-going Culture can be disentangled in our survey data. As it turns out, over 40 percent of the variance in
admissions can be explained broadly in a logistic regression model by these two
constructs. Roughly 19 percent can be understood uniquely in terms of Rigorous Curriculum. Another 10 percent can be explained in terms of College-going
Culture alone and a significant 24 percent from a combination of the two that
cannot be disentangled statistically. Whereas 10 percent can be thought of as the
least that College-going Culture contributes to the equation, much of this shared
portion of the variance can also be attributed to College-going Culture, given

FIGURE 2.9
The Contribution of College-going Culture to UC and CSU Admissions

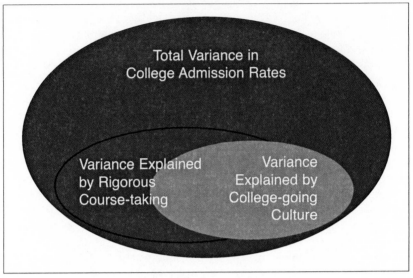

the logical assumption that course-taking patterns mediate much of the relationship between College-going Culture and college admission.

The fact that together, these constructs explain only 40 percent of the variation in admissions makes clear that even taking the right courses and being encouraged to go to college can not guarantee that students will actually apply to schools for which they are eligible or even choose to apply at all. As is the case with most educational outcomes, the college-going equation is extremely complex, so models explaining more than a small fraction of total variation are rare. One's decision to apply to college—and one's likelihood of being admitted—can be affected by a vast range of factors beyond the scope of this study, from early school experiences to health and family issues. In light of this complexity, the strength of association between college-going school culture and college admission is remarkable. Importantly, these factors predict college-going for both represented and underrepresented students, although not always in the same ways.

## IS A COLLEGE-GOING SCHOOL CULTURE
## AVAILABLE EQUALLY?

Returning to the question of whether California schools provide a comparable college-going culture to all groups, figures 2.10 and 2.11 suggest that they do

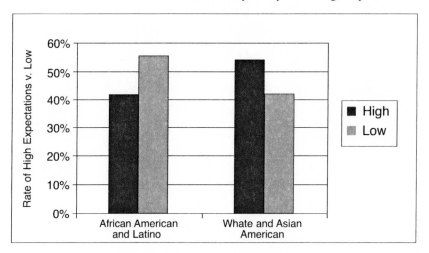

FIGURE 2.10
African Americans and Latinos are Less Likely to Experience High Expectations

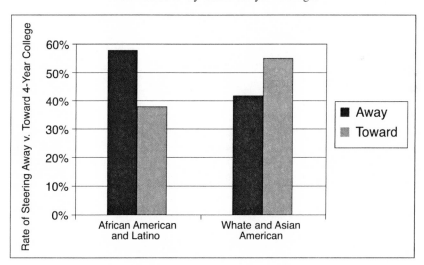

FIGURE 2.11
African Americans and Latinos are More Likely
to be Steered Away from Four-year Colleges

not, at least in the case of Assistance and Steering. African Americans and Latinos are more than 40 percent more likely to be in the lowest quartile of Expectations than in the highest.

We see the same pattern on the Steering index, with underrepresented students 50 percent more likely to be steered away from college by school adults than to be steered toward UC or CSU.

Additionally, students from college-educated families report higher levels of college-going support at school. They are two to three times *more* likely to have information and assistance, and they are two to three times *less* likely to be "steered" away from four-year colleges. Compounding their school advantages, the survey found that these students also have more support outside of school: more private tutoring—more than two times as likely (32 percent to 14 percent); extra classes from a private school or company—almost two times as likely (9 percent to 5 percent); and access to private college counselors to help with applications—almost two times (13 percent to 7 percent).

## WHAT LIES AHEAD?

Over time, UC ACCORD's goal is to build an Indicator System that will paint a comprehensive portrait of the trajectories that various subgroups of California students take through the K-12 system into college and the university. It will place students' accomplishments in the context of critical transitions from childhood to college and the schooling conditions described previously.

California has recent experience showing that such indicators could actually prompt constructive action. Take the experience of Grant High School, one of the two schools displayed on the GIS map in figure 2.5 (see appendix), for example. The map shows significant disparities in the rates at which two schools serving very similar populations, Grant High and neighboring North Hollywood High, produce college-ready graduates (23 percent versus 7 percent). Beneath these indicators is a story of the success of a concrete policy intervention that one might recommend in response to our College-going Culture indicators. Grant High School has a program (Project College Bound) designed specifically for the purpose of generating a stronger College-going School Culture. Students of color are ushered toward college eligibility from the time they enter the ninth grade. They are given clear information about the requirements and are followed closely by college counselors. Students and their parents are notified if they fail to register for important courses or if their performance puts them at risk for falling off the college-prep trajectory. In the first cohort of the program, the number of African Americans in the district who were admitted to the University of California more than doubled. This is surely an intervention that indicators of a College-going Culture could both prompt and track.

What we have described in this chapter is just the tip of the iceberg of a comprehensive project to develop a set of California Opportunity Indicators. However, we believe that our work so far demonstrates its promise. The COR indicator has been widely received as compelling and useful, even though it only represents a new way to array simple, pre-existing state data. Our College-going Culture indicators make clear that constructing useful indicators is possible, feasible, and helpful. A few questions added to the annual survey of teachers by the California Basic Educational System could provide valuable data for the construction of indicators of conditions and opportunities in California schools. So, too, could a questionnaire for high school students attached to California's High School Exit Exam.

Neither collecting data nor constructing and reporting indicators will guarantee equity. But surely, both processes can clarify problems, identify points of intervention and ultimately prompt action and track progress. Good indicators can inform and move a serious and badly needed public discussion and action to advance California's efforts to achieve diversity and equity in college access for all. UC ACCORD's indicators work is meant to prompt just such discussion and action.

## NOTES

1. The fact that a considerable number of undergraduates do not declare themselves as one of these common racial categories does not diminish the disparities. Analyses by Saul Geiser show that most of the UC students who decline to state are either White or Asian—groups not under represented (Saul Geiser, personal communication, 2003).

2. UC ACCORD, a multi-campus research institute housed at UCLA, is the research arm of this outreach strategy. Established in 2001, ACCORD's charge is to engage UC faculty in research that could assist the university and the state to better understand and alter the state's glaring racial disparities in access to higher education. ACCORD's goal is to produce research that is useful as policy makers, educators, and the public struggle to make college-going in California more equitable.

3. In addition to the authors, ACCORD's indicators team includes Daniel Solorzano, Walter Allen, and John Rogers.

4. Note that we use the term "underrepresented" students to refer to African American, Latino, and American Indian students, since these groups are underrepresented in the group of students admitted each year to the University of California.

5. Number includes all ninth graders, including students who were retained.

6. In a few cases, the graduating class was slightly larger than the ninth grade class. In those cases, we report that for every 100 ninth graders there were 100 graduates.

7. These are courses, known as the "A–G" subject requirements, that include: 2 years of history/social science, 4 years of English, 3 years of mathematics, 2 years of laboratory science, 2 years of foreign language, and 2 years of college-preparatory electives.

8. Note that California has a two-tiered system of public four-year universities. Both systems require successful completion of the A–G requirements. Eligibility for the more competitive University of California system requires higher grades in the courses as well as qualifying scores on the SAT I and II.

9. The data come from the California Basic Educational Data System. Since the state does not collect data in a way that allows us to follow individual students over time, some portion of the drop in the numbers between ninth grade and graduation may reflect students who move as well as those who do not graduate. Such student mobility may affect an individual school's COR, but the statewide trends are conservative estimates, since California had a net increase in the number of high school age underrepresented students over the course of the study. One important aspect of ACCORD's work is to improve the breadth and quality of the state's data about its schools and colleges.

10. For this analysis we calculate CORs only for comprehensive public high schools that have college preparation as one of their goals. Thus, small alternative schools that do no offer college preparation are not included.

11. Contrary to what one might expect, a larger bar does not portray a "better" score on the COR.

12. While the importance of these conditions is supported by a large number of studies with consistent findings across locations, populations, educational outcomes, et cetera, we provide only illustrative examples here.

13. Regarding the use of dichotomous variables in factor analysis, the SPSS manual warns: "Interval data are assumed. However, Kim and Mueller (1978) note that . . . dichotomous data may be used if the underlying metric correlations between the variables are thought to be moderate (.7) or lower" (pp. 74–75). Most of the items used in our factor analysis are Likert-scale measures. In some cases, such as the measurement of course-taking, dichotomous variables are used. Since the correlation between any two items is affected by both their substantive similarity and by the similarities of their statistical distributions (Nunnaly & Bernstein, 1994), factors defined by dichotomous items were given additional scrutiny. The primary concern is that items with similar distributions tend to correlate more strongly with one another than do with items with dissimilar distributions. For instance, test items with similar levels of difficulty are predisposed to load on the same factor (Nunnaly & Bernstein, 1994, p. 318). Similarly, two courses with similar rates of student enrollment may be more likely to load on the same factor. Several steps were taken to insure that this was not a problem in our data. Initially, factors were scrutinized for face validity. The course-taking clusters appear to measure, uncontroversially, participation in remedial, mid-level, and advanced courses. Second, factor analysis with full information (SEM) was applied to confirm the robustness of the SPSS findings. This approach avoids the prob-

lems associated with correlation matrixes and uses all of the information contained in the response pattern frequencies (Swygert, McLeod, & Thissen, 2001)—in essence, relating the constructs that are assumed to underlie the data (e.g., likelihood of enrolling in rigorous courses), which are assumed to be continuous and normally distributed (Muthen, 1978; Panter, Swygert, Dahlstrom, & Tanaka, 1997).

14. In this chapter, we focus only on the bivariate relationships. However, other work reports the more complex statistical modeling that demonstrates the independent effects of these variables—which are generally substantial, both in terms of significance and magnitude.

## REFERENCES

Adelman, C. (1999). *Answers in the tool box: Academic intensity, attendance patterns, and bachelor's degree attainment.* Washington, DC: U.S. Department of Education.

Astor, R., Meyer, H., & Behre, W. (1999). Unowned places and times: Maps and interviews about violence in high schools. *American Educational Research Journal, 36*(1), 3–42.

Auerbach, S. (2002). Why do they give the good classes to some and not to others? Latino parent narratives of struggle in a college access program. *Teachers College Record, 104*(7), 1369–1393.

Betts, J. R., Rueben, K. S., & Danenberg, A. (2000). *Equal resources, equal outcomes? The distribution of school resources and student achievement in California.* San Francisco: Public Policy Institute of California.

Bowers, J., & Charles, W. (1989). Effects of physical and school environment in students and faculty. *The Educational Facility Planner, 26*(1), 28–29.

Carter, K., & Doyle, W. (1987). Teachers' knowledge structures and comprehension processes. In J. Calderhead (Ed.), *Exploring Teacher Thinking* (pp. 147–160). London: Cassell.

Cooper, C. R. (1999). Multiple selves, multiple worlds: Cultural perspectives on individuality and connectedness in adolescent development. In A. Masten (Ed.), *Cultural Processes in Child Development, 29* (pp. 161–185). New Jersey: Erlbaum.

Cooper, C. R., Denner, J., & Lopez, E. M. (1999). Cultural brokers: Helping Latino children on pathways to success. *The Future of Children, 9,* 51–57.

Cooper, C. R., & Gándara, P. (2001). When diversity works: Bridging families, peers, schools and communities. *Journal for the Education of Students Placed at Risk, 6,* 1–2.

Cooper, C. R., Jackson, J. F., Azmitia, M., Lopez, E. M., & Dunbar, N. (1995). Bridging students' multiple worlds: African-American & Latino youth in academic outreach programs. In R. F. Macias & R. G. Garcia Ramos (Eds.), *Changing Schools for Changing Students* (pp. 245–268). Santa Barbara, CA: University of California Linguistic Minority Research Institute.

Corcoran, T. B., Walker, L. J., & White, J. L. (1988). *Working in urban schools.* Washington, DC: Institute for Educational Leadership.

Darling-Hammond, L., & Youngs, P. (2002). Defining "highly qualified teachers": What does "scientifically-based research" actually tell us? *Education Researcher 31*(9), 13–25.

Davidson, A., & Phelan, P. (1999). Students' multiple worlds. *Advances in Motivation and Achievement, 11*, 233–73.

Doyle, W. (1986). Content representation in teachers' definitions of academic work. *Journal of Curriculum Studies, 18*, 365–379.

Earthman, G. (1997). The impact of school buildings on student achievement and behavior: A review of the research. *PEB Exchange, 30*, 11–15.

Education Trust. (1988). *Education watch 1998: State and national data book, 2.* Washington, DC: Author.

Ferguson, R. (1988). Teachers' perceptions and expectations and the test score gap. In C. Jencks & M. Phillips (Eds.), *The Black-White Test Score Gap* (pp. 273–317). Washington, DC: The Brookings Institute.

Fetler, M. (1997). Where have all the teachers gone? *Education Policy Analysis Archives, 5*(2). Retrieved on January 18, 2004, from http://olam/ed.asu.ed/epaa/v5n2

Fine, M. (1991). *Framing dropouts.* Albany: State University of New York Press.

Gándara, P., & Bial, D. (2001). *Paving the way to postsecondary education: K-12 intervention programs for underrepresented youth.* Washington DC: National Center for Education Statistics.

Kahne, J., & Bailey, K. (1999). The role of social capital in youth development: The case of 'I have a dream' programs. *Educational Evaluation and Policy Analysis, 21*(3), 321–343.

Kim, J., & Mueller, C. (1978). *Factor Analysis: Statistical methods and practical issues.* Thousand Oaks, CA: Sage Publications.

Krop, C., Brewer, D., Gates, S. M., Gill, B. P., Reichardt, R. E., Sundt, M., & Throgmorton, D. (1998). *Potentially eligible students: A growing opportunity for the University of California.* Santa Monica: The RAND Corporation.

Ladson-Billings, G. (1994). The dreamkeepers: Successful teachers of African American children._San Francisco, CA: Jossey-Bass.

Lee, V. E., & Smith, J. B. (2001). *Schools that work.* New York: Teachers College Press.

McDonough, P. (1997). *Choosing colleges.* Albany: State University of New York Press.

Maxwell, L. (2000). A safe and welcoming school. *Journal of Architecture and Planning Research, 17*(4), 271–282.

Mehan, H., Okamota, D., & Adam, J. (1997). *Constructing school success: The consequences of untracking low achieving students.* Cambridge: Cambridge University Press.

Mitchell, R. E. (2002). *Segregation in California's K-12 public schools: Biases in implementation, assignment, and achievement with the multi-track year-round calendar.* Report prepared for *Williams et al. v. State of California et al.*, Superior Court, San Francisco, California.

Muthen, B. (1978). Contributions to factor analysis of dichotomized variables. *Psychometrika, 43*, 551–560.

Newmann, F. M., Wehlage, G. G., Secada, W., Marks, H., Gamoran, A., King, B., & Associates (Eds.). (1996). *Authentic achievement: Restructuring schools for intellectual quality.* San Francisco: Jossey-Bass.

Noguera, P. A. (2001). Transforming urban schools through investments in the social capital of parents. In S. Saegert, J. P. Thompson, & M. R. Warren (Eds.), *Social Capital and Poor Communities* (pp. 189–212). New York, NY: Russell Sage Foundation.

Nunnaly, J., & Bernstein, I. (1994). *Psychometric theory.* New York: McGraw-Hill.

Oakes, J. (1986). *Educational indicators: A guide for policymakers.* Center for Policy Research in Education, Santa Monica: The RAND Corporation.

Oakes, J. (2000). Grouping and tracking. In A. E. Kazdin (Ed.), *Encyclopedia of Psychology 4* (pp. 16–20). Washington, DC: American Psychological Association.

Oakes, J. (1996). Two cities: Tracking and within-school segregation. In E. C. Lagemann & L. Miller (Eds.), *Brown v. Board of Education: The Challenge for Today's Schools* (pp. 81–90). New York: Teachers College Press.

Oakes, J., Muir, K., & Joseph, R. (in press). Access and achievement in mathematics and science: Inequalities that endure and change. In J. A. Banks & C. M. Banks (Eds.), *Handbook of Research on Multicultural Education.* San Francisco: Jossey-Bass.

Oakes, J., Quartz, K. H., Ryan, S., & Lipton, M. (2000). *Becoming good American schools: The struggle for civic virtue in education reform.* San Francisco: Jossey-Bass.

Oakes, J., Rogers, J., Lipton, M., & Morell, E. (2001). The social construction of college access: Confronting the technical, cultural, and political in eligibility. In W. G. Tierney & L. S. Hagedorn (Eds.), *Extending Our Reach: Strategies For Increasing Access to College* (pp. 105–122). Albany, NY: State University of New York Press.

Panter, A. T., Swygert, K. A., Dahlstrom, W. G., & Tanaka, J. S. (1997). Factor analytic approaches to personality item-level data. *Journal of Personality Assessment, 68*, 561–589.

Phillips, M. (Winter 1997). What makes school effective? A comparison of the relation of communitarian climate and academic climate to math achievement and attendance during middle school. *American Educational Research Journal, 34*(4), 633–662.

Rivera-Batiz, F. L., & Marti, L. (1995). *A school system at risk: A study of the consequences of overcrowding in New York City public schools*. New York: Institute for Urban and Minority Education, Teachers College, Columbia University.

Sanders, W. L., & Rivers, J. C. (1996). *Cumulative and residual effects of teachers on future student academic achievement*. Knoxville: University of Tennessee Value-Added Research and Assessment Center.

Shavelson, R., McDonnell, L. M., & Oakes, J. (Eds.). (1989). *Indicators for monitoring mathematics and science education: A sourcebook*. Santa Monica: The RAND Corporation.

Stanton-Salazar, R. D. (1997). A social capital framework for understanding the socialization of racial minority children and youth. *Harvard Educational Review, 67*, 1–40.

Steele, C. (1997). A threat in the air: How stereotypes shape intellectual identity and performance, *American Psychologist, 52*(6), 613–629.

Steinberg, L. (1996). *Beyond the classroom*. New York: Simon & Schuster.

Swygert, K. A., McLeod, L. D., & Thissen, D. (2001). Factor analysis for items or testlets scored in more than two categories. In D. Thissen & H. Wainer (Eds.), *Test Scoring* (pp. 217–250). New Jersey: Lawrence Earlbaum Associates, Inc.

The College Board. (1993). *The advanced placement challenge: Providing excellence and equity for the future*. New York: author.

Tomás Rivera Center. (2001). *College knowledge: What Latino parents need to know and why they don't know it*. Claremont, CA: author.

Wenglinsky, H. (2002, February 13). How schools matter: The link between teacher classroom practices and student academic performance. *Education Policy Analysis Archives, 10*(12). Retrieved on January 7, 2004, from http://epaa.asu.edu/epaa/v10n12/

Valenzuela, A. (1999). *Subtractive schooling: U.S.-Mexican youth and the politics of caring*. Albany: State University of New York Press.

Vasquez, O., Stanton-Salazar, R., & Mehan, H. (2000). Engineering success through institutional support. In S. T. Gregory (Ed.), *The Academic Achievement of Minority Students* (pp. 214–247). Lanham, NY: University Press of America.

---

APPENDIX FOLLOWS

---

# FIGURE 2.4

## 2002 College Opportunity Ration (COR):
### California Public High Schools Prepare Few Underrepresented Ninth Graders for College

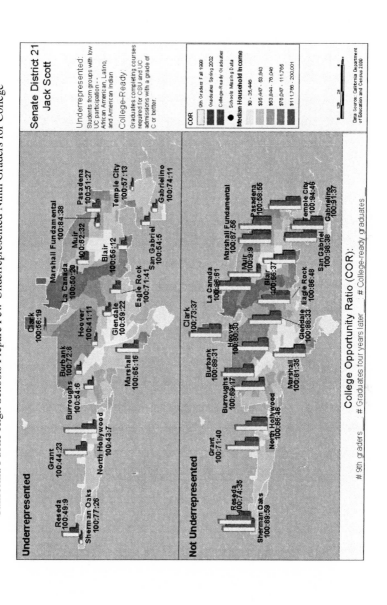

FIGURE 2.5
2002 College Opportunia Ration (COR): California Public
High Schools Prepare Few Underrepresented Ninth Graders for College

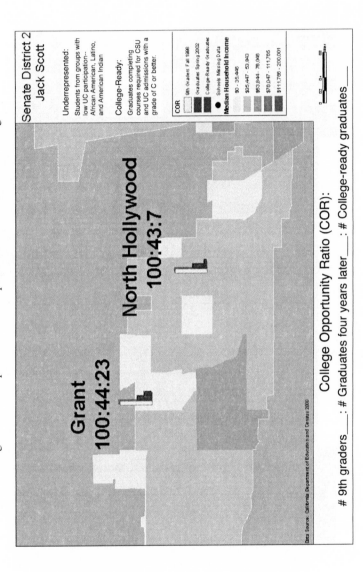

BRIAN K. FITZGERALD

Chapter Three

*Lowering Barriers to College Access:*
*Opportunities for More Effective*
*Coordination of State and*
*Federal Student Aid Policies*

INTRODUCTION

Nearly forty years ago, the federal and state governments initiated policies and
programs—through a legislative partnership—in an effort to ensure access to
higher education regardless of student and family economic circumstances. As
a result, millions of students who otherwise could not have afforded college
were able to enroll in higher education and attain degrees, which in turn pro-
pelled economic growth in the late 20th century (Advisory Committee, 2001).

However, progress toward closing the opportunity gap that continues to
exist for low- and moderate-income families remains elusive. Gaps in college
participation rates are as great now as in the 1970s and appear to be widening
despite rising economic returns to a college education (College Board, 2002b;
Fitzgerald & Delaney, 2002; Kane, 2001). In addition, significant barriers to
college enrollment exist, including the lack of accurate, timely information
about college and financial aid; complex forms and financial aid processes;

and shortfalls in student aid, especially grant aid (Ellwood & Kane, 2000; Advisory Committee, 2002, 2003).

Better coordination of federal and state policies and more effective utilization of resources and programs can mitigate access barriers and increase enrollment opportunities for low- and moderate-income students. Aligning federal and state policies can significantly simplify the process by which low-income students demonstrate eligibility for aid. This can create transparency and certainty for students, especially if the shared eligibility standards are common to federal means-tested programs, and can permit identification of eligible populations in middle school. Linking assurances of financial aid with early intervention and support services can have powerful, positive effects on the academic preparation, college enrollment, and persistence of low-income students (St. John et al., 2002).

This chapter documents these enrollment gaps and identifies the barriers to college enrollment that confront low-income, first generation, and minority students. The chapter explores and analyzes short- and long-term opportunities for improved policy making and coordination between states and the federal government in order to improve college access.

## The Federal Commitment to Access

Ensuring equal educational opportunity for all citizens represents the most important federal role in higher education. Since the passage of the Higher Education Act (HEA) in 1965, need-based student financial aid has served as the primary federal postsecondary policy instrument, attempting to ensure that students who otherwise could not afford college have the financial resources to enroll and persist through degree completion. The 1965 Act also created early intervention programs, commonly known as the TRIO programs, which promote college awareness and assist students in preparing for college.[1]

Student aid in general, and grant aid in particular, are essential to the college enrollment of low- and moderate-income students. Grants are generally acknowledged as a more effective means of encouraging students to enroll and persist in postsecondary education, especially at a four-year institution, than loan or work aid (Wolanin, 2003).

Today, the federal investment in student aid totals $55 billion a year, including almost $12 billion in grants, which, augmented by need-based grant aid from states and institutions, lowers the price of college for needy students (College Board, 2002a). The Federal Pell Grant program (Pell Grant), created in the 1972 Amendments to the HEA as a voucher program, currently provides 4.5 million low- and moderate-income recipients with grants up to a maximum of $4,050 (Department of Education, 2002a). The 1972 Amendments also created the State Student Incentive Grant program (SSIG), now the Leveraging Educational Assistance Partnership (LEAP) program, which consists of incentive grants to states that encourage creation and expansion of grant and work-study programs (Wolanin, 2003). State grants, which in some states can exceed the Pell Grant maximum award, are key access tools for low- and moderate-income students.

*States' Commitment to Access*

In the second half of the 20th century, states have made fundamental commitments to college access by creating and dramatically expanding public universities. By 2002–2003, state postsecondary appropriations reached nearly $64 billion (Palmer, 2002). As a result of these investments, 82 percent of all students and 75 percent of full-time students are enrolled in public sector institutions (College Board, 2002b). States have also supported need-based grant programs, and early outreach and intervention programs. In 2002, states collectively provided $6 billion in student aid, of which $3.9 billion was need-based. California, Illinois, New York, New Jersey, and Pennsylvania support the largest state need-based grant programs (NASS-GAP, 2003).

California provides over $1 billion in grant aid to students. The Cal Grant, the largest state need-based grant program, has existed since the 1960s; the program provides over $639 million in grants to California students and represents the second largest source of grant aid for California students. In addition, the state appropriates $561 million to public institutions for student aid (Legislative Analyst's Office, 2003). California students received $7 billion in student aid from all sources in 2001–2002 (CSAC, 2003).

In 2000, the Cal Grant program was changed from a competitive awards program to an entitlement to students who meet both financial and academic merit eligibility criteria. It now provides as much as full tuition and fee coverage for public sector students or $9,708 for students attending independent institutions (Wellman, 2002; CSAC, 2003).

In addition to providing grant funding, some states also have implemented programs to increase both academic preparation and college enrollment, most recently, combining program services with early guarantees of financial aid. In 1978, the California legislature created the nation's first such program, the California Student Opportunity and Access Program (CPEC, 2002). More recently, Indiana and Oklahoma implemented programs in the early 1990s that guarantee access and provide intervention services, and Washington State also implemented a similar program late in the decade (Advisory Committee, 2002). The Indiana program combines an effective early intervention program with an access guarantee; the program provides an in-state tuition grant to all low-income students who successfully participate. Evaluations of the Indiana 21st Century Scholars Program have documented significant improvements in the academic preparation, college attendance, and persistence rates of low-income students. Successful participants in the 21st Century Scholars program are 4.43 times more likely to enroll in a public four-year college than non-participants and persist at the same rate as all other students (St. John et al., 2002).

However, recent fiscal crises have caused many states to back away from commitments to affordable access to higher education. In particular, decreases in appropriations have resulted in significant increases in tuition in dozens of states and smaller state grants, making college less affordable (National Center for Public Policy and Higher Education, 2002; Russakoff & Argetsinger, 2003). As a result, state legislatures have initiated fundamental reexaminations of access policy and explorations of a wide range of alternatives, which include high tuition-high aid policies, student vouchers in lieu of institutional subsidies, and the wholesale replacement of fees with a post-graduation income-contingent payment mechanism (Hebel, 2002, 2003). These events suggest that barriers to college access may be rising throughout the nation.


## THE PROBLEM OF OPPORTUNITY IN AMERICA

Low-income, first-generation, and minority youth today face many barriers to college access, including inadequate academic preparation, insufficient information about college and the student aid application process, rising tuition, and shortfalls in student aid, especially grant aid. These barriers are compounded by current demographic trends in the United States, which will increase the low-income and minority college-going population and the challenge of providing college access.

### The College Participation Gap

The participation of low-income and minority youth in postsecondary education continues to lag far behind that of their middle- and upper-income peers and appears to be widening (Kane, 2001). Although the college-going rate of all students has risen, large differences, over 30 percentage points, persist. Gaps between low-income families, below $25,000, and high-income families, above $75,000, are as wide as the gaps that existed three decades ago (College Board, 2002b). Family income also determines where students enroll. Table 3.1 indicates that substantially lower percentages of low- and moderate-income students attend four-year colleges after high school, by nearly forty percentage points, than do their middle- and high-income peers.

The college-going rates in the 18 to 29-year-old population differ by race and ethnicity as well. In 1996, the nationwide college-going rate of Hispanics was 60 percent the rate of Whites, and the participation rate of African Americans was slightly more than three-quarters that of Whites. Equally troubling, the bachelor's degree attainment gaps between Whites, Hispanics, and African Americans are wider; Hispanics attain bachelor's

TABLE 3.1

Proportion of Students from Families in Each Income Quartile Who Enroll in
Postsecondary Schools within 20 Months of High School Graduation (Class of 1992)

| Parental Income Quartile | Total | Any Postsecondary Schooling | | |
|---|---|---|---|---|
| | | Vocational, Technical | 2-Year College | 4-Year College |
| Bottom | 0.60 | 0.10 | 0.22 | 0.28 |
| 3rd | 0.70 | 0.07 | 0.25 | 0.38 |
| 2nd | 0.79 | 0.06 | 0.25 | 0.48 |
| Top | 0.90 | 0.05 | 0.19 | 0.66 |
| Total | 0.75 | 0.07 | 0.23 | 0.45 |

*Source:* Ellwood and Kane (2000).

degrees at only 40 percent the rate of Whites, and African Americans at 55
percent the rate of Whites (Heller, 2001).

*Demographic Trends*

The United States will experience powerful demographic changes as the population grows from 275 million in 2000 to more than 400 million by mid-cen-
tury (Swail, 2002). By 2015, the projected national growth in the traditional
college-age population will exceed 16 percent, which, in absolute terms,
approaches 5 million youth and will rival the size of the baby boom generation. But this new cohort will be more ethnically diverse than previous cohorts
or the general population; 80 percent of this cohort will be non-White and
almost 50 percent will be Hispanic (Carnevale & Fry, 2000). California will
experience the greatest population increase, a significant portion of which will
occur among minority populations; by 2015 over 65 percent of 18 to 24 year
olds will be minorities (Swail et al., 2001).

As is the case today, it is reasonable to assume that nearly half of tomorrow's minority students will be from the lowest income families and will be
the most dependent on student aid for college access. This trend will greatly
increase the total financial aid required to ensure access and will leave public
budgets stretched thin (Advisory Committee, 2001; Kane, 2001). The strain
on the federal student aid programs today is a harbinger of future demand for
student aid. Over the past two years, the Pell Grant program has faced a shortfall in excess of a billion dollars as eligibility for grants has exceeded appropriated funds (Morgan, 2002). The Department of Education reported a 16
percent rise in Pell Grant applications and a 19 percent rise in Pell Grant
recipients between 2000–2001 and 2002–2003 (King, 2003).

## Academic Preparation

Academic preparation is key to college attendance and persistence. However, data from the 1992 National Educational Longitudinal Study (NELS) indicate that nearly a third of low-income eighth graders drop out of high school. In addition, only about half of low-income high school graduates are qualified to attend four-year colleges; only half of these college-qualified students attend four-year colleges and a quarter attend no college at all (NCES, 1997).

Inadequate academic preparation, including the failure to graduate from high school, is a significant barrier to access for minorities, who fail to graduate from high school at significantly higher rates than Whites. Currently, the percentage of 18 to 24 year olds nationwide who did not complete high school is twice as high for African Americans as Whites and more than four times as high for Hispanics (NCES, 2002). This pattern is also reflected in the 25 and older population. The percentage of this population that did not earn a high school diploma is nearly twice as high for African Americans as for Whites and three and a half times as high for Hispanics (Heller, 2001).

This pattern of under-preparation exists even in states with high rates of high school graduation. While overall high school completion rates for California are significantly higher than the national average, the state has the second highest minority dropout level in the nation; three out of four California dropouts are minority students. Nationwide, approximately one out of every six African American, Latino, and Native American students drops out of high school before graduation, which is double the rate of White or Asian students (Swail et al., 2001). Although the rate of high school diploma attainment for African Americans is nearly equal that of Whites, the rate for Hispanics is only slightly more than half that of Whites (Heller, 2001).

## Complexity

The impact of financial aid can be seen in two distinct outcomes. First, sending clear and unequivocal messages that adequate aid will be available upon graduation from high school can make college seem possible for low-income students in middle school. Second, financial aid can make college a reality for high school graduates by providing adequate funds to permit enrollment and persistence. Yet, for several reasons, the current system of financial aid falls short on both counts. First, the student aid system is so opaque that no student can determine the amount of need-based aid for which she is eligible until quite late in the process—only after completing an application—which limits the effectiveness of aid in increasing families' investment in higher education (Kane, 2003). Second, the application process itself is complex and burdensome, especially for the most at-risk students for whom the eventual outcome—maximum eligibility—is a virtual certainty, creating an unnecessary barrier (Advisory Committee, 2002).

Third, federal and state application requirements are inconsistent, especially for the lowest income applicants.

Issues of student aid complexity and lack of reliable, early information about eligibility have plagued the federal and state student aid programs since their inception. The HEA of 1965 and the HEA Amendments of 1972 put into place an array of individual programs with different eligibility rules and, indeed, different application processes. For example, in creating what is now the Pell Grant program, Congress created a unique, more highly targeted eligibility formula than either of the models controlled by the American College Testing (ACT) and College Scholarship Service (CSS) of the College Board *and* a separate, free application form[2] processed by what is now the U.S. Department of Education (Fitzgerald, 1990, 1991). The 1972 Amendments also created the SSIG program, which encouraged virtually every state to create or expand state need-based grant programs (Wolanin, 2003). However, this expansion produced additional, unique application requirements in virtually every state. The new reality of student aid in the 1970s became a maze of multiple forms, eligibility models that produced conflicting results, and annual student fees that shrouded the programs in impenetrable complexity.

Although steps toward simplification were taken in the 1980s, the first major simplification occurred in 1992 when Congress created an integrated eligibility model for all federal programs and a single, free national application form, the Free Application for Federal Student Aid (FAFSA), which included data needed to award state aid. In addition, Congress expanded a little-used "Simple Needs Test" (SNT), which eliminated the requirement for applicants to provide assets and created a new automatic eligibility process for families with incomes below $15,000—the "automatic zero" or auto-zero—simplifying application and making eligibility more certain. These changes created a true national delivery system for the first time, as well as a streamlined application process.

Despite these statutory changes, by the late 1990s all students were required to complete the entire FAFSA because the Department of Education had eliminated the simplified application. When implementing FAFSA on the web, which customizes forms for different types of applicants, the Department nonetheless required completion of the entire application. The Department altered FAFSA on the Web in 2003 to create simplified applications for students who qualify for the SNT or auto-zero for academic year 2003–2004. Although 47 states have adopted FAFSA as the application for state grants, only 18 states have adopted federal eligibility standards (e.g., auto-zero) and permit use of the simplified application. The remaining 29 states determine eligibility differently, requiring students to complete the entire FAFSA, including additional state questions, in order to apply for state aid. These differing eligibility standards and application requirements make the student aid system more complex and opaque and limit the ability of student aid to promote aspirations, academic preparation, and, ultimately, enrollment.

*Financial Barriers*

Research has consistently demonstrated the importance of net price (college costs remaining after student aid) and particularly net price adjusted for the family's ability to pay for college on decisions regarding college attendance.[3] In particular, this body of literature has indicated that low-income students are most price sensitive and are most dependent on student aid to overcome financial barriers.

Despite wide recognition of the need to reduce financial barriers to ensure the enrollment of low-income students, the net price of higher education for low-income student has risen to record heights. Indeed, over the past thirty years the share of family income necessary to pay for enrollment in a four-year public college has risen from 42 to 63 percent for low-income families, while the share has risen only slightly for middle-income families and is unchanged for high-income families (College Board, 2002b). In contrast, financial aid, especially grant aid, has failed to keep pace with the rise in college prices, producing large gaps between college cost of attendance and available financial aid and creating significant barriers for those who can least afford college.

*Empty Promises: The Myth of College Access in America* (Advisory Committee, 2002) analyzed the impact of financial barriers on academically qualified low-income high school graduates. The report demonstrated that two decades of under-funded grant aid has erected substantial financial barriers to college for low- and moderate-income students, the most price sensitive of all students. As a result, table 3.2 demonstrates that unmet need[4] has reached unprecedented levels. On average, annual unmet need for low-income families in the late 1990s reached $3,200 at community colleges, $3,800 at four-year public colleges, and $6,200 at four-year private colleges. By contrast, high-income families face only $400 in unmet need at four-year public colleges.

TABLE 3.2

Average Annual Unmet Need Facing High School Graduates by
Family Income and Type of College (Full-time, Dependent Students)

| | Type of College | | |
| --- | --- | --- | --- |
| *Family Income* | *Public 2-Year* | *Public 4-Year* | *Private 4-Year* |
| 0–$24,999 | $3,200 | $3,800 | $6,200 |
| $25,000–$49,999 | $2,700 | $3,000 | $4,900 |
| $50,000–$74,999 | $600 | $1,500 | $4,500 |
| $75,000–above | $100 | $400 | $3,000 |

*Source:* U.S. Department of Education, NCES (1999).

However, this gap between college expenses and financial aid belies the true magnitude of the financing challenges facing these families. Most low-income families are able to contribute only a small portion of college expenses and, consequently, the real financial barrier is total college expenses minus all grant aid. Yet, as figure 3.1 indicates, grants comprise about one-third of total student aid, and the work and borrowing required to make enrollment a reality can be substantial.

High levels of unmet need even after work-study and loans cause large numbers of low-income students to fill the gap with additional work. Excessive work, often as high as 35 hours a week or more, can reduce persistence and degree completion (Advisory Committee, 2001; NCES, 1997). In addition, annual borrowing among low-income students increased throughout the 1990s by 65 percent to $3,000 in annual borrowing and cumulative debt increased by 50 percent to $15,000. Low-income minority students borrow at much higher rates than high-income students and often much more than all other students; 71 percent of low-income students graduate with debt compared to 44 percent of high-income students. African American students borrow $2,000 more than other students, and over half of both African American and Hispanic students graduate with debt levels that are considered unmanageable by student loan industry standards (US PIRG, 2002).

FIGURE 3.1

Work and Loan Burden Facing Low-income Families
with High Unmet Need at a Typical Four-year Public College

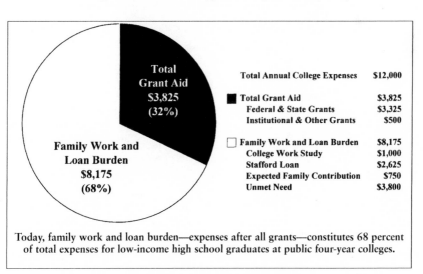

| Total Annual College Expenses | $12,000 |
|---|---|
| ■ Total Grant Aid | $3,825 |
| Federal & State Grants | $3,325 |
| Institutional & Other Grants | $500 |
| ☐ Family Work and Loan Burden | $8,175 |
| College Work Study | $1,000 |
| Stafford Loan | $2,625 |
| Expected Family Contribution | $750 |
| Unmet Need | $3,800 |

Today, family work and loan burden—expenses after all grants—constitutes 68 percent of total expenses for low-income high school graduates at public four-year colleges.

*Source:* Advisory Committee on Student Financial Assistance (2002).

Like low-income students, moderate-income students (family income between $25,000 and $50,000) confront similar financial barriers: $2,700 in unmet need at community colleges; $3,000 at four-year public colleges; and $4,900 at four-year private colleges (see table 3.2).

*Impact on Student Enrollment Behavior*

Financial barriers represent key factors in determining whether academically prepared low-income students have access to a four-year public institution and a bachelor's degree. Focusing on these students provides an opportunity to isolate the effects of finances from academic preparation and other factors on college-going behavior.

Clearly, while academic preparation plays a role in determining whether students will go on to college, the differences in college-going rates of even those low-income students who graduate from high school academically prepared to attend four-year colleges lag behind those of students from middle- and high-income families. Ellwood and Kane (2000) found that although some differences in academic preparation are accounted for by family background, very large gaps remain between students from high- and low-income families and between high and low levels of parental education. Youth who appear to be similarly prepared academically when emerging from high school enroll in college at very different rates depending on their parent's income and education.[5] Their analysis indicates that even after controlling for academic preparation and parental education, the odds that a low-income student will attend college are considerably lower than a high-income student due to the greater sensitivity of low-income families to net price.

Ellwood and Kane's analysis in table 3.3 also finds differences in college-going rates by students' scores on a standardized test of basic math skills administered in the 12th grade. Among students with test scores in the bottom third of the class of 1992, the differences in enrollment by family income are particularly large; 72 percent of youths from the highest income category went on to postsecondary schooling despite low test scores, while only 48 percent of low-income students with such test scores went on to college. However, differences remain even among students with test scores in the top third of their class; 96 percent of high-income, high-test-score students went on to postsecondary schooling compared with 82 percent of low-income, high-test-score youths. The differences in four-year college entry are particularly striking. Only 68 percent of the low-income, high-test-score youths went on to a four-year college within 20 months of high school graduation compared to 84 percent of high-income, high-test-score youths.[6]

The Advisory Committee (2002) used a complementary means of assessing the impact of financial barriers on student behavior, analyzing

TABLE 3.3

Percent of Students Enrolling in Postsecondary Institutions within 20 Months
by Parental Income Quartile and Test Scores (Class of 1992)

| Parental Income Quartile | Enrollment | Math Test Tertile | | | Overall Average |
|---|---|---|---|---|---|
| | | *Bottom* | *Middle* | *Top* | *Average* |
| Lowest | | 48% (1.6) | 67% (1.8) | 82% (2.1) | 60% (1.1) |
| Second | Any | 50% (1.9) | 75% (1.6) | 90% (1.2) | 71% (1.0) |
| Third | Postsecondary | 64% (2.1) | 83% (1.3) | 95% (0.8) | 82% (0.8) |
| Highest | Institution | 72% (2.4) | 89% (1.2) | 96% (0.6) | 90% (0.7) |
| Overall Average | | 55% (1.0) | 79% (0.8) | 93% (0.6) | 76% (0.5) |
| Lowest | | 15% (1.1) | 33% (1.8) | 68% (2.5) | 30% (1.0) |
| Second | 4-Year | 14% (1.3) | 37% (1.8) | 69% (1.8) | 39% (1.1) |
| Third | College | 21% (1.8) | 47% (1.8) | 78% (1.5) | 52% (1.1) |
| Highest | | 27% (2.3) | 59% (2.0) | 84% (1.1) | 67% (1.0) |
| Overall Average | | 17% (0.7) | 44% (0.9) | 77% (0.8) | 47% (0.5) |

*Note:* Standard errors in parentheses. Figures based on tabulation of 8,313 observations from the National Education Longitudinal Study of 1988.

*Source:* Ellwood and Kane (2000).

the enrollment patterns of those students who graduate from high school academically prepared, and, therefore, more likely to attend a four-year college.

Although high financial barriers affect college-qualified, low-income students at many steps leading up to college enrollment, their clearest effect is on college enrollment decisions. Table 3.4 reports that 48 percent of low-income, college-qualified students do not attend a four-year college within two years of graduation and 22 percent attend no college at all. As in the case of low-income high school graduates, the financial barriers confronting college-qualified, moderate-income high school graduates have a substantial and comparable impact on their expectations, plans, and enrollment behavior; 43 percent do not enroll in a four-year college within two years of graduation and 16 percent do not attend any college at all (Advisory Committee, 2002).

Consistent with the findings of Ellwood and Kane (2000), the Advisory Committee (2001) analysis indicates that these enrollment differences do not narrow, even among the most highly qualified students. Among those high school graduates who are rated as highly and very highly qualified, high-income students attend four-year colleges at a rate that is 43 percent higher than their low-income counterparts—67 percent versus 47 percent.

TABLE 3.4

Access Pipeline: Impact of Family Income and Unmet Need on the College-going
Behavior of College Qualified High School Graduates by Family Income

| Family Income | Unmet Need at a 4-year Public College | Expect to Finish College | Plan to Attend a 4-year College | Take Entrance Exam and Apply | Enroll in a 4-year College | Do Not Enroll in Any College |
|---|---|---|---|---|---|---|
| 0–$24,999 | $3,800 | 70% | 63% | 62% | 52% | 22% |
| $25,000– $49,999 | $3,000 | 78% | 68% | 68% | 57% | 16% |
| $50,000– $74,999 | $1,500 | 90% | 80% | 82% | 73% | 7% |
| $75,000– above | $400 | 95% | 88% | 91% | 83% | 4% |

*Source:* Calculated from data in U.S. Department of Education, NCES (1997).

The highest achieving poor students attend college at the same rate, 78 percent, as the lowest achieving wealthy students, 77 percent[7] (Advisory Committee, 2001).

The substantial proportion of college-qualified, low- and moderate-income high school graduates who are unable to enroll in a four-year college—or any college at all—suggests that large numbers of students were denied access to college in 2001–2002; that is, 406,000 college-qualified high school graduates from low- and moderate-income families were prevented from enrolling in a four-year college, and 168,000 of them did not enroll in any college at all (Advisory Committee 2002). These annual figures portend very substantial losses over the course of this decade. Figure 3.2 suggests that 4.4 million students will not attend a four-year college and 2 million students will not attend any college at all.

## POLICY OPTIONS FOR
## IMPROVING ACCESS AND OPPORTUNITY

Reauthorization of the Higher Education Act provides an opportunity to make key changes to the student aid programs that can enhance access to higher education, particularly for the lowest-income students, and to coordinate these

FIGURE 3.2
Cumulative Impact of High Unmet Need on
Low- and Moderate-income High School Graduates from 2001-2010

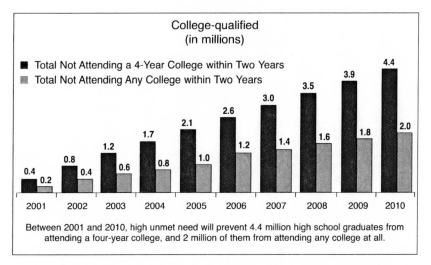

College-qualified
(in millions)

■ Total Not Attending a 4-Year College within Two Years
▒ Total Not Attending Any College within Two Years

Between 2001 and 2010, high unmet need will prevent 4.4 million high school graduates from attending a four-year college, and 2 million of them from attending any college at all.

*Source:* Calculated from data in U.S. Department of Education, NCES (1997) and (2001).

changes at the federal and state levels. The challenge in the 2004 reauthorization, however, is to implement systemic and long-lasting solutions to the nation's core college access and persistence problems through a national access and persistence partnership that will coordinate federal and state access policies, including student aid.

The Advisory Committee recommended to Congress in May, 2003, the creation of a national partnership that links the federal government, states, colleges, and K-12 schools through the existing Title IV programs, in pursuit of an increase in access and persistence rates for the nation's neediest students and an increase in academically qualified students. To be as successful as possible, the partnership should provide an early assurance of financial access, simplify the application process, provide adequate grant aid, and enhance the likelihood of persistence. A key goal of the partnership should be to ensure that states and institutions hold low-income students harmless against increases in tuition by increasing their financial aid as tuition or fees rise. Federal legislation is necessary as a catalyst to encourage states to make such policy changes.

Senator Jack Reed (D-RI) introduced SB 2477 in May, 2004, with a bipartisan group of co-sponsors. This bill restructures the Leveraging Educational Access Partnerships program (LEAP) to provide additional funds to states that join in such an access and persistence partnership. These partnerships include early notification of students regarding their eligibility for federal and state aid and encouragement of states to grant free-lunch-eligible students maximum state grants. However, such federally sponsored partnerships could be years away from passage and implementation.

Perhaps the most immediate and promising approach to enhancing access could come from simplifying the application process for low-income students and providing an early assurance of access, if only through greater certainty of eligibility and improved information. Some steps could be taken immediately. At the federal level, the Department of Education could increase the number of applicants who use the simplified Web applications. In addition, the department could reintroduce a simplified paper application, dropped in the late 1990s, and could introduce, for the first time, an FAFSA EZ for more than a million filers. The department could reduce overall application burden for all Web applicants by eliminating those state questions that are not required by the applicant's state of residence. Use of a "smart" application could present applicants only with those questions necessary to determine eligibility for federal aid and their state's need-based program.

The department could better manage the application process and encourage states to make administrative or statutory changes in order to adopt these simpler forms for purposes of state need-based aid. For example, statutes in some states require financial and other data that force students to complete the entire FAFSA even though federal rules permit their completing a simplified application. Yet, in several states that do not have such statutory requirements, including one that does not have a state grant program, students complete the entire FAFSA. In addition, some states are changing statutes to permit the use of simplified applications. In 2003, California passed Senate Bill 728 that, for the first time, permitted nearly half a million applicants to use the simplified forms in 2005–2006.

A more aggressive approach involves federal statutory changes. At the federal level, increasing the income threshold on the auto-zero[8] from $15,000 to $25,000 or beyond would expand eligibility, although this requires amending the HEA. The Reed Bill, S 2477, not only makes this change, but also includes a host of other changes designed to simplify the federal and state aid application processes.

Reconsidering the income threshold on the auto-zero provides the opportunity to link student aid eligibility to those programs that serve low-income students while they are in middle school and high school. This alignment would project federal and state aid eligibility into middle school, providing low-income families with better information about financial programs and greater certainty about financial award amounts. It would also lower application barriers by allowing earlier application completion to meet state and institutional deadlines, thereby increasing the aid awarded to low-income students, who can miss state deadlines for completed applications and, therefore, receive no state aid.

*Expanding the Auto-zero*

Expanding the auto-zero by increasing the income threshold has two effects, increasing the number of applicants who can utilize the auto-zero application for federal and state aid and increasing the cost to the programs. In 2003–2004, the auto-zero income threshold was $15,000. Over 1.5 million or about a third of Pell Grant recipients qualified for the auto-zero and were awarded approximately $3.5 billion in Pell Grants. In 2005 the auto-zero was increased to $20,000 and table 3.5 shows the approximate increase in recipients as a result of this congressional action.

A range of options exists for further increasing the income threshold. For example, table 3.5 shows the nationwide impact of raising the threshold to $25,000. This would result in a 34 percent increase in students eligible for auto-zero from the prior income threshold of $15,000. Of the more than 2.2 million students eligible for auto-zero, less than 1 percent would be newly Pell eligible. Raising the income threshold to $25,000 would increase total awards to auto-zero qualified recipients by 2.5 percent, with 72 percent of the additional funds going to previously Pell-eligible students.

TABLE 3.5
Effects of Raising the Automatic Zero Income Threshold
Nationwide for Pell Grant Applicants Academic Year 2003–2004

| *Effects on Auto-zero Eligibility and Program Costs* | | *Income Threshold* | | | |
|---|---|---|---|---|---|
| | | $20,000 | $25,000 | $30,000 | $35,000 |
| Auto Zero Eligibility | Current Pell Recipients | 1,916,544 | 2,235,517 | 2,485,120 | 2,663,641 |
| | New Pell Recipients | 11,165 | 28,753 | 51,369 | 75,407 |
| | Total Auto-zero Eligible | 1,927,709 | 2,264,270 | 2,536,489 | 2,739,048 |
| Program Costs | To Current Pell Recipients | $77 m. | $214 m. | $383 m. | $548 m. |
| | To New Pell Recipients | $30 m. | $79 m. | $141 m. | $210 m. |
| | Total Increase in Costs | $107 m. | $293 m. | $524 m. | $758 m. |

*Source:* U.S. Department of Education, Office of Postsecondary Education, Pell Grant Cost Estimation Model, Update.

Table 3.5 indicates that at an income threshold of $35,000, 76.8 percent, more students, or more than 2.7 million, are eligible for auto-zero, with 2.75 percent of those newly Pell eligible. Total awards would increase by 21.6 percent, and 72 percent of that increase would go to current Pell recipients. Overall, increasing the income threshold could provide significant benefits to students who are currently eligible for Pell with modest to moderate increases in program cost depending on the income threshold selected.

### Aligning the Auto-zero with Federal Benefit Programs

Selecting a new income threshold for the auto-zero provides policy makers with an opportunity to go beyond a narrow assessment of costs and increases in recipients. Indeed, improving early information and certainty of awards should be a key consideration in the calculus of selection. Consequently, linkages with means-tested federal benefit programs that target the Pell-eligible population should be explored; in particular, the eligibility income ranges of means-tested federal programs should be a central consideration in selecting a higher auto-zero income threshold.

Aligning eligibility for the auto-zero with the eligibility requirements for federal means-tested benefit programs, which target low-income populations and use of a national eligibility standard, can increase not only application benefits, but early information and early award notification as well. Two federal programs, the Free or Reduced Lunch Program and Food Stamps, both administered by the U. S. Department of Agriculture, meet these criteria. Both provide benefits to families earning 130 percent of the poverty threshold, although the Reduced Lunch Program serves families who earn up to 180 percent of the poverty threshold. In 2003, families of four with an income up to $23,530 are eligible for both Food Stamp and Free Lunch benefits, and families with income up to $33,485 are eligible for reduced price lunches.

Utilizing the Free or Reduced School Lunch program has an added benefit: local schools determine eligibility for benefits and, consequently, possess rosters of eligible students that can be used to target information and intervention services. Existing programs of this type, including the federal TRIO and GEAR UP programs, currently use Free or Reduced Lunch to reach and qualify students for services. For example, the Indiana 21st Century Scholars program sends program notices and applications to all Free or Reduced School Lunch eligible students.

In addition, several bills introduced in the 108th Congress, for example, HR 2956, would permit applicants and their families who receive benefits under certain federal means-test benefit programs, including Free or Reduced School Lunch, to utilize the auto-zero application process. These provisions would expand eligibility for the auto-zero and ensure that students so identified in middle or high school would qualify for a maximum Pell Grant. Thus, the number of students benefiting from the auto-zero could be higher than the estimates discussed previously.

## IMPLICATIONS FOR ACCESS AND OPPORTUNITY

The current under-participation of low-income students and minorities in higher education and accompanying lower rates of bachelor's degree attainment represent some of the most important education policy problems confronting federal and state governments. The demographic wave that will swell the numbers of these students makes the problem more pressing, especially in states such as California and Texas. This chronic under-participation is the result of many factors: non-completion of high school or failure to meet academic requirements for college enrollment; the lack of early, reliable information about the net price of college; the complexity associated with application for student aid; and, finally, financial barriers that inhibit enrollment and persistence to degree attainment. Better coordination of federal and state policies and more effective use of resources could have multiple, positive effects on low- and moderate-income and minority students across each of these problem areas. In addition, as state policy makers explore a range of access policy alternatives, including high tuition-high aid, these barriers must serve as key variables in the calculus of decision making.

Nationwide, a long-term strategy of developing broad federal-state access partnerships designed to achieve this coordination could address each of these barriers to the success of low-income and minority students by complementing efforts to boost middle and high school achievement and enhancing college enrollment and degree attainment by lowering financial barriers. Such partnerships, which would differ according to state problems and resources, would link the federal government, states, colleges, schools, and early intervention programs to the academic preparation and college enrollment of low-income and minority students.

Narrower approaches, including simplifying federal and state aid application processes and aligning eligibility criteria, could address some parts of the problem in a significant fashion. Creating greater certainty about eligibility for at least federal and state aid could minimize the opacity of the current system and make academic and financial planning for college more straightforward. Simplifying the application process could lower barriers to college, even without a full-fledged access partnership.

In the long run, better coordination of federal and state aid policies, and integration of access assurances with aid information and intervention programs, can improve access for low- and moderate-income and minority students. However, federal-state access partnerships that could encourage these efforts may take several years to create because they require federal legislation. Nevertheless, making shorter term administrative changes and amending state statutes can advance these goals.

Fiscal conditions at the federal and state levels pose serious challenges to making progress on this agenda. At the federal level, the half-trillion dollar budget deficit and the $1.2 billion shortfall in the Pell Grant program two years running place tremendous strains on the program's finances and perhaps limit the ability to expand the auto-zero beyond $25,000. This financial backdrop places significant constraints on the process of reauthorizing the HEA, which may preclude broadening the LEAP program to establish new federal-state access partnerships.

Likewise, state deficits and the potential need to limit enrollments in all public sectors has confronted lawmakers in many states with the challenge of fundamentally restructuring statewide access policies. In order to maintain, at a minimum, the current level of access, the process of examining policy alternatives must address the current barriers to access confronting low-income and minority students. Alternatives that increase the real net price of higher education for low-income students will exacerbate the under-participation of these students, even the highly qualified among them. Even raising the "sticker price" at public institutions, that is, a high tuition/fee policy, without an enhanced commitment to need-based grants/high aid coupled with a strong "guarantee" of access likely will discourage many students from becoming prepared for college and enrolling. They may perceive the new, higher cost of college as out of their reach. Notwithstanding these fiscal and political constraints, the degree of opportunity afforded the next generation of low- and moderate-income and minority youth over the current decade will not only represent a telling insight into the nation's and states' commitments to their citizens, but also will determine the economic future of the nation and many states for decades to come. Coordination of eligibility policy and application processes at the federal and state levels can eliminate the opacity of the current aid system and provide greater certainty for low-income and minority students, which will enhance college access and opportunity.

## NOTES

The authors would like to acknowledge the contributions of several individuals to this chapter. Steve Carter at the U.S. Department of Education ran the Pell Grant simulations analyzed in this chapter. Kirstin McCarthy and Nicole Barry of the Advisory Committee, and Jeneva Stone provided editorial assistance. The views expressed in this chapter are those of the author and should not be attributed to the Advisory Committee on Student Financial Assistance, the University of California at Los Angeles, or any other organization.

1. In addition to the Pell Grant program, federal allocations are made for Supplemental Educational Opportunity Grants (SEOG), which are matching grants provided to participating institutions, generally used to supplement Pell Grants for needy students. Other Federal student aid programs include the Federal Family Education Loan Program, the William D. Ford Direct Loan Program, the Work-study Program,

TRIO, Gaining Early Awareness and Readiness for Undergraduate Programs (GEAR UP), High School Equivalency Programs, and College Assistance Migrant Programs.

2. ACT and the CSS charged fees to process their forms, which were used to determine eligibility for the campus-based programs created by the 1965 HEA.

3. For reviews of literature and analyses of the effects of net price and student aid on college enrollment see, for example, Fitzgerald and Delaney (2002), Ellwood and Kane (2000), and McPherson and Schapiro (1999).

4. Unmet need is the portion of college expenses not covered by what the family can reasonably pay, otherwise known as the expected family contribution (EFC), and student aid, including work-study and loans.

5. Ellwood and Kane (2000) note that parental education picks up some of the effects of income on enrollment through measurement error and may more closely measure the family's long-term wealth than a single year of income.

6. Although table 3.3 accounts for only one difference between high- and low-income youths (math test scores), Ellwood and Kane (2000) included a longer list of student characteristics in attempting to control for other differences in academic preparation between high- and low-income students. Although the differences in college enrollment rates can be partially attributed to differences in measured academic preparation among high school seniors, a substantial difference in college entry remains.

7. See also Lee (1999) and McPherson and Schapiro (1999).

8. The auto-zero is a special statutory provision for very low-income families that assigns a zero expected family contribution (EFC)(ensuring a maximum Pell Grant and other aid(based only on the parents' income. In contrast, the calculation of eligibility for other families involves dozens of items including student income and family assets. The auto-zero both reduces complexity and increases certainty regarding eligibility.

## REFERENCES

Advisory Committee on Student Financial Assistance. (2001). *Access denied: Restoring the nation's commitment to equal educational opportunity.* Washington, DC: Author.

Advisory Committee on Student Financial Assistance. (2002). *Empty promises: The myth of college access in America.* Washington, DC: Author.

Advisory Committee on Student Financial Assistance. (2003). *Efforts to Improve College Access.* Washington, DC: Author.

California Postsecondary Education Commission (CPEC). (2002). *The California Postsecondary Education Commission's Public Agenda: Priorities for Action.* Commission Report 02–5. Sacramento, CA: Author.

California Student Aid Commission (CSAC). ( 2003). *Facts at Your Fingertips: Grant & Loan Programs 2000–2001.* Sacramento, CA: Author.

Carnevale, A. P., & Fry, R. A. (2000). *Crossing the great divide: Can we achieve equity when Generation Y goes to college?* ETS Leadership 2000 Series. Princeton, NJ: Educational Testing Service.

College Board. (2002a). *Trends in student aid, 2002.* Washington, DC: Author.

College Board. (2002b). *Trends in college pricing, 2002.* Washington, DC: Author.

Ellwood, D. T., & Kane, T. J. (2000). Who is getting a college education? Family background and the growing gaps in enrollment. In S. Danziger & J. Waldfogel (Eds.), *Securing the Future: Investing in Children from Birth to College.* New York: Russell Sage Foundation.

Fitzgerald, B. K. (1990). Equity and efficiency: An analysis of simplifying the Pell Grant eligibility formula. Unpublished doctoral thesis, Harvard University.

Fitzgerald, B. K. (1991). Simplification of need analysis and delivery: Imperatives and opportunities. In J. Merisotis (Ed.), *The Changing Dimensions of Student Aid.* San Francisco: Jossey-Bass.

Fitzgerald, B. K., & Delaney, J. A. (2002). Educational opportunity in America. In D. Heller (Ed.), *Condition of Access. Higher Education for Lower Income Students.* Westport, CT: Praeger.

Hebel, S. (2002, November 8). Colorado eyes voucher system to ease financial strain. *The Chronicle of Higher Education, 49*(11).

Hebel, S. (2003, October 10). California budget woes lead colleges to limit access. *The Chronicle of Higher Education, 50*(7).

Heller, D. E. (2001). *The effects of tuition prices and financial aid on enrollment in higher education: California and the nation.* Cordova, CA: EdFund.

H.R. 4911, the "Higher Education Extension Act of 2006," which extends programs authorize Higher Education Act of 1965 through June 30, 2006.

Kane, T. J. (2001). Assessing the American financial aid system: What we know, what we need to know. In M. Devlin (Ed.), *Forum Futures 2001: Exploring the Future of Higher Education.* Cambridge, MA: Forum for the Future of Higher Education.

Kane, T. J. (2003). *A Quasi-experimental estimate of the impact of financial aid on college-going.* Working Paper No. 9703. Cambridge, MA: National Bureau of Economic Research.

King, J. E. (2003). *2003 Status Report on the Pell Grant Program.* Washington, DC: The American Council on Education.

Lee, J. B. (1999). How do students and families pay for college? In J. E. King (Ed.), *Financing a College Education: How It Works, How It's Changing.* Phoenix, AZ: The American Council on Education and The Oryx Press.

Legislative Analyst Office. (2003). *California spending plan 2003–04.* Sacramento, CA: Author.

McPherson, M. S., & Schapiro, M. O. (1999, May). *Reinforcing stratification in American higher education: Some disturbing trends.* St. Paul, MN: Macalester Forum on Higher Education Conference, Diversity and Stratification in American Higher Education.

Morgan, R. (2002, August 16). Pell grant program may still face $1 billion shortfall. *The Chronicle of Higher Education, 48*(49).

National Association of State Student Grant and Aid Programs (NASSGAP). (2003). *33rd Annual NASSGAP Survey.* Springfield, IL: Author.

National Center for Educational Statistics. (1997). *Access to postsecondary education for the 1992 high school graduates.* Washington, DC: Author.

National Center for Educational Statistics. (2002). *Digest of educational statistics.* Washington, DC: Author.

National Center for Public Policy and Higher Education. (2002). *Losing ground: A national status report on the affordability of American higher education.* San Jose, CA: Author.

Palmer, J. C. (2002). *Grapevine: A national database of tax support for higher education.* Normal, IL: Illinois State University Press.

Russakoff, D., & Argetsinger, A. (2003, July 22). States plan big tuition increases. *The Washington Post.*

St. John, E. P., Musoba, D. G, Simmons, A. B., & Chung, C. G. (2002). *Meeting the access challenge: Indiana's twenty-first century scholars program.* Bloomington, IA: Indiana Education Policy Center.

Swail, W. S., Gladieux, L. E., & Lee, J. B. (2001). *The California dream and its future: indicators of educational and economic opportunity in the golden state.* Cordova, CA: EdFund.

Swail, W. S. (July 2002). Higher education and the new demographics: Questions for Policy. *Change Magazine.* Washington, DC: American Association for Higher Education.

US PIRG. (2002). *The burden of borrowing. A report on the rising rates of student loan debt.* Washington, DC: Author.

Wellman, J. (2002). *Accounting for student aid: How state policy and student aid connect.* Washington, DC: The Institute for Higher Education Policy.

Wolanin, T. R. (2003). *Reauthorizing the Higher Education Act: Issues and options.* Washington, DC: The Institute for Higher Education Policy.

SAUL GEISER
VERONICA SANTELICES

Chapter Four

# The Role of Advanced Placement and Honors Courses in College Admissions

## THE EXPANDING ROLE OF ADVANCED PLACEMENT IN COLLEGE ADMISSIONS

Begun in 1955, the original intent of the Advanced Placement (AP) program was to provide students the opportunity to take college-level coursework and earn college credit while still in high school. Initially AP was used almost exclusively for purposes of college credit and placement, as distinct from admissions. One difficulty in using AP in admissions decisions is that students ordinarily do not take advanced courses until their junior and senior years in high school, and their scores on the end-of-course AP exams are not available in many cases until well after the admissions process is completed. For that reason, colleges and universities first used AP exam scores mainly to award course credits, allowing high-achieving students to place out of introductory courses and move directly into more advanced college work (Commission on the Future of the Advanced Placement Program, 2001).

The expansion of AP into the area of admissions began only gradually and did not accelerate until the 1980s. This development appears to be confined to highly selective colleges and universities, reflecting those institutions' need to make increasingly fine distinctions among growing numbers of applicants (National Research Council, 2002a). According to a recent survey of deans of admission from 264 colleges and universities conducted by the National Research Council (2002a), the primary rationale for increased emphasis on AP and other honors courses in admissions is to assist in identifying highly qualified students.

> Because past performance is deemed a strong predictor of student performance, admissions officers carefully review applicants' transcripts to determine how well and to what extent the applicants have taken advantage of the school- and community-based opportunities available to them in high school. Admissions personnel generally view the presence of AP or IB [International Baccalaureate] courses on a transcript as an indicator of the applicant's willingness to confront academic challenges. (p. 55)[1]

AP courses are useful to admissions officers at selective colleges and universities for other reasons as well. Such courses may serve as indicators of the quality of the academic program offered by the applicant's high school and thereby assist in comparing students from different schools. Moreover, consideration of AP and honors courses in admissions decisions can serve an important incentive or "signaling" function in driving needed changes in the schools (Kirst, 1998). Especially for leading public universities, emphasis on AP and honors as admissions criteria can set de facto standards for public schools in their states, creating pressure on the schools to upgrade curricula and instruction. At the same time, students have the incentive to challenge themselves to attempt more rigorous coursework, knowing that this will be viewed favorably in their college applications. The incentive or signaling effect of college admissions criteria for students and schools was one of the primary considerations leading to the adoption of AP as an admissions criterion at the University of California, as described later in this chapter.

Today, almost all selective colleges and universities give special consideration to AP and honors courses in admissions decisions, although the manner in which this information is used varies from institution to institution.[2] Some, like UC, recalculate an applicant's high school grade point average (HSGPA) to give additional "bonus points" for approved AP/honors coursework. Others do not recalculate HSGPA but use the HSGPA reported on an applicant's transcript, thus implicitly accepting the school or district weighting of AP/honors; about 69 percent of American high schools now grant bonus grade points for AP/honors, according to a 2003 survey by the National Association for College Admission Counseling (NACAC, 2004). But beyond the recalculation of HSGPA, the most widespread practice among admissions officers is to consider the number of AP/honors courses as part of the comprehensive review of an applicant's high school record. Institutions that use a more quantitative form of comprehensive review often assign extra points to

AP and IB courses, which are considered more rigorous than other honors-level courses. Institutions that use a more qualitative form of comprehensive review tend to use AP/honors in other ways, such as comparing the records of applicants from the same high school or comparing the extent to which applicants from different schools have taken advantage of the curricular opportunities available to them.

Given its expanding role in college admissions, the AP program grew dramatically during the 1980s and 1990s. According to figures from the College Board, which owns and operates the program, the total number of students taking AP exams (no national data are available on the number of students taking AP courses) increased from 133,702 in 1980–1981 to 1,017,396 in 2003–2004, a 660 percent increase, and the total number of AP exams taken increased from 178,159 to 1,737,231, a 750 percent increase, during the same period (College Board, 2004).

## PROBLEMS WITH AP AS AN ADMISSIONS CRITERION

Yet the growing prominence of AP in "high stakes" admissions has also highlighted a number of problematic features. Disparities in availability and access to AP courses among underrepresented minorities and others from disadvantaged backgrounds have been well documented (Doran, Dugan, & Weffer, 1998; Ekstrom, Goertz, & Rock, 1988; Gamoran, 1992; Oakes, 1990; Oakes, Gamoran, & Page, 1992). Because students from poorer schools typically have less access to AP courses than those from schools with higher college-going rates, emphasis on AP coursework as a selection factor can adversely affect their chances of college admission. Although many states, including California, have adopted policies encouraging expansion of AP coursework in disadvantaged schools (Santoli, 2003; Hurwitz & Hurwitz, 2003), participation in AP and other honors-level courses remains sharply skewed along socioeconomic and racial/ethnic lines. One reason for these persistent group disparities may lie in the fact that, even within the same schools, low-income and underrepresented minority students tend to be tracked into non-college preparatory work and thus enroll in AP and honors-level courses at much lower rates than other students (CSU Institute for Education Reform, 1999, 2001; Oakes, 1985).

The growing emphasis on AP in "high stakes" admissions has had unintended consequences. Like many other aspects of the admissions process at highly selective institutions, AP has become a significant factor in what former UC President Richard Atkinson has called the "educational arms race," as applicants and their parents seek every advantage to improve their chances of acceptance (Atkinson, 2001). For example, it is now common for upper-middle-class parents to evaluate and choose high schools for their children based on the number of AP courses offered at those schools, thereby placing great pressure on schools to expand their AP offerings (Mathews, 1998). According to a recent evaluation of AP and International Baccalaureate (IB) programs by the National Research Council, this pressure can lead schools to offer more advanced courses than they are able to support adequately with trained teachers and other resources (National Research Council, 2002a). There are other unintended consequences as well.

> Some schools use the results of AP or IB examinations to evaluate teachers, the consequence of which may be to discourage potentially low-scoring students from taking the courses or the examination. It is not uncommon for selective colleges to view the existence of AP or IB courses on an applicant's transcript as an important part of their evaluation of the student's intellectual and academic motivations. Without any measure of the quality of the student's achievement in such courses, however, this emphasis on the number of AP or IB courses on a transcript leads many students to enroll in the courses without a commitment to mastering the material. (National Research Council, 2002b, p. 536)

A large and apparently growing number of students now enroll in AP course-work without taking the associated AP exams. AP differs considerably in this respect from the IB program, in which examinations are considered an integral part of the coursework and virtually all students take the exams (Campbell, 2000). The Commission on the Future of the Advanced Placement Program estimated in 2001 that over a third of AP students do not sit for the examinations, although this is a rough, overall estimate and varies both from subject to subject and from state to state (CFAPP, 2001). The National Research Council (2002a) has commented pointedly on the differing expectations of the IB and AP programs regarding test completion.

> It is interesting to note that a far larger percentage of IB than AP students take the final examinations. The IBO [International Baccalaureate Organization] promotes the idea that IB courses prepare students for success in college and in real life. The examinations, students are told, are an integral part of the course and are the best way for them to demonstrate to themselves and others that they have achieved competence. In contrast, AP materials focus primarily on the usefulness of AP test scores for college credit and placement. If students lose interest in earning credit or placement or the colleges at which they plan to matriculate do not accept AP credits, they may choose not to sit for the examinations. . . . [W]e believe that sitting for the examinations should become an integral part of AP courses. Otherwise, students will miss an important opportunity to validate their performance, colleges and universities will lack information that can be highly useful in deciding upon appropriate placements, and AP will be less credible as a rigorous program for high school students. (p. 170)

Another unintended consequence of the emphasis on AP coursework in college admissions is grade inflation. Many high schools and colleges give "bonus points" or extra credit for AP and other honors courses so that, for example, a "B" grade in an AP course is counted as the equivalent of an "A" grade in a regular course, thereby increasing the grade points from three to four. With so many students now taking substantial numbers of AP and other honors courses in order to improve their chances of admission to college, high school grade point averages have soared. Among freshmen admitted to UC Berkeley in 2003, for example, the *mean* HSGPA was 4.31.

But perhaps the most problematic aspect of AP's expanding role in "high stakes" admissions is the extent to which this development has occurred largely unexamined and with little hard evidence of the validity of AP coursework as a selection criterion. Although the College Board and others have conducted research on the relationship between students' AP exam scores and their subsequent performance in college, little research has been done on the predictive validity of AP coursework per se. Probably the most frequently cited research in support of employing AP coursework as an admissions criterion is Adelman's influential study, *Answers in the Toolbox*, which concluded that the most powerful predictor of college graduation is the "academic intensity" of a student's high school curriculum (Adelman, 1999). Yet while Adelman did include AP courses as one of several components of his composite index of "academic intensity," the study was never intended as a systematic examination of AP per se, and in fact Adelman's data suggest that, compared to other indicators of "academic intensity," AP courses were among the weaker predictors of college outcomes (Adelman, 1999).

In its recent review of the Advanced Placement and International Baccalaureate programs, the National Research Council (2002b) noted the paucity of systematic research on the predictive or "consequential" validity of these programs.

> [L]ittle evidence is available for evaluating the long-term effects of the AP and IB programs. For instance, the panel could not find systematic data on how students who participate in AP and IB fare in college mathematics relative to other students. . . . While the College Board and a few colleges that receive IB students have conducted some isolated studies addressing how AP or IB students perform in college . . . , the inferences that can accurately be drawn from the findings of these studies are ambiguous. . . . (p. 495)

Extant studies have typically examined the validity of using AP exam scores to place students out of introductory college courses (see, for example, Morgan & Ramist, 1998), but few, if any, have examined the validity of AP and other honors-level coursework as admissions criteria. The present study is intended to fill that void.

## AP AND HONORS-LEVEL COURSES IN UC ADMISSIONS

The University of California first began using AP examination scores for purposes of college placement in 1961, but did not recognize AP coursework as a factor in admissions until 1982.

> To encourage students to take demanding advanced academic courses, grades in up to four units taken in the last two years of high schools will be counted on a scale of A = 5, B = 4, C = 3, if these courses are certified by the high school as offered at an honors level. These courses must be in the areas of history, English, advanced mathematics, laboratory science, and foreign language. Courses in these fields designed to prepare students for the Advanced Placement Examinations of the College Board are considered to be examples of honors courses. (University of California, 1982)

Several aspects of this policy are noteworthy. First is the policy rationale: encouraging students to take more rigorous courses in high school. For the Board of Admissions and Relations with Schools (BOARS), the UC faculty committee responsible for formulating admissions policy, the primary reason for granting extra credit for AP and honors courses was to provide an incentive for prospective UC students to challenge themselves to take more rigorous classes in high school, thereby assuring the university of a well-prepared and high-achieving student body.

A second noteworthy feature is the formulaic character of UC's policy, or what has become known as the "bonus point" for AP and honors courses. While as noted earlier other institutions tend to consider AP and honors coursework more "holistically" in admissions decisions as one factor among many, UC chose to assign such courses a fixed, numeric weight. In part this policy choice reflected the requirements of California's Master Plan for Higher Education, which provides that students must rank within the top one-eighth, or 12.5 percent, of the state's public high school graduates in order to be "eligible" for admission to UC. Incorporating the "bonus point" within the calculation of HSGPA provided a straightforward method for determining whether an applicant's high school grades were sufficient to achieve eligibility.[3]

Even at the time, however, BOARS recognized that there were marked socioeconomic and racial/ethnic disparities in AP enrollments, which helps explain a third feature of the policy: giving equal weight to other honors-level courses, in addition to AP, BOARS' intent was to ensure that students attending schools with limited AP course offerings would not be unduly disadvantaged by the "bonus point" policy insofar as other honors-level courses offered at those schools were given equal credit.[4] For much the same reason, BOARS would later add International Baccalaureate courses, as well as concurrent Community College courses taken while students were still in high school, to the list of courses that could receive the "bonus point."

Last but not least, perhaps the most important feature of the 1982 policy was its severance of the link between AP coursework and the AP examinations: "Courses . . . designed to prepare students for the Advanced Placement Examinations" were credited with the "bonus point" whether or not students actually completed the exams.

## EXPANSION OF AP AND HONORS IN CALIFORNIA SCHOOLS

Spurred in part by UC's policy as well as by the increasingly competitive environment of college admissions, student participation in AP and other honors-level courses in California grew rapidly after 1982. As California does not have a K-12 student-level data system with which to track course-taking patterns, it is difficult to determine the precise extent of this growth, although it is clearly substantial. Based on historical data from the College Board on AP exam-takers in California (no trend data are available on AP course-takers), the number of students who took at least one AP exam increased from 21,572 in 1982 to 163,581 in 2002, about a 760 percent increase, and the total number of AP exams taken increased from 25,137 to 291,945, almost a twelvefold increase, over this same twenty-year period. California's growth rate outpaced the national growth rate on both measures. Moreover, since these data do not include large numbers of students who took AP courses but did not sit for the exams, or who took honors-level coursework other than AP, total growth in AP and other honors-level course enrollments was undoubtedly much greater.[5]

Yet the expansion of AP and honors in California has been highly uneven and varies substantially across socioeconomic and demographic lines. Currently two main sources of data are available with which to examine access to AP and other honors courses in California schools. The first is UC Doorways, a database on California high schools maintained by the university that lists all approved coursework required for UC admission, including AP and honors courses. Although the UC Doorways database unfortunately does not indicate how many times a given course was offered or how many students participated, it does at least provide a general picture of the distribution of courses across schools. Table 4.1 was developed from the UC Doorways database and shows the number of Advanced Placement, International Baccalaureate, and other honors-level courses offered by California public high schools in 2002–2003. The schools are categorized by Academic Performance Index (API), using a school-ranking system developed by the California Department of Education. School API rankings are closely associated with socioeconomic, racial/ethnic, and other demographic differences among students who attend them. For example, 87 percent of students attending schools in the lowest API quintile are underrepresented minorities,[6] compared to only 17 percent among schools in the top quintile.[7]

TABLE 4.1
Average Number of AP, IB, and Other Honors Courses
Offered per School by API Quintile, 2002–2003

| | Advanced Placement | | International Baccalaureate | | Other Honors-level Courses | | Total Honors-level Courses | |
|---|---|---|---|---|---|---|---|---|
| School API Quintile | # | % | # | % | # | % | # | % |
| Quintile 5 (high) | 14.5 | 74% | 1.2 | 6% | 4.5 | 23% | 19.7 | 100% |
| Quintile 4 | 12.0 | 73% | 1.1 | 7% | 3.9 | 24% | 16.5 | 100% |
| Quintile 3 | 11.1 | 70% | 1.2 | 7% | 4.1 | 26% | 15.8 | 100% |
| Quintile 2 | 11.3 | 73% | 0.7 | 4% | 3.6 | 24% | 15.4 | 100% |
| Quintile 1 (low) | 10.2 | 72% | 0.6 | 4% | 3.5 | 25% | 14.2 | 100% |
| All Schools | 11.3 | 72% | 1.1 | 7% | 3.5 | 23% | 15.5 | 100% |

*Source:* UC Doorways and California Department of Education.

AP, IB, and "other" honors courses offered by particular schools are not necessarily exclusive of one another and may be counted within more than one category.

As table 4.1 indicates, AP courses are by far the predominant type of honors-level courses offered in California public high schools, accounting for about 72 percent of all such course offerings, while IB and other honors-level courses account for the remaining share.[8] This pattern is evident not only for the schools overall, but also within each quintile of California public schools. Looking across school quintiles, moreover, it is evident that there are fewer AP and other honors-level courses offered in low-quintile than high-quintile schools, although the differences are not as great as perhaps might be expected. Offerings of AP courses, for example, ranged from 10.2 courses per school in the bottom quintile of schools to 14.5 courses per school in the top quintile. And looking at all honors-level courses combined, the number of offerings ranged from 14.2 courses per school in the bottom quintile to 19.7 per school at the top.

However, because the UC Doorways data shown in table 4.1 do no necessarily indicate how many times a course was offered or, if offered, how many students actually enrolled, they may understate differences in student participation in AP and honors courses. To get a better sense of the numbers and types of students who participate in honors-level courses, it is necessary to turn to a second main source of data. Table 4.2 presents data from the statewide SAT database, which includes all college-bound seniors who took the SAT in 2002. Almost half of California high school seniors take the SAT each year, including the great majority of the college-bound population. When students take the SAT, they complete a Student Data Questionnaire (SDQ), and table 4.2 shows SDQ results on the number of subjects in which students reported taking at least one honors course.

TABLE 4.2

Demographic Profile of California College-bound Seniors by Number of AP/Honors Subjects Taken, 2002

| Number of AP/Honors Subjects Taken | Number of Students | Percent of Sample | Percent Underrepresented Minority | Percent First-generation College | Percent from Low-performing Schools | Percent from Low-income Families |
|---|---|---|---|---|---|---|
| 0 | 64,577 | 54.9% | 32.3% | 46.4% | 31.2% | 23.2% |
| 1–4 | 30,947 | 26.3% | 30.5% | 47.4% | 31.8% | 24.0% |
| 5–8 | 13,872 | 11.8% | 23.7% | 40.1% | 30.0% | 21.3% |
| 9–16 | 8,137 | 6.9% | 17.4% | 31.6% | 25.2% | 17.3% |
| 17+ | 117 | 0.1% | 14.5% | 23.9% | 23.1% | 17.9% |
| TOTAL | 117,650 | 100.0% | 29.8% | 44.9% | 30.8% | 22.8% |

*Source:* College Board file on all California college-bound seniors who took the SAT I in 2002.

"Number of AP/Honors Subjects Taken" is the number of subjects in which students report having taken at least one honors course. "Low-performing Schools" are those within the bottom two API quintiles according to the California Department of Education. "Low-income" indicates families with incomes <$30,000.

Table 4.2 shows that there are substantial demographic and socioeconomic differences between students who take many honors courses and those who take few or none. Approximately half of all California SAT-takers reported taking no honors-level courses in high school. Underrepresented minorities comprise almost a third (32.3 percent) of this group, but their proportion falls to only 17.4 percent among the group who report taking honors courses in 9 to 16 subjects. Differences of similar magnitude are evident for first-generation college students and those from low-performing schools and low-income families.[9]

These disparities in student participation in AP and honors courses became the focus of a class-action lawsuit filed by the American Civil Liberties Union in 1999 against the State of California (*Daniel v. California*, 1999). The suit challenged the state for not providing sufficient access to AP courses in all schools and led to a major state-funded initiative supporting expansion of AP course offerings in low-performing schools, rural areas, and other underserved regions of the state. It is unclear, however, whether this initiative will substantially reduce disparities in AP participation among underrepresented groups, since such disparities may owe at least as much to patterns of tracking within schools as to differences between schools in the number of AP courses they offer. A recent statewide study of the AP program conducted by the California State University's Institute for Education Reform found that, even in schools with extensive AP offerings, Latino and African American students enrolled in these courses much less often than other students; availability of AP coursework appeared to be less an issue than participation in the courses that were available (CSU Institute for Education Reform, 1999).

Such disparities in student participation in AP and honors coursework make it especially important that their use as an admissions criterion can be empirically validated. Without evidence that participation in such courses is a valid indicator of success in college, it would seem difficult to rationalize continued reliance on a criterion with adverse effects on groups that have been historically underrepresented in higher education.

## DATA AND METHODOLOGY

The present study examined the role of AP and other honors courses in predicting college performance for four cohorts of students who entered UC between Fall 1998 and Fall 2001 inclusive. The sample included a total of 81,445 students who enrolled as first-time freshmen at UC's eight undergraduate campuses during that four-year period.[10]

Two sources of data were available for the sample. The primary source was the UC Corporate Student System, which provided both admissions data (e.g., HSGPA, SAT/ACT scores, number of AP/honors courses taken in high school) as well as longitudinal data (e.g., college persistence and GPA) for each student. The UC Corporate data also included other relevant information needed for purposes of multivariate analysis, such as parents' income and education, UC campus of enrollment, and student major.

A second data source was statewide information on California AP test-takers made available through a data-sharing agreement between UC and the College Board. Those data were matched against the UC Corporate data file in order to enrich the latter file with information on students' AP test history and their scores, if any, on the AP exams.

The study employed several indicators of student performance in college. Freshman grade-point average is the most frequently used performance indicator in studies of the predictive validity of college admissions criteria, and that measure was employed in the present study as well. However, because of concerns that first-year grades might mask important differences among students—e.g., some students who took AP/honors courses in high school might repeat the same courses in their first year in college and thus boost their freshman GPA or, alternatively, others might take more advanced college courses and possibly lower their freshman GPA—the study also employed second-year college GPA as an outcome measure. This indicator was based on second-year grades only, not calculated cumulatively with first-year grades, in order to minimize possible confounding effects of repeat course-taking. In addition, the study employed both first-year and second-year college persistence as outcome measures. By far the most attrition occurs, if it occurs at all, within students' first two years at UC, so that student persistence through their first and second years is a very strong indicator of the likelihood that students will continue on through graduation.[11]

Regression analysis was used to study the extent to which students' grades and persistence in college could be predicted or explained by AP and honors coursework in high school when other factors were held constant. For example, because students from highly educated families and better-performing schools are more likely to take AP and honors courses than other students, it is important to separate the effects of parents' education and school quality from the effects of AP and honors per se, and regression analysis permits one to do so. The main predictor variables examined in the analysis, in addition to AP and honors coursework, were HSGPA, SAT I and SAT II scores, AP exam scores, school API quintile, parents' education, student major, and UC campus of enrollment. Ordinary linear regression was used to study the relationship between these predictor variables and first- and second-year UC grade point average (UCGPA), which is a continuous numerical variable, while logistic regression was employed in the analysis of first- and second-year college persistence, which is a dichotomous (persistence/attrition) outcome variable.[12]

The following analysis proceeds from the simple to the complex. We begin by examining the extent to which the "bonus point" for AP/honors, as used in calculating students' HSGPA at point of admission, is related to their subsequent performance in college. Finding that the "bonus point" bears little or no relationship to college performance, we then introduce additional variables into the analysis in an attempt to identify factors that might explain or account for the initial null relationship.

## PREDICTIVE VALIDITY OF THE AP/HONORS "BONUS POINT"

Table 4.3 examines the relationship between student performance at UC and their high school grades and test scores at point of admission. HSGPA SAT I and SAT II scores are the three primary factors considered in UC's "eligibility index," which sets minimum requirements for admission to UC's multi-campus system. The table shows the percentage of explained variance ($R^2$) in freshman and sophomore grades that is predicted by a regression equation that considers HSGPA and SAT I and SAT II scores.[13]

$$UCGPA = \alpha \; HSGPA + \beta \; SAT \; I + \varphi \; SAT \; II$$

The HSGPA variable used in this analysis was an "academic" GPA and included students' grades in college-preparatory subjects only. HSGPA was calculated in three different ways: (1) unweighted, that is, with no bonus points for AP and honors courses; (2) half-weighted, with an additional half grade point for AP and honors; and (3) fully weighted, with an additional full grade point for AP and honors.[14] Table 4.3 displays the percentage of variance in first- and second-year college grades that is predicted when each of these different HSGPA calculations is substituted within the regression equation, holding SAT I and SAT II scores constant. The table also shows the rank order of the three HSGPA calculations with respect to the percentage of variance they explain.

Examining the results in table 4.3, it is evident that an unweighted HSGPA—a GPA that does *not* grant additional points for honors—is consistently the best predictor of both first- and second-year college grades for each of the three cohorts in the sample. The greater the weight given to AP and honors, moreover, the weaker the prediction. Thus, the half-weighted HSGPA is the second-best predictor, after unweighted HSGPA, in all cases, while the HSGPA weighted with a full bonus point for AP and honors is invariably the worst predictor of college performance, at least within this specific regression equation. This finding is consistent with earlier UC studies (Kowarsky, Clatfelder, & Widaman, 1998), and the same general pattern is also evident in disaggregated, campus-level data for each UC undergraduate campus.[15] The complete lack of predictive power associated with an honors-weighted HSGPA came as somewhat of a surprise and led us to expand the analysis in several ways in an effort to try to account for that finding. First, a number of

TABLE 4.3

Percent of Variance in UCGPA Predicted by HSGPA and Test Scores
with and without Bonus Points for AP/Honors

Regression equation: UCGPA = αHSGPA + βSAT I + φSAT II

*Explained Variance in First-year UCGPA*

| *HSGPA* | *1998* | | *1999* | | *2000* | |
| *Weighting* | *R²* | *Rank* | *R²* | *Rank* | *R²* | *Rank* |
| No Bonus Point | 21.32% | 1 | 21.46% | 1 | 23.54% | 1 |
| Half Bonus Point | 20.67% | 2 | 21.10% | 2 | 22.87% | 2 |
| Full Bonus Point | 19.22% | 3 | 19.82% | 3 | 21.19% | 3 |

*Explained Variance in Second-year UCGPA*

| *HSGPA* | *1998* | | *1999* | | *2000* | |
| *Weighting* | *R²* | *Rank* | *R²* | *Rank* | *R²* | *Rank* |
| No Bonus Point | 14.91% | 1 | 13.88% | 1 | 16.37% | 1 |
| Half Bonus Point | 14.33% | 2 | 13.34% | 2 | 15.79% | 2 |
| Full Bonus Point | 13.16% | 3 | 12.28% | 3 | 14.65% | 3 |

*Source:* UC Corporate admissions and longitudinal data for first-time California resident freshmen entering in Fall 1998, 1999, and 2000.

N = 50,472

demographic variables were introduced into the regression analysis to determine whether they might be artificially masking the relationship between AP/honors and college performance. A second concern was the possibility that students who take more honors-level courses in high school may also take more difficult coursework in college, which might obscure the relationship between AP/honors and college performance. To address this concern, we disaggregated the analysis by student major to examine differences between the "harder" versus "softer" academic disciplines in the extent to which AP/honors predict college performance. Third, the analysis was expanded to include outcome variables other than college grades, namely, first- and second-year persistence rates, which are known to be highly correlated with college graduation. Fourth, because UC policy treats AP, IB, Community College, and other honors-level courses as equivalent for purposes of awarding the honors "bonus point," which could mask important differences, we examined separately the predictive validity of each of these specific types of honors-level courses. And finally, the analysis examined the role of AP test scores in order to assess the extent to which student mastery of AP coursework, as distinct from mere enrollment in such courses, contributed to the prediction of college performance.

## EXPANDED REGRESSION RESULTS

Table 4.4 displays standardized regression coefficients, by discipline, for six variables in predicting students' college grades: unweighted HSGPA, school API quintile, parents' education, SAT I and SAT II scores, and total number of AP/honors courses. Standardized regression coefficients, or "beta weights," show the relative strength of different predictor variables within a regression equation. The weights represent the number of standard deviations that an outcome variable, in this case UCGPA, changes for each standard-deviation change in any given predictor variable, all other variables held constant. Number of AP/honors courses is considered separately from HSGPA in this analysis in order to isolate the role of AP/honors courses.[16]

Table 4.4 shows that, controlling for school API quintile and parents' education as well as unweighted HSGPA and test scores, the number of AP/honors courses that students take in high school bears almost no relationship to their college grades. Second-year UCGPA is used as the outcome variable in the analysis shown here, although the beta weights are virtually identical for first-year UCGPA. Looking at the coefficients for the overall UC sample, shown in the bottom row of table 4.4, HSGPA has by far the strongest predictive weight (.25), followed by SAT II scores (.16), parents' education (.08), school API quintile (.05), and SAT I scores (.04)—all of which are statistically significant at the 99 percent confidence level—but number of AP/honors courses (.01) has no statistically significant predictive weight. Introduction of additional demographic variables into the regression analysis does not, in short, help to improve or explain the null relationship between AP/honors coursework and college grades.[17]

This same general pattern of regression coefficients holds, moreover, across all major disciplines shown in table 4.4. Although the weight for AP/honors is statistically significant in one disciplinary area, math/science, the size of the effect is extremely small: the regression coefficient of .05 for math/science translates into an effect size of only about three one-hundredths of a grade point, or the difference between a college GPA of 3.01 and 3.04.[18] If it is true that students who take more AP/honors courses in high school tend to enter more difficult academic fields in college, where grading standards are tougher, then one would expect to find larger differences across disciplines in the predictive weight associated with AP/honors. But this is not the case. The predictive weight associated with AP/honors is uniformly small across all disciplinary areas.

TABLE 4.4

Standardized Regression Coefficients for Specified Variables in Predicting Second-year UCGPA by Major Disciplinary Area

Regression equation: UCGPA = αHSGPA + βSchool API + φParents' Ed + θSAT I + μSAT II + ψAP/Honors

| | | | | Standardized Regression Coefficients | | | | |
|---|---|---|---|---|---|---|---|---|
| Major Field | Unweighted USGPA | School API Quintile | Parents' Education | SAT I Scores | SAT II Scores | Number of AP/Honors | $R^2$ | N |
| Biological Sciences | 0.24* | 0.03 | 0.06* | 0.09 | 0.22* | 0.00 | 21.2% | 2,283 |
| Math & Physical Sci | 0.32* | 0.00 | 0.06* | 0.05 | 0.19* | 0.05* | 23.5% | 3,038 |
| Social Sci/Humanities | 0.26* | 0.07* | 0.08* | 0.08* | 0.17 | 0.01 | 22.3% | 4,069 |
| General/Undeclared | 0.24* | 0.06* | 0.08* | 0.09* | 0.14* | 0.00 | 18.3% | 7,122 |
| Other Professions | 0.34* | 0.01 | 0.07 | 0.04 | 0.13* | -0.08* | 17.8% | 729 |
| All | 0.25* | 0.05* | 0.08* | 0.04* | 0.16* | 0.01 | 17.4% | 17,245 |

*Source:* UC Corporate admissions and longitudinal data for first-time California resident freshmen entering in Fall 2000 who completed second year.

"Number of AP/Honors" includes only courses taken in 10th or 11th grade and known at point of UC admission. "Other Professions" includes majors such as Physical Education, Education, Law, Social Work, and Journalism.

* = statistically significant at .01 level.

## COLLEGE PERSISTENCE AS AN OUTCOME VARIABLE

Table 4.5 examines the relationship between AP/honors and another outcome variable, college persistence. Both first- and second-year college persistence rates are considered. Dropouts, or non-persisters, were defined as those who left school in academic difficulty, that is, with a college GPA below 2.0. Logistic regression results are shown for each of the three freshman cohorts entering UC between 1998 and 2000:

The pattern of regression weights for college persistence is very similar to that observed previously for college grades. HSGPA and SAT II scores have by far the greatest predictive weight, followed by school API quintile and parents' education, but AP/honors courses (and SAT I scores) have little relationship with either first-or second-year college persistence in any of the three freshman cohorts studied.[19]

## PREDICTIVE VALIDITY OF SPECIFIC TYPES
## OF HONORS-LEVEL COURSES

One potential criticism of the findings presented thus far is that we have treated AP, IB, and other honors courses interchangeably and so may have failed to discern important differences among them. Even though AP courses account for the great majority of honors-level courses offered in California schools, it is nevertheless possible that disaggregating these different types of courses could reveal significant variations in their capacity to predict college performance.

Although disaggregated, course-specific data were not available for our main sample of freshmen entering UC between 1998 and 2000, such data were available from electronic application files for the freshman cohort entering in 2001. First-year outcome data were also available for this cohort, and table 4.6 displays that data. The first column in table 4.6 shows standardized coefficients and percentage of explained variance in first-year college grades for a regression equation *without* AP, IB, Community College, and other honors-level courses. The following columns then show the results when AP, IB, and other honors courses are successively added in to the equation, thus allowing one to isolate the contribution of each to the prediction.

Table 4.6 indicates that none of the specific types of honors-level coursework adds substantially to the prediction of college grades. Though it is true that the regression weights for AP and IB courses are statistically significant, this result is due primarily to the large size of the UC sample, which permits more precise estimates of even very small statistical effects. That AP and IB and other honors courses have little practical significance or effect in predicting college grades is shown by the findings on explained variance at

# TABLE 4.5

Standardized Regression Coefficients for Specified Variables in Predicting First- and Second-year Persistence

Equation: Persistence = $\alpha$HSGPA + $\beta$School API + $\varphi$Parents' Ed + $\theta$SAT I + $\mu$SAT II + $\psi$AP/Honors

## First-year Persistence

Standardized Regression Coefficients

| Freshman Cohort | Unweighted HSGPA | School API Quintile | Parents' Education | SAT I Scores | SAT II Scores | Number of AP/Honors | N |
|---|---|---|---|---|---|---|---|
| 1998 | 0.24* | 0.11* | 0.07* | −0.04 | 0.27* | 0.03 | 17,287 |
| 1999 | 0.26* | 0.15* | 0.10* | −0.08 | 0.17* | 0.06 | 15,086 |
| 2000 | 0.33* | 0.11* | 0.13* | −0.03 | 0.20* | 0.04 | 18,099 |

## Second-year Persistence

Standardized Regression Coefficients

| Freshman Cohort | Unweighted HSGPA | School API Quintile | Parents' Education | SAT I Scores | SAT II Scores | Number of AP/Honors | N |
|---|---|---|---|---|---|---|---|
| 1998 | 0.25* | 0.12* | 0.09* | −0.09* | 0.25* | 0.03 | 17,013 |
| 1999 | 0.28* | 0.17* | 0.10* | −0.12* | 0.21* | 0.06 | 15,016 |
| 2000 | 0.32* | 0.13* | 0.11* | −0.02 | 0.19* | 0.05 | 18,018 |

Source: UC Corporate admissions and longitudinal data for first-time California resident freshmen.

"Number of AP/Honors" includes only courses taken in 10th or 11th grade and known at point of UC admission.

* = statistically significant at .01 level.

TABLE 4.6

Standardized Coefficients and Explained Variance for Specified Regression Models/Equations in Predicting First-year UCGPA

| Predictor Variables | Standardized Regression Coefficients for Specified Prediction Models/Equations | | | | |
|---|---|---|---|---|---|
| Unweighted HSGPA | 0.31* | 0.31* | 0.31* | 0.31* | 0.31* |
| School API Quintile | 0.09* | 0.10* | 0.10* | 0.10* | 0.10* |
| Parents' Education | 0.06* | 0.06* | 0.06* | 0.06* | 0.06* |
| Family Income | 0.02* | 0.02* | 0.02* | 0.02* | 0.02* |
| SAT I Scores | 0.05* | 0.05* | 0.05* | 0.05* | 0.05* |
| SAT II Scores | 0.15* | 0.15* | 0.15* | 0.15* | 0.15* |
| AP Courses | | 0.02* | 0.02* | 0.02* | 0.02* |
| IB Courses | | | 0.02* | 0.02* | 0.02* |
| Other Honors Courses | | | | 0.02 | 0.02 |
| Community College Courses | | | | | 0.00 |
| % Explained Variance ($R^2$) | 23.7% | 23.8% | 23.8% | 23.8% | 23.8% |

*Source:* UC Application Processor data and UC Corporate admissions and longitudinal data for first-time California resident freshmen entering in Fall 2001 for whom complete data were available for all variables.

N = 16,455.

* = statistically significant at .01 level.

the bottom of Table 4.6. Adding AP, IB, Community College, and other honors courses into the regression equation increases the percentage of explained variance in college grades by only one-tenth of one percentage point, from 23.7 percent to 23.8 percent. Whether individually or in combination, AP, IB and other honors-level coursework contributes little to the prediction of college performance.

## PREDICTIVE VALIDITY OF AP EXAMINATION SCORES

The final set of regression results to be considered here concerns the predictive validity of AP examination scores, as distinct from AP coursework. Although the AP exams were originally intended as end-of-course tests, a large and apparently growing number of students now enroll in AP coursework without taking the associated AP exams. It is difficult to estimate the extent of this trend due to the fact that, while the number of AP test-takers is known, the number of AP course enrollments is not. Based on test data for California, an educated guess is that only about 55 to 60 percent of students enrolled in AP courses go on to take the AP exams.[20] This is unfortunate, because there is research to suggest that performance on the AP exams may be a good indicator of students' performance in college (Morgan & Maneckshana, 2000; Morgan & Ramist, 1998).

Our regression results support this conclusion. Whereas AP coursework, by itself, contributes almost nothing to the prediction of college performance, AP examination scores are relatively strong predictors, according to the UC data. Table 4.7 shows standardized regression coefficients for all of the predictor variables examined previously, but with AP examination scores now added into the regression equation:

As table 4.7 demonstrates, students' scores on the AP exams are remarkably strong predictors of performance in college. In contrast to the number of AP/honors courses taken, which carries little or no predictive weight, AP scores have greater predictive weight than any other factor except high school grades, and this pattern holds not only for the total UC sample, but also for every major disciplinary area with the exception of "Other Professions." Overall, introducing AP exam scores into the regression equation improves the percentage of explained variance in second-year college GPA by 1.4 percentage points, from 17.4 percent to 18.8 percent.[21]

This finding is consistent with previous research on the superiority of curriculum-based achievement tests over tests of generalized reasoning ability or aptitude in predicting college performance (Crouse & Trusheim, 1988; Geiser with Studley, 2003). Contrary to the conventional wisdom, research has shown that tests that measure students' mastery of specific, college-preparatory subjects, such as the SAT II, are consistently better predictors of college performance than tests that are designed to assess students' general reasoning capacity or aptitude for learning, such as the SAT I. The subject-specific, curriculum-intensive AP exams are the epitome of "achievement tests," in this sense, and their validity in predicting college performance should not be surprising from that standpoint.

## SUMMARY AND POLICY IMPLICATIONS

Originally developed for purposes of college placement, AP is increasingly emphasized as a factor in "high stakes" admissions at leading colleges and universities. The main finding of this study, however, is that, controlling for other academic and socioeconomic factors, the number of AP and other honors-level courses taken in high school bears little or no relationship to students' later performance in college. This finding holds consistently for each of the four cohorts in the UC sample; for outcome measures including college persistence as well as first- and second-year college grades; for every major disciplinary area; and for all major types of honors coursework, including AP,

TABLE 4.7

Standardized Regression Coefficients for Specified Variables in Predicting Second-year UCGPA by Major Disciplinary Area

Regression equation: UCGPA = $\alpha$HSGPA + $\beta$School API + $\varphi$Parents' Ed + $\theta$SAT I + $\mu$SAT II + $\psi$AP/Honors + $\omega$AP Scores

| Major Field | Unweighted HSGPA | School API Quintile | Parents' Education | SAT I | SAT II | Number of AP/Honors | AP Exam Scores | $R^2$ | N |
|---|---|---|---|---|---|---|---|---|---|
| | | | | Standardized Regression Coefficients | | | | | |
| Biological Sciences | 0.21* | 0.01 | 0.05 | 0.07 | 0.14* | 0.01 | 0.19* | 23.7% | 2,038 |
| Math & Physical Sci | 0.29* | -0.02 | 0.05 | 0.03 | 0.08 | 0.06* | 0.22* | 25.8% | 2,816 |
| Social Sci/Humanities | 0.26* | 0.06* | 0.08* | 0.08* | 0.09* | 0.02 | 0.11* | 22.9% | 3,480 |
| General/Undeclared | 0.23* | 0.04* | 0.09* | 0.07* | 0.06 | 0.01 | 0.15* | 19.7% | 6,030 |
| Other Professions | 0.35* | 0.04 | 0.06 | 0.03 | 0.13 | -0.06 | 0.01 | 20.3% | 558 |
| All | 0.24* | 0.03* | 0.08* | 0.03 | 0.08* | 0.02 | 0.15* | 18.8% | 14,926 |

*Source:* UC Corporate admissions and longitudinal data for first-time California resident freshmen entering in Fall 2000 who completed second year and for whom data on AP exam scores was available.

* = statistically significant at .01 level.

IB, and other honors-level courses. While AP exam scores are strongly related to college performance, many students who enroll in AP courses do not complete the associated AP exams, and merely taking AP or other honors-level courses in high school is not a valid indicator of the likelihood that students will perform well in college. If the UC sample is representative of other selective colleges and universities, admissions officers need to reconsider the manner in which AP and honors courses are treated in "high stakes" admissions. Such reconsideration assumes special importance in light of the disparity in AP and honors participation among groups that have been historically underrepresented in higher education.

In the concluding paragraphs, we discuss several policy options for changing the manner in which AP and honors coursework is treated in admissions decisions. For each option, the discussion considers issues not only of predictive validity, but also of educational equity, the incentive or signaling effect of admissions policy on students and schools, practicality, and possible unintended consequences. As will be seen, there appears to be no one, perfect solution that simultaneously addresses all of these issues and that might be equally appropriate for all institutions.

*Require Minimum AP Examination Scores*

A first policy option is to give extra weight to AP coursework in admissions decisions only where students take the associated end-of-course AP examinations and achieve exam scores sufficient to demonstrate their mastery of the subject matter. This option would, in effect, extend the AP program model from the area of college placement to the area of admissions. Such a policy is well justified on grounds of predictive validity, since, as we have seen, AP exam scores are demonstrably related to college performance. With respect to its incentive or signaling function, however, the exam-score option is more equivocal. On the one hand, it would continue to provide an incentive for students not only to enroll in advanced courses, as under present policy, but also to master the course content and take the end-of-course exams, for which present policy provides no incentive. On the other hand, the exam-score option could serve as a *dis*incentive for some students to take AP coursework if they believed they might do poorly on the AP exams, since they might earn better GPAs in non-AP courses in the same subjects.

From the standpoint of educational equity as well, the exam-score option is also equivocal. On the one hand, disadvantaged and underrepresented minority students tend to score lower than others, on average, on the AP exams, requiring a minimum exam score would greatly reduce the *total* number of additional credits granted for AP coursework. At the same time, however, requiring a minimum AP score of four, for example, would reduce the total number of additional AP credits granted by over 90 percent, according to simulations based on UC applicant data. With so many fewer applicants receiving AP credits, the gap between disadvantaged or under-represented minority students and other applicants might be substantially smaller than under present policy.[22]

The main issues with an exam-score requirement concern its practicality and possible unintended consequences. By design, AP and other higher-level coursework are most appropriate for students in their later years in high school, after they have completed the necessary introductory and prerequisite courses. But because students apply to college in the middle of their senior year, exam scores for AP courses that students take as seniors are not available at the point that colleges make admissions decisions.

Exam scores are available at point of admission for AP courses taken in the tenth and eleventh grades, but this raises other concerns. Many have questioned whether courses taken in the tenth grade or earlier can be legitimately considered "advanced" work. The competition for admission to elite colleges has led many students to take AP courses in earlier and earlier grades, and the National Research Council (2002a) has noted the perverse effect of this trend in creating "curriculum compression" within the schools:

> Compression of the curriculum also can occur when students are allowed to skip prerequisite courses and take an AP course as a first course. Among the sciences, AP physics is the course students most frequently select as the first course in the discipline. Data obtained from the College Board indicate that almost half of all physics-test takers had had no prior experience with physics before enrolling in the AP course. Thus, the AP course had to cover both a year of high school physics and a year of college physics, making in-depth examination of any topic nearly impossible. (p. 190)

A possible unintended consequence of an exam-score requirement could be to reinforce and perhaps even accelerate this trend toward offering "advanced" coursework in earlier grades. And such a requirement could add significantly to the already heavy burden of standardized tests imposed upon K-12 students.

Finally, the exam-score option also poses problems with respect to honors-level courses other than AP, for which standardized, end-of-course examinations may not be available. Requiring students who take other types of honors-level courses to sit for the AP exams would violate a fundamental principle of testing, namely, that assessment should be aligned with curriculum (American Educational Research Association et al., 1985).[23] But to deny extra credit entirely for students who take honors-level courses other than AP would also seem fundamentally unfair.

In short, although an exam-score requirement seems initially attractive in many respects, there are a variety of reasons why it might prove problematic in practice.

## Consider AP/Honors Coursework in Local Context

A second policy option is to consider students' AP and honors coursework in a local context, that is, within the context of the available curriculum at each student's particular school. Some colleges and universities already follow this practice as part of the process of comprehensive admissions review. In addition, this option might be useful in states such as California, Florida, and Texas, which emphasize students' class rank in school as a criterion for admission to their public university systems.[24] Rather than looking simply at the number of AP/honors courses that applicants have completed, the local-context option focuses on the extent to which applicants have taken advantage of available opportunities within their individual schools.

The primary rationale for considering students' AP/honors coursework in local context is that it "levels the playing field" and eliminates unfair comparisons between students who attend schools with many AP/honors courses and those who attend schools with few or none. Admissions officers may take a very different view of two applicants who both have four AP courses on their transcripts, knowing that one attends a school with a broad range of AP offerings and the other is from a school with only four. And for students, the local-context option preserves the incentive to take as many advanced-level courses as possible from among the available offerings at their school.

A key problem with the local-context option, however, is the lack of any demonstrable relationship between AP/honors courses and students' later performance in college. This objection is not necessarily fatal, as colleges and universities can and do frequently employ other admissions criteria with little or no predictive validity (e.g., criteria designed to promote geographic, socioeconomic, or demographic diversity). The lack of predictive validity becomes problematic only where such criteria can be shown to have an adverse impact on groups that have been historically underrepresented in higher education. But that is precisely the case here. Educational research provides abundant evidence that *even within the same schools*, underrepresented minority students tend to be tracked out of college-preparatory coursework and to enroll in AP/honors courses at much lower rates than other students. According to a recent study of the AP program in California conducted by California State University's Institute for Education Reform (1999),

> [E]ven when Hispanics and African-Americans are in schools with large AP programs, their rate of participation is lower than their proportionate share of enrollment. In short, for Hispanics and African-Americans, the crucial problem is not availability . . . but participation in the classes that are offered. (p. 6)

Given persistent patterns of tracking in the schools, admissions officers cannot safely assume that, even for students from the same school, different levels of AP/honors participation reflect different levels of ability or commitment to education. Though the local-context option may help to "level the playing field" *between* schools, it does little to address concerns about equity *within* schools and, to the contrary, could serve inadvertently to preserve and reinforce existing disparities at the K-12 level.

## Reduce the Weight for AP/Honors Coursework

A final policy option to be considered here is to reduce the weight given to AP and honors coursework in college admissions. This option would be most practical for institutions, such as UC, that assign quantitative weights for AP/honors within their admissions processes. One variant of the reduced-weight option, for example, would be to assign only a half point rather than a full "bonus point" for AP/honors classes in calculating HSGPA. Another would be to impose a cap restricting the total number of AP/honors courses for which students could receive extra credit.[25] A more extreme variant, of course, would be to stop giving any additional weight to AP/honors courses in admissions decisions.

Short of eliminating consideration of AP/honors entirely, the primary rationale for the reduced-weight option is to strike a balance between two fundamental, but competing, policy concerns: maintaining an incentive for students to take rigorous, higher-level coursework while minimizing disparities among disadvantaged and underrepresented minority students. The issue is often simplified as a question of balance between "academic quality" and "fairness," and the reduced-weight option "splits the difference," in effect, between these two core values. Granting only a half point for AP/honors, for example, preserves an incentive for students to take advanced coursework in high school but at the same time is intended to mitigate the adverse impact of such coursework as a criterion for college admission.

Although "splitting the difference" is understandable as a way of balancing the competing values at stake, the question remains whether this represents an internally coherent and defensible educational policy. It is not clear that halving the "bonus point" for AP/honors, for example, would have any effect in ameliorating group disparities in admissions, since the result might be simply to restrict the HSGPA range without any change in the relative standing of individuals or groups within the applicant pool. But even if the reduced-weight option did have this effect—and this is the important point—at least some residual disparity would remain. By what standards or principles does one decide how much residual disparity is acceptable as the price for realizing other educational values?

The standard normally employed in answering this question is the legal standard applied in "disparate impact" analysis (National Research Council, 1999a, 1999b). As it has evolved from case law on employment discrimination into the area of educational testing and college admissions, this standard holds that standardized tests and other selection criteria may have a disparate impact on protected groups only to the extent that can be justified by "educational necessity." The determination of educational necessity, in turn, involves a two-part test: Do the criteria have a significant relationship with the educational purpose intended, and are there alternative criteria that could achieve the same purpose with less disparate impacts?

For selective colleges and universities, the primary purpose of admissions criteria is to select a high-achieving student body (and in the case of public institutions, one that is broadly representative of the populations they serve). The present study, however, provides no grounds for believing that use of AP/honors as a selection criterion is necessary or valid for this purpose, as AP/honors coursework bears virtually no relationship to student achievement in college. The case for reducing the weight for AP/honors but accepting some residual disparate impact thus rests on a secondary and more diffuse purpose of college admissions criteria, that is, their incentive or signaling effect upon K-12 students and schools.

Whether the incentive function of giving at least partial credit for AP/honors courses rises to the level of "educational necessity" is an open question and one that is difficult to answer on purely empirical grounds. While college admissions criteria clearly do have a substantial impact on students and schools, many other influences at the local, state, and federal levels also affect the extent to which schools offer, and students enroll in, advanced-level coursework. It is therefore difficult to isolate the impact of college and university admissions criteria in this regard. Moreover, the educational necessity test also requires colleges and universities to consider whether they might achieve the same purpose by other means—such as expanded outreach to K-12 schools—without giving extra weight to AP/honors in admissions. Indeed, a case can be made that there are already strong incentives, both intrinsic and extrinsic, for students to take honors-level courses—more interesting learning experiences, improved performance on college entrance exams, better references from teachers—so that additional incentives may be unnecessary.

In sum, like both the exam-score and local-context options discussed previously, the rationale for reducing the weight for AP/honors in college admissions, while initially plausible, on closer analysis seems more equivocal.

## CONCLUSION

It is important to emphasize that the present study is not intended as an assessment of the value or effectiveness of the Advanced Placement or International Baccalaureate programs, nor of other honors-level coursework offered by high schools in either the United States or California. Given the decentralized system of educational governance in the United States and the lack of national curricular standards, programs such as AP and IB appear to offer one of the most promising strategies for improving the academic rigor of school curricula nationwide, while remaining responsive to state and local standards (National Research Council, 2002a). Participation in rigorous, advanced-level coursework may be especially strategic for disadvantaged and underrepresented minority students if our society is to make inroads in reducing pervasive disparities in educational achievement (Adelman, 1999).

The present study has focused on a different issue, namely, the use of AP and other honors-level coursework as a criterion for admission at elite colleges and universities. Developed originally for purposes of college placement, AP is increasingly emphasized as a factor in "high stakes" admissions, but this evolution has occurred largely unexamined and with little systematic study of the extent to which its use for that purpose is valid. The UC data indicate that AP/honors coursework has little, if any, validity with respect to the prediction of college outcomes.

Lacking an empirical rationale, it is probably inevitable that discussions of the future role of AP/honors in admissions may devolve into the familiar value conflict between those who would emphasize "academic quality" and those who would emphasize "fairness" in college admissions. Yet closer analysis of the various options for recasting the role of AP/honors in admissions suggests that there is an imbalance, in this case, between those competing values. The primary purpose of admissions criteria is to select a high-achieving student body, but the predictive-validity findings raise doubts whether the academic quality of admitted students, as measured by their actual performance in college, would in any way suffer if AP/honors coursework were not considered in admissions. The argument for academic quality thus turns on a secondary and more diffuse purpose of college admissions criteria, their incentive or signaling effect on K-12 students and schools. Balanced against that generalized and hard-to-measure effect is the specific, immediate, and disparate impact of AP/honors on admissions of those who have been historically underrepresented at elite colleges and universities. Different observers may strike this balance differently, but the preponderance of both data and policy considerations would appear to favor a fundamental reconsideration of the role of AP and honors in "high stakes" admissions.

## NOTES

1. The International Baccalaureate program was developed in the late 1960s to provide an international standard of secondary education for children of diplomats and others stationed outside their countries, but is now also offered by many schools in the United States during the last two years of high school. In contrast to the AP program, which aims to provide discrete college-level courses for students in high school, IB courses are part of an integrated program designed to prepare students for college. The IB program is much smaller than the AP program and was offered in 255 U.S. high

schools in 2000, whereas AP classes were offered in approximately 62 percent of the nation's schools (National Research Council, 2002a).

2. The following generalizations about how student enrollment in AP/honors courses are treated in admissions decisions at selective colleges and universities are based on an e-mail survey of a purposive sample of admissions officers at 18 AAU institutions conducted by the authors in early 2003. Twelve institutions responded to the survey, including Harvard, Michigan State, Penn State, Purdue, State University of New York–Buffalo, University of Colorado–Boulder, University of Illinois–Urbana, University of Michigan–Ann Arbor, University of Oregon, University of Texas–Austin, University of Washington, and Yale.

3. UC's admissions process involves two stages: "eligibility" and "admissions selection." Eligibility establishes minimum requirements for admission to the UC system as a whole, while admissions selection is the process employed to select students at individual campuses with more eligible applicants than places available. AP and other honors courses are considered as part of both eligibility and admissions selection.

4. BOARS establishes standards for all courses that UC will accept for admissions, including honors-level courses, and oversees an administrative process for approving individual course descriptions submitted by each high school.

5. Estimates of the number of students who take AP courses but do not sit for the exams or who take honors-level coursework other than AP are provided further on.

6. Underrepresented minorities are defined as those whose proportion of college enrollments are substantially below their proportion of high school graduates. In California, these groups include Chicano/Latino, African American, and American Indian students.

7. Percentages of underrepresented minorities by school API quintile are calculated from 2003 data on California public high schools available at the California Department of Education website (http://api.cde.ca.gov/datafiles.asp).

8. Table 4.1 includes only honors courses recognized by UC and thus may differ from what a given school or school district considers "honors-level" coursework.

9. Similar demographic and socioeconomic differences in AP/honors participation are evident within the pool of applicants to UC. Such differences tend to be slightly smaller within the UC applicant pool than in the statewide pool of SAT-takers because of the highly selective nature of UC admissions. Nevertheless, within the pool of UC applicants, participation both in AP/honors coursework and on AP tests remains sharply stratified along racial/ethnic and socioeconomic lines; see appendix 4.1.

10. Descriptive statistics for the study sample and variables employed in the following analysis are provided in appendix 4.2. The main sample used in this analysis was comprised of the three freshman cohorts entering UC between Fall 1998 and Fall 2000. However, because data on the specific types of AP/honors courses taken by students were not available for those cohorts, the sample was augmented with information from UC's electronic application system for the freshman cohort entering in Fall 2001, for whom such data were available; see table 4.6.

11. Based on the most recent available data (for the freshman cohort entering UC in 1997), UC's 6-year graduation rate is 78 percent. Among the 22 percent of the cohort who failed to graduate, 16 percent dropped out within their first two years.

12. A correlation matrix of all of the predictor and outcome variables employed in this analysis is provided in appendix 4.3.

13. The SAT I score used in this analysis is the student's composite score from the math and verbal sections combined. The SAT II score is a composite of the three SAT II tests required for UC admissions: SAT II Math, Writing, and a third subject selected by the student.

14. UC employs a "capped" variant of the fully weighted HSGPA for purposes of calculating eligibility. Though a full bonus point is awarded for AP/honors courses, the total number of courses for which students can receive bonus points is capped at eight. For reasons of simplicity, that specific variant of the bonus-point calculation is not shown here; regression results for the "capped" HSGPA variant employed by UC are very similar to the fully weighted, "uncapped" variant shown in table 4.3.

15. HSGPA weighted with a full bonus point for AP and honors courses is the worst predictor of both first and second-year college grades at all eight UC undergraduate campuses, while HSGPA with no additional weighting for AP or honors is the best predictor in almost all cases. See appendix 4.4 for campus-level data.

16. The number of AP/honors courses shown in table 4.4 represents courses taken in the 10th and 11th grades only. Only 10th and 11th grade transcript data are available at point of UC admission, and for that reason, only 10th and 11th grade AP/honors courses are included in this analysis. Analyses including 12th grade AP/honors (senior-year courses that students planned to take, as indicated on their college application) were also performed and produced virtually identical results to those shown here.

17. Socioeconomic (SES) variables were included in the regression analyses for two reasons. First, UC explicitly takes such factors into consideration in its admissions process, although these factors are known to correlate negatively, to some degree, with student performance at UC. And second, recent research indicates that academic predictors such as SAT scores often serve as a "proxy" for SES and other student background variables, so that omission of such variables from validity analyses can lead to significant overestimation of the SAT's predictive weight (Rothstein, 2004). The data were examined for multicollinearity to determine whether the effect of AP/honors courses on college performance might be accounted for through their correlation with other predictor variables, but there was no evidence that this was the case. In fact, only 17 percent of the variance in AP/honors was shared with the other predictor variables shown here; see appendix 4.3 for correlations among predictor variables. In addition, the data were also examined for curvilinearity, but there was no evidence of a non-linear relationship between AP/honors and college performance.

18. Data with which to calculate effect sizes for all variables employed in this study are shown in appendix 4.2.

19. This finding is consistent with other UC research that has failed to find any significant relationship between AP credits and time to graduation (Eykamp, 2003).

20. Based on data California college-bound seniors who took the SAT I in 2002, about 40 percent of students who reported taking honors-level courses on the SDQ had AP test scores on file. However, this sample includes students enrolled in honors-level courses other than AP. The UC Doorways database indicates that AP accounts for about 72 percent of all honors-level courses offered in CA schools (see table 4.1). Dividing the 40 percent estimate from the SAT database by the 72 percent estimate from UC Doorways, we can calculate that about 56 percent (40%/72%) of AP students sit for the AP exams, although this estimate must be considered very rough. The California data also suggest that there are substantial variations across AP subjects with respect to test completion, with Calculus and History having among the highest rates of test completion and English Language and Spanish Literature having among the lowest.

21. Compare table 4.8 with table 4.4. It should be noted that, because not all students take the AP exams, the sample upon which the regression findings in table 4.7 are based is smaller (N = 14,922) and more selective than the sample upon which the earlier findings in table 4.4 were based (N = 17,245).

22. Proportionately, compared to their 18–percent share under UC's current policy of granting "bonus points" for merely taking AP/honors courses, underrepresented minorities would receive about 17 percent of all points awarded under a policy that required a minimum AP test score of four, according to simulations based on UC applicant data. But because so many fewer applicants would receive "bonus points" under a minimum-score policy, the deficit in the absolute number of points awarded to underrepresented minorities versus other applicants would be reduced approximately tenfold.

23. Most states have K-12 assessment systems that might be adapted for this purpose, but it is not clear that such systems have sufficient psychometric rigor for use in "high stakes" admissions. For example, California's K-12 assessment system, called the California Standards Test, is geared toward the general K-12 population and, based on preliminary studies conducted jointly by UC and the State of California, appears to lack sufficient reliability and predictive validity at the high end of the achievement distribution to be useful for purposes of admissions at highly selective institutions such as UC.

24. UC currently employs a "local context" approach both in determining students' eligibility under UC's "Top 4% Plan" and also in admissions selection, where many campuses group together and rank applicants from the same high school as part of their comprehensive admissions review process. However, UC also considers AP/honors coursework in comparing applicants from different schools, such as when an "honors-weighted" HSGPA is used to rank applicants across schools. Under a strict "local-context" approach, the latter use would not be permitted.

25. UC policy already caps the total number of honors at eight. The reduced-weight option might, for example, lower this number to four.

## REFERENCES

Adelman, C. (1999). *Answers in the toolbox: Academic intensity, attendance patterns, and bachelor's degree attainment.* Washington, DC: U.S. Department of Education, Office of Educational Research and Improvement.

American Educational Research Association, American Psychological Association, and National Council on Measurement in Education. (1985). *Standards for educational and psychological testing.* Washington, DC: American Psychological Association.

Atkinson, R. C. (2001). Standardized tests and access to American universities. The 2002 Robert H. Atwell Distinguished Lecture, delivered at the 83rd Annual Meeting of the American Council on Education, Washington, DC.

Campbell, P. (2000). International Baccalaureate program. Paper presented to the Committee on Programs for Advanced Study of Math and Science in American Schools meeting, March 26, Irvine, CA.

College Board. (2004). AP central—Participation in AP: Annual participation. Retrieved on June 28, 2005, from http://apcentral.collegeboard.com/article/0, 3045,150–156–0–2055,00.html

Commission on the Future of the Advanced Placement Program (CFAPP). (2001). *Access to excellence: A report of the Commission on the Future of the Advanced Placement program.* New York: College Entrance Examination Board.

Crouse, J., & Trusheim, D. (1988). *The case against the SAT.* Chicago: University of Chicago Press.

CSU Institute for Education Reform. (1999). *The Advanced Placement program: California's 1997–98 experience.* Sacramento: California State University.

CSU Institute for Education Reform. (2001). *Characteristics and performance of Advanced Placement classes in California.* Sacramento: California State University.

*Daniel v. California.* (1999). Case No: RDVSOC174397, Superior Court of the State of California.

Doran, B. J., Dugan, T., & Weffer, R. (1998). Language minority students in high school: The role of language in learning biology concepts. *Science Education, 82*(3), 311–331.

Ekstrom, R. B., Goertz, M., & Rock, D. A. (1988). *Education and American youth.* Philadelphia: Falmer Press.

Eykamp, P. (2003). The effect of Advanced Placement credit on time to degree at the University of California. Paper presented at American Institutional Research 2003 Forum. Oakland, CA: UC Office of the President.

Gamoran, A. (1992). The variable effects of high school tracking. *Sociology of Education, 57*(4), 812–828.

Geiser, S., with R. Studley. (2003). UC and the SAT: Predictive validity and differential impact of the SAT I and the SAT II at the University of California. *Educational Assessment, 8*(1), 1–26.

Hurwitz, N., & Hurwitz, S. (2003). Is the shine off the AP apple? *American School Board Journal*, March.

Kirst, M. W. (1998). *Improving and aligning K-14 standards, admissions, and freshman placement policies.* Stanford, CA: Stanford University, National Center for Postsecondary Improvement.

Kowarsky, J., Clatfelder, D., & Widaman, K. (1998). *Predicting university grade-point average in a class of University of California freshmen: An assessment of the validity of a-f GPA and test scores as indicators of future academic performance.* Institutional research paper. Oakland, CA: UC Office of the President.

Mathews, J. (1998, March 30). 100 best high schools in America. *Newsweek.*

Morgan, R., & Maneckshana, B. (2000). *AP students in college: An investigation of their course-taking patterns and college majors.* Princeton, NJ: Educational Testing Service.

Morgan, R., & Ramist, L. (1998). *Advanced placement students in college: An investigation of course grades at 21 colleges.* Princeton, NJ: Educational Testing Service.

National Association for College Admission Counseling. (2004). *National school counselor survey.* Alexandria, VA: NACAC.

National Research Council. (1999a). *High stakes: Testing for tracking, promotion, and graduation.* Washington, DC: National Academies Press.

National Research Council. (1999b). *Myths and tradeoffs: The role of tests in undergraduate admissions.* Washington, DC: National Academies Press.

National Research Council. (2002a). *Learning and understanding: Improving advanced study of mathematics and science in U.S. high schools.* Washington, DC: National Academies Press.

National Research Council. (2002b). *Learning and understanding: Improving advanced study of mathematics and science in U.S. high schools—Report of the content panel on mathematics.* Washington, DC: National Academies Press.

Oakes, J. (1985). *Keeping track: How schools structure inequality.* New Haven, CT: Yale University Press.

Oakes, J. (1990). *Multiplying inequalities: Race, social class, and tracking students' opportunities to learn mathematics and science.* Santa Monica: RAND.

Oakes, J., Gamoran, A., & Page, R. N. (1992). Curriculum differentiation: Opportunities, outcomes and meanings. In P. Jackson (Ed.), *Handbook of Research on Curriculum* (pp. 570–608). New York: Macmillan.

Rothstein, J. (2004). College performance predictions and the SAT. *Journal of Econometrics*, volume 121, 297–317.

Santoli, S. (2003). Is there an Advanced Placement advantage? *American Secondary Education, 30*(3), Summer.

University of California. (1982). May 5, 1982, Academic Senate, Northern Section: Notice of Meeting of the Representative Assembly. Berkeley: UC Academic Council.

APPENDIX 4.1

Demographic Profile of UC Applicants by Number of AP/Honors Subjects Taken

| Number of AP/Honors Subjects Taken | Number of Students | Percent of Sample | Percent of Total | | | |
| --- | --- | --- | --- | --- | --- | --- |
| | | | Underrepresented Minorities | First-generation Students | Students from Low-performing Schools | Low Income |
| 0 | 4,343 | 8.5% | 23.2% | 34.5% | 13.8% | 22.1% |
| 1–4 | 9,305 | 18.2% | 22.9% | 34.7% | 16.1% | 23.1% |
| 5–8 | 10,024 | 19.6% | 19.9% | 33.1% | 18.4% | 22.0% |
| 9–16 | 18,169 | 35.6% | 17.5% | 29.8% | 19.5% | 20.6% |
| 17–24 | 7,578 | 14.8% | 12.6% | 23.7% | 15.4% | 18.7% |
| 25 or more | 1,677 | 3.3% | 11.2% | 19.6% | 15.3% | 17.1% |
| TOTAL | 51,096 | 100% | 18.5% | 30.5% | 17.4% | 21.1% |

(continued on next page)

APPENDIX 4.1 (continued)

Demographic Profile of UC Applicants by Number of AP Exams Taken

| Number of AP Exams Taken | Number of Students | Percent of Sample | Percent of Total | | | |
| --- | --- | --- | --- | --- | --- | --- |
| | | | Underrepresented Minorities | First-generation Students | Students from Low-performing Schools | Low Income |
| 0 | 27,302 | 53.4% | 20.1% | 30.2% | 13.5% | 19.9% |
| 1 | 4,820 | 9.4% | 20.4% | 37.0% | 23.3% | 24.8% |
| 2 | 4,940 | 9.7% | 18.9% | 33.8% | 24.8% | 24.1% |
| 3 | 4,318 | 8.5% | 17.8% | 31.4% | 23.4% | 23.7% |
| 4 | 3,344 | 6.5% | 15.7% | 29.2% | 21.0% | 21.2% |
| 5 or more | 6,372 | 12.5% | 12.1% | 24.3% | 18.0% | 19.3% |
| TOTAL | 51,096 | 100% | 18.5% | 30.5% | 17.4% | 21.1% |

Source: College Board and UC Admissions data, Fall 1998.

Population includes only California residents. Number of honors-level courses includes those completed by applicants in 10th, 11th, and 12th grades.

APPENDIX 4.2
Descriptive Statistics for Study Sample and Variables

### 1998 Fall UC Freshman Cohort

| Variable | N | Mean | Median | SD |
|---|---|---|---|---|
| Unweighted HSGPA | 19,772 | 3.53 | 3.57 | 0.34 |
| SAT I Composite | 18,965 | 1191 | 1200 | 165 |
| SAT II Composite | 18,800 | 1748 | 1750 | 245 |
| Number of AP/Honors | 19,820 | 6.6 | 6.0 | 4.6 |
| AP Exam Scores | 14,031 | 3.0 | 3.0 | 0.9 |
| Parents' Education | 18,701 | 15.7 | 16.0 | 3.3 |
| 1st-Year UCGPA | 19,074 | 2.90 | 2.98 | 0.65 |
| 2nd-Year UCGPA | 17,772 | 3.00 | 3.06 | 0.64 |
| 1st-Year Persistence | 18,682 | n/a | n/a | n/a |
| 2nd-Year Persistence | 18,390 | n/a | n/a | n/a |

### 1999 Fall UC Freshman Cohort

| Variable | N | Mean | Median | SD |
|---|---|---|---|---|
| Unweighted HSGPA | 16,934 | 3.55 | 3.60 | 0.33 |
| SAT I Composite | 16,907 | 1204 | 1210 | 164 |
| SAT II Composite | 16,791 | 1797 | 1800 | 249 |
| Number of AP/Honors | 16,981 | 7.6 | 8.0 | 4.9 |
| AP Exam Scores | 14,328 | 3.0 | 3.0 | 1.0 |
| Parents' Education | 16,350 | 15.6 | 16.0 | 3.3 |
| 1st-Year UCGPA | 16,560 | 2.92 | 3.00 | 0.64 |
| 2nd-Year UCGPA | 15,487 | 3.03 | 3.11 | 0.63 |
| 1st-Year Persistence | 16,122 | n/a | n/a | n/a |
| 2nd-Year Persistence | 16,045 | n/a | n/a | n/a |

*(continued on next page)*

APPENDIX 4.2 *(continued)*

| *2000 Fall UC Freshman Cohort* | | | | |
|---|---|---|---|---|
| *Variable* | *N* | *Mean* | *Median* | *SD* |
| Unweighted HSGPA | 20,376 | 3.54 | 3.58 | 0.34 |
| SAT I Composite | 20,441 | 1192 | 1200 | 167 |
| SAT II Composite | 20,065 | 1789 | 1790 | 250 |
| Number of AP/Honors | 20,471 | 7.7 | 8.0 | 5.2 |
| AP Exam Scores | 17,347 | 2.9 | 3.0 | 1.0 |
| Parents' Education | 19,624 | 15.4 | 16.0 | 3.4 |
| 1st-Year UCGPA | 20,041 | 2.89 | 2.97 | 0.67 |
| 2nd-Year UCGPA | 18,724 | 3.03 | 3.11 | 0.62 |
| 1st-Year Persistence | 19,714 | n/a | n/a | n/a |
| 2nd-Year Persistence | 19,626 | n/a | n/a | n/a |

| *2001 Fall UC Freshman Cohort* | | | | |
|---|---|---|---|---|
| *Variable* | *N* | *Mean* | *Median* | *SD* |
| Unweighted HSGPA | 24,363 | 3.53 | 3.58 | 0.34 |
| SAT I Composite | 24,502 | 1195 | 1210 | 165 |
| SAT II Composite | 24,177 | 1809 | 1810 | 251 |
| Number of AP Courses | 24,292 | 3.0 | 2.0 | 2.8 |
| Number of IB Courses | 24,305 | 0.2 | 0.0 | 1.3 |
| Number of CCC Courses | 24,292 | 0.5 | 0.0 | 1.4 |
| Number of Other Honors | 24,291 | 3.5 | 3.0 | 3.1 |
| Parents' Education | 23,622 | 15.5 | 16.0 | 3.4 |
| Family Income | 20,189 | $79,319 | $60,928 | $76,779 |
| 1st-Year UCGPA | 24,424 | 2.92 | 3.00 | 0.65 |

Correlation Matrix for AP/Honors Study Variables
(Fall 2000 cohort of first-time CA resident freshmen)

| | | SAT I composite | SAT II composite | honors 10th & 11th grade | 1st yr UCGPA | 2nd yr UCGPA | HSGPA unweighted | HSGPA semi weighted | parents education | AP exam mean scr | API quintile | HSGPA fully weighted | 1st yr persistence | 2nd yr persistence |
|---|---|---|---|---|---|---|---|---|---|---|---|---|---|---|
| SAT I composite | Pearson Correlation | 1 | .847** | .351** | .370** | .314** | .302** | .380** | .431** | .578** | .440** | .415** | .114** | .136** |
| | Sig. (2-tailed) | | .000 | .000 | .000 | .000 | .000 | .000 | .000 | .000 | .000 | .000 | .000 | .000 |
| | N | 20441 | 20059 | 20441 | 20011 | 18705 | 20349 | 20349 | 19597 | 17330 | 20056 | 20349 | 19684 | 19596 |
| SAT II composite | Pearson Correlation | .847** | 1 | .344** | .383** | .330** | .333** | .406** | .327** | .653** | .385** | .436** | .112** | .136** |
| | Sig. (2-tailed) | .000 | | .000 | .000 | .000 | .000 | .000 | .000 | .000 | .000 | .000 | .000 | .000 |
| | N | 20059 | 20065 | 20065 | 19657 | 18401 | 19981 | 19981 | 19240 | 17120 | 19691 | 19981 | 19318 | 19231 |
| honors 10th & 11th grade | Pearson Correlation | .351** | .344** | 1 | .142** | .111** | .114** | .403** | .095** | .120** | -.021** | .604** | .043** | .050** |
| | Sig. (2-tailed) | .000 | .000 | | .000 | .000 | .000 | .000 | .000 | .000 | .003 | .000 | .000 | .000 |
| | N | 20441 | 20065 | 20471 | 20041 | 18724 | 20376 | 20376 | 19624 | 17347 | 20085 | 20376 | 19714 | 19626 |
| 1st yr UCGPA | Pearson Correlation | .370** | .383** | .142** | 1 | .590** | .402** | .414** | .223** | .397** | .204** | .395** | .478** | .524** |
| | Sig. (2-tailed) | .000 | .000 | .000 | | .000 | .000 | .000 | .000 | .000 | .000 | .000 | .000 | .000 |
| | N | 20011 | 19657 | 20041 | 20041 | 18567 | 19952 | 19952 | 19208 | 17085 | 19667 | 19952 | 19441 | 19371 |
| 2nd yr UCGPA | Pearson Correlation | .314** | .330** | .111** | .590** | 1 | .330** | .338** | .192** | .332** | .169** | .321 | .008 | .342** |
| | Sig. (2-tailed) | .000 | .000 | .000 | .000 | | .000 | .000 | .000 | .000 | .000 | .000 | .260 | .000 |
| | N | 18705 | 18401 | 18724 | 18567 | 18724 | 18636 | 18636 | 17939 | 16087 | 18380 | 18636 | 18141 | 18141 |
| HSGPA unweighted | Pearson Correlation | .302** | .333** | .114** | .402** | .330** | 1 | .952** | .083** | .314** | .023** | .848** | .141** | .168** |
| | Sig. (2-tailed) | .000 | .000 | .000 | .000 | .000 | | .000 | .000 | .000 | .001 | .000 | .000 | .000 |
| | N | 20349 | 19981 | 20376 | 19952 | 18636 | 20376 | 20376 | 19554 | 17281 | 19992 | 20376 | 19620 | 19532 |
| HSGPA semi weighted | Pearson Correlation | .380** | .406** | .403** | .414** | .338** | .952** | 1 | .101** | .327** | .007 | .970** | .143** | .169** |
| | Sig. (2-tailed) | .000 | .000 | .000 | .000 | .000 | .000 | | .000 | .000 | .349 | .000 | .000 | .000 |
| | N | 20349 | 19981 | 20376 | 19952 | 18636 | 20376 | 20376 | 19554 | 17281 | 19992 | 20376 | 19620 | 19532 |

(continued on next page)

# APPENDIX 4.3 (continued)

| | | SAT I composite | SAT II composite | honors 10th & 11th grade 11th grade | 1st yr UCGPA | 2nd yr UCGPA | HSGPA unweighted | HSGPA semi weighted | parents education | AP exam mean scr | API quintile | HSGPA fully weighted | 1st yr persistence | 2nd yr persistence |
|---|---|---|---|---|---|---|---|---|---|---|---|---|---|---|
| parents education | Pearson Correlation | .431** | .327** | .095** | .223** | .192** | .083** | .101** | 1 | .243** | .456** | .109** | .088** | .103** |
| | Sig. (2-tailed) | .000 | .000 | .000 | .000 | .000 | .000 | .000 | | .000 | .000 | .000 | .000 | .000 |
| | N | 19597 | 19240 | 19624 | 19208 | 17939 | 19554 | 19554 | 19624 | 16625 | 19248 | 19554 | 18895 | 18812 |
| AP exam mean scr | Pearson Correlation | .578** | .653** | .120** | .397** | .332** | .314** | .327** | .243** | 1 | .339** | .315** | .106** | .126** |
| | Sig. (2-tailed) | .000 | .000 | .000 | .000 | .000 | .000 | .000 | .000 | | .000 | .000 | .000 | .000 |
| | N | 17330 | 17120 | 17347 | 17085 | 16087 | 17281 | 17281 | 16625 | 17347 | 17059 | 17281 | 16689 | 16622 |
| API quintile | Pearson Correlation | .440** | .385** | -.021** | .204** | .169** | .023** | .007 | .456** | .339** | 1 | -.007 | .084** | .105** |
| | Sig. (2-tailed) | .000 | .000 | .003 | .000 | .000 | .001 | .349 | .000 | .000 | | .321 | .000 | .000 |
| | N | 20056 | 19691 | 20085 | 19667 | 18380 | 19992 | 19992 | 19248 | 17059 | 20085 | 19992 | 19341 | 19254 |
| HSGPA fully weighted | Pearson Correlation | .415** | .436** | .604 | .395** | .321** | .848** | .970** | .109** | .315** | -.007 | 1 | .135** | .159** |
| | Sig. (2-tailed) | .000 | .000 | .000 | .000 | .000 | .000 | .000 | .000 | .000 | .321 | | .000 | .000 |
| | N | 20349 | 19981 | 20376 | 19952 | 18636 | 20376 | 20376 | 19554 | 17281 | 19992 | 20376 | 19620 | 19532 |
| 1st yr persistence | Pearson Correlation | .114** | .112** | .043** | .478** | .008 | .141** | .143** | .088** | .106** | .084** | .135** | 1 | .805** |
| | Sig. (2-tailed) | .000 | .000 | .000 | .000 | .260 | .000 | .000 | .000 | .000 | .000 | .000 | | .000 |
| | N | 19684 | 19318 | 19714 | 19441 | 18141 | 19620 | 19620 | 18895 | 16689 | 19341 | 19620 | 19714 | 19626 |
| 2nd yr persistence | Pearson Correlation | .136** | .136** | .050** | .524** | .342** | .168** | .169** | .103** | .126** | .105** | .159 | .805** | 1 |
| | Sig. (2-tailed) | .000 | .000 | .000 | .000 | .000 | .000 | .000 | .000 | .000 | .000 | .000 | .000 | |
| | N | 19596 | 19231 | 19626 | 19371 | 18141 | 19532 | 19532 | 18812 | 16622 | 19254 | 19532 | 19626 | 19626 |

**Correlation is significant at the 0.01 level (2-tailed).

# APPENDIX 4.4
## By Campus Results

Regression equation: UCGPA = $\alpha$HSGPA + $\beta$SAT I + $\varphi$SAT II

### UC Berkeley

| HSGPA Weighting for AP/Honors | Dependent Variable | | | |
|---|---|---|---|---|
| | 1st-year GPA | | 2nd-year GPA | |
| | $R^2$ | Rank | $R^2$ | Rank |
| No Bonus Point | 0.154 | 1 | 0.141 | 1 |
| Half Bonus Point | 0.145 | 2 | 0.134 | 2 |
| Full Bonus Point | 0.129 | 3 | 0.120 | 3 |

### UC Davis

| HSGPA Weighting for AP/Honors | Dependent Variable | | | |
|---|---|---|---|---|
| | 1st-year GPA | | 2nd-year GPA | |
| | $R^2$ | Rank | $R^2$ | Rank |
| No Bonus Point | 0.269 | 1 | 0.187 | 1 |
| Half Bonus Point | 0.259 | 2 | 0.178 | 2 |
| Full Bonus Point | 0.236 | 3 | 0.161 | 3 |

### UC Irvine

| HSGPA Weighting for AP/Honors | Dependent Variable | | | |
|---|---|---|---|---|
| | 1st-year GPA | | 2nd-year GPA | |
| | $R^2$ | Rank | $R^2$ | Rank |
| No Bonus Point | 0.141 | 1 | 0.081 | 1 |
| Half Bonus Point | 0.139 | 2 | 0.077 | 2 |
| Full Bonus Point | 0.124 | 3 | 0.067 | 3 |

### UC Los Angeles

| HSGPA Weighting for AP/Honors | Dependent Variable | | | |
|---|---|---|---|---|
| | 1st-year GPA | | 2nd-year GPA | |
| | $R^2$ | Rank | $R^2$ | Rank |
| No Bonus Point | 0.233 | 1 | 0.190 | 1 |
| Half Bonus Point | 0.224 | 2 | 0.182 | 2 |
| Full Bonus Point | 0.206 | 3 | 0.167 | 3 |

(continued on next page)

APPENDIX 4.4 (continued)

## UC Riverside

| HSGPA Weighting for AP/Honors | Dependent Variable | | | |
|---|---|---|---|---|
| | 1st-year GPA | | 2nd-year GPA | |
| | $R^2$ | Rank | $R^2$ | Rank |
| No Bonus Point | 0.136 | 1 | 0.103 | 1 |
| Half Bonus Point | 0.140 | 2 | 0.106 | 2 |
| Full Bonus Point | 0.130 | 3 | 0.097 | 3 |

## UC San Diego

| HSGPA Weighting for AP/Honors | Dependent Variable | | | |
|---|---|---|---|---|
| | 1st-year GPA | | 2nd-year GPA | |
| | $R^2$ | Rank | $R^2$ | Rank |
| No Bonus Point | 0.198 | 1 | 0.142 | 1 |
| Half Bonus Point | 0.183 | 2 | 0.136 | 2 |
| Full Bonus Point | 0.147 | 3 | 0.117 | 3 |

## UC Santa Barbara

| HSGPA Weighting for AP/Honors | Dependent Variable | | | |
|---|---|---|---|---|
| | 1st-year GPA | | 2nd-year GPA | |
| | $R^2$ | Rank | $R^2$ | Rank |
| No Bonus Point | 0.212 | 1 | 0.144 | 1 |
| Half Bonus Point | 0.204 | 2 | 0.132 | 2 |
| Full Bonus Point | 0.179 | 3 | 0.110 | 3 |

## UC Santa Cruz

| HSGPA Weighting for AP/Honors | Dependent Variable | | | |
|---|---|---|---|---|
| | 1st-year GPA | | 2nd-year GPA | |
| | $R^2$ | Rank | $R^2$ | Rank |
| No Bonus Point | 0.152 | 1 | 0.093 | 1 |
| Half Bonus Point | 0.151 | 2 | 0.094 | 2 |
| Full Bonus Point | 0.140 | 3 | 0.090 | 3 |

Source: College Board and UC admissions and longitudinal data for new UC freshmen entering in Fall 2000.

CHARLES A. RATLIFF

Chapter Five

# *K-12 and the Pipeline*
# *to Higher Education*

## INTRODUCTION

Access to higher education is dependent in very large part on the quality of
the K-12 schooling to which students are exposed, and California, like the rest
of the nation, is taking a long look at what it means to provide a high quality
education to elementary and secondary school students. Long before enactment of the No Child Left Behind Act (NCLB), many states were engaged in
a series of reform efforts aimed at improving a public education system that
was described by the renowned *A Nation at Risk* report (1983) as equivalent
to "an act of war" if designed and implemented by a foreign power. The
NCLB act goes one step further than the *Nation at Risk* report in its efforts to
shore up the nation's education system. It asserts that the nation's future
depends on not being deceived by measures of average achievement; that educators and policy makers should monitor the achievement of subgroups of students to ensure we do not deprive any student of a quality education and, by
extension, not overlook or devalue the potential contribution of any American
citizen. This is a bold and far-reaching step for the federal government and, in
the minds of some, it may be overreaching a bit. Education is primarily a state
responsibility. Amendment X of the United States Constitution assigns to

states all rights and responsibilities not explicitly assigned to the federal government by the Constitution nor prohibited by it to the states. Article IX, Section 5 of the California Constitution requires the legislature to set up a system of free common schools throughout the state.

California's commitment to public education was clear as far back as its second constitutional convention in 1879. Article IX of the revised state constitution read, "A general diffusion of knowledge and intelligence being essential to the preservation of the rights and liberties of the people, the Legislature shall encourage by all suitable means the promotion of intellectual, scientific, moral, and agricultural improvement" by providing "a system of common schools by which a free school shall be kept up . . . in each district. . . ." By 1879, the legislature had also enacted a compulsory attendance law for the state's youth (Education Code Section 48200). The state also supported a "normal school" to prepare teachers for the common schools, and the state constitution established the University of California as a public trust.

Despite this longstanding commitment to public education, available data indicate that California has failed to provide a quality education to all of its students. In 1986, California's State Board of Education adopted a set of model high school graduation requirements and called upon all public school districts to adopt similar high school graduation standards. That call did not have the force of law, however, and districts were free to adopt whatever standards they deemed to be appropriate. This deferral to local district choice led to growing disparity in expectations of students and, not surprisingly, to very different levels of student achievement. In 1999, California sought to shore up this weakness by enacting the Public Schools Accountability Act (PSAA), which defined academic content standards for what should be taught to every student at every grade level in four subject areas and seeks to hold schools accountable for steady growth in the proportions of students who meet state performance standards in each of these areas.

While California made an initial misstep by relying on a commercially available norm-referenced test to measure student achievement, it took steps shortly thereafter to design and implement a criterion-referenced test (the California Standards Test, CST) that actually measures the extent to which students have mastered what teachers are expected to be teaching, as defined by California's academic content standards. By this measure, California has been experiencing success in improving student achievement levels in recent years. However, this improvement has not been uniform across different student groups. For instance, based on the 2003 administration of the CST, only one in five Black and Latino students earned scores of proficient or advanced in the CST measure of English/Language Arts compared to more than half of their White and Asian peers in third, fifth, and seventh grades. In the area of mathematics, roughly one of three third-grade Black and Latino students demonstrated desired levels of proficiency, and the proportion demonstrating proficiency declined consistently in grades five and seven. In contrast, six of ten White and seven of ten Asian third-grade students demonstrated desired levels of proficiency in mathematics. However, similar to their Black and Latino peers, the proportion of Asian and White students scoring at the proficient or advanced levels in mathematics declined in grades five and seven (see table 5.1).

Other measures of student performance—demonstrated proficiency in Algebra 1, completion of college preparatory coursework, attainment of eligibility for selective universities in the state—reveal similar achievement gaps between Black, Latino, and American Indian students when compared to their White and Asian peers and between students from more and less affluent families.

Studies conducted in California and other states reveal that these observed achievement gaps are strongly correlated with something we have come to label as the opportunity gap. Fewer of the students whose test scores document achievement below desired levels have the opportunity to be exposed to quality preschool experiences, to be taught by fully credentialed and experienced teachers, to attend well maintained and equipped schools, to receive the learning support they need to meet expectations, or to be challenged to push the limits of their respective intellectual abilities. Virtually all of the resources that matter most in a quality education environment are least available to students attending our lowest performing schools.

TABLE 5.1
Percent Scoring Proficient or Advanced on the 2003 California Standards Test

|  | *3rd Grade* | *5th Grade* | *7th Grade* |
|---|---|---|---|
| *African American* | | | |
| English/Language Arts | 23% | 23% | 20% |
| Mathematics | 29% | 20% | 12% |
| *Latino* | | | |
| English/Language Arts | 19% | 20% | 20% |
| Mathematics | 33% | 22% | 16% |
| *Asian* | | | |
| English/Language Arts | 56% | 56% | 54% |
| Mathematics | 72% | 63% | 60% |
| *White* | | | |
| English/Language Arts | 52% | 54% | 54% |
| Mathematics | 61% | 49% | 44% |

*Source:* California Department of Education, 2004.

## THE CALIFORNIA CONTEXT

California's public school system now enrolls approximately 6.2 million students, distributed in more than 1,000 school districts and 6,000 schools throughout the state. The school districts in which California students are enrolled range from fewer than 50 students to more than 700,000, reflecting California's geographic diversity. The vast majority of them are served in traditional elementary, middle, and high schools sited within local communities. However, nearly 250,000 students received their education from a variety of non-traditional educational settings ranging from home schooling to continuation schools to education provided within the corrections system.

California provides a unique opportunity to think comprehensively, even systemically, about the challenges of providing access to quality education to an ever expanding and increasingly diverse group of students. The state population increases 500,000 to 600,000 people each year, driven by the combined impact of new immigrants declaring California as their place of residence and families continuing to have children. Recent estimates by the California Department of Finance's Demographic Research Unit indicate that the state population has now exceeded 36 million and may well reach 40 million by 2010 (California Department of Finance, 2004).

The challenge of this population growth is more than a simple matter of numbers; it is profoundly affected by the diversity of this growth. The sheer size and diversity of California's population magnifies the problems and challenges faced by public schools. The Department of Finance estimates that public school enrollment in academic year 2010–2011 is expected to be 6,405,550, a growth of 438,380 or 7.34 percent over the actual 2000–2001 public school enrollment (California Department of Finance, 2004).

*Looking different . . .*

Public school enrollment growth will not be equal across all racial/ethnic groups, however. For instance, Latino students enrolled in public schools will likely increase by 27.6 percent between 2000–2001 and 2010–2011, while White students are expected to decline by 16.7 percent and Black students are expected to decline by 9.7 percent over the same time period. The data in table 5.2 also reveal that in the 1990–1991 academic year, no racial/ethnic group constituted 50 percent or more of the public school enrollment, a fact that has been true since 1988–1989 in elementary schools, providing a mix of cultures, languages, and learning styles that have created extremely rich educational environments but that have also presented daunting challenges to California's public schools.

The diversity of California's population has also generated multiple opinions about how California should go about meeting the educational, social, and health needs of its people. The diversity of the school age popula-

TABLE 5.2
K-12 Graded Public School Enrollment by Ethnicity History and Projection

| | Year | Total | Amer. Indian | Asian | Black | Filipino | Hispanic | Pacific Island | White |
|---|---|---|---|---|---|---|---|---|---|
| Actual | 1990–91 | 4,842,174 | 37,263 | 382,985 | 411,868 | 108,319 | 1,661,799 | 26,358 | 2,213,582 |
| | 1992–93 | 5,089,808 | 40,471 | 417,957 | 432,709 | 120,984 | 1,836,757 | 28,427 | 2,212,503 |
| | 1994–95 | 5,242,078 | 45,118 | 435,311 | 450,078 | 127,772 | 1,982,161 | 29,565 | 2,172,073 |
| | 1996–97 | 5,512,155 | 47,479 | 456,537 | 473,948 | 132,681 | 2,187,148 | 32,496 | 2,181,866 |
| | 1998–99 | 5,748,344 | 49,380 | 470,483 | 492,299 | 137,963 | 2,373,881 | 36,303 | 2,188,035 |
| | 2000–01 | 5,967,170 | 51,641 | 483,958 | 498,694 | 144,365 | 2,585,676 | 38,489 | 2,164,347 |
| | 2002–03 | 6,176,698 | 53,906 | 504,394 | 508,217 | 156,815 | 2,802,800 | 41,497 | 2,109,069 |
| Projected | 2004–05* | 6,308,289 | 55,307 | 521,359 | 507,068 | 164,444 | 2,974,115 | 42,834 | 2,043,162 |
| | 2006–07* | 6,398,098 | 55,336 | 538,208 | 495,105 | 172,734 | 3,124,755 | 44,113 | 1,967,847 |
| | 2008–09* | 6,413,707 | 54,373 | 552,812 | 472,972 | 179,318 | 3,230,097 | 45,004 | 1,879,131 |
| | 2010–11* | 6,405,580 | 53,469 | 566,949 | 450,153 | 185,257 | 3,300,298 | 46,159 | 1,803,295 |
| 2000–01 to 2010–11 Change | | 7.34% | 3.53% | 17.15% | -9.73% | 28.32% | 27.63% | 19.93% | -16.68% |

Source: Department of Finance, Demographic Research Unit, 2003 Projection Series.

tion of students has and will continue to fuel debate about the extent to which English should be the only language of instruction and whether bilingual approaches should be embraced as a legitimate strategy to address the learning needs of students for whom English is not the primary language spoken in their homes. Is fluency in a second language a specialty skill that should be highly valued and in which the state should invest, particularly among education and social service providers, or is it another demand on public expenditures that should be avoided as much as possible?

Racial and ethnic diversity also challenges states to examine the desirable balance between pushing a common American culture for all residents of the United States and fostering an awareness, understanding, and respect for multiple world cultures. California is a bellwether state in this regard. Located on the Pacific Rim of the United States and with a population comprised of individuals and families from around the world, California wrestles daily with the question of whether its population diversity should be addressed as a liability or an asset.

In 1999, the California legislature created a joint committee to carefully examine public education at all levels in an effort to craft a coherent master plan for education that would encompass the entire education system from preschool through university levels. What they learned during the course of this examination and discussions with literally thousands of people was that while numerous educational reforms and promising practices could be identified, there was an alarming misdirection of efforts to address differences in achievement among students from different racial/ethnic and income groups. The growth in the numbers of students for whom English was a second language and in the numbers of students of color fostered a series of political battles over many of the issues delineated in the foregoing paragraphs, as well as debates about equal opportunity and elimination of affirmative action. At no time was the recognition of growing numbers of nonwhites and diversity among students viewed as an asset that could be used to enrich the educational experiences of all students.

Missing from the policy discussions were a focus on using the state's growth and diversity as a catalyst for encouraging literacy in multiple languages, for encouraging more students to consider teaching as a career (until school overcrowding created crises in some districts), for modifying the preparation requirements of prospective teachers, or for encouraging the state's colleges and universities to produce more educational leaders to staff burgeoning schools. The final Master Plan for Education transmitted to the legislature in 2002[1] sought to address these omissions in a systemic fashion by focusing on a coherent educational system that places a priority on meeting students' needs. Other states would be well advised to learn from California's experiences and view student diversity as an asset that can enrich the educational experiences of all students and indeed the social cohesiveness of the state.

*Voting Differently . . .*

California is home to some of the wealthiest people in the country as well as some of the poorest; it takes pride in the respected reputation of its public colleges and universities while wringing its hands over the uneven quality of its public schools. The quality of public schools was once as highly regarded as the state's postsecondary education system but the combined impact of demographics, economics, and politics has served to reduce California's investment in public education. That is not a statement that education is valued any less than prior decades. In fact, polls conducted by the Public Policy Institute of California reveal that Californians continue to place a high value on education and are even willing to pay additional tax to ensure accessibility to high quality public schools and postsecondary education.

Increasingly, public schools are the primary vehicle for educating the children of immigrant parents, children from low-income families, children of families who have fled political and racial oppression in other countries, and children suffering from the adverse impact of drug and alcohol abuse. However, the cost of addressing all of the needs that such children bring with them competes directly with the cost of providing roads, health care and medicine for a growing population of elderly, staffing for a corrections system bursting at the seams from an electorate intent on being tough on crime, and debt service. Even in the best of economic times, it is tough for California's policy makers to balance demands for public General Fund support with the actual revenue the state receives from various forms of taxes and fund transfers. It is particularly difficult when the state experiences recessionary pressures, prompting efforts by various stakeholder groups to capture the attention, if not the hearts, of policy makers and voters through such vehicles as opinion polls, demonstrations, and voter initiatives.

The combined impact of demographics and economics has also had a profound influence on the political environment in California. Roughly 80 percent of the voters in California are over 50 and White, many of whom have no children enrolled in public schools, while almost the same proportion of Californians dependent on public schools are young and from communities of color. Nearly six of every ten students enrolled in public schools today are students of color, a precursor for what lies ahead for the state as a whole.

The fallout from these demographic shifts and cyclical economic pressures are manifest in the decisions of California's electorate. In 1978, voters elected to contain their property tax burden by passing Proposition 13, which reduced property taxes to one percent of assessed value and limited property tax growth to a maximum of 2 percent each year, indexed to 1978 property tax values. Three years later, voters approved Proposition 101, which limited growth in public spending. The impact on education of these decisions has been profound, shifting funding for public schools from primarily local districts to the state. This shift, in turn, has led to increased scrutiny of the state's public schools and the extent to which schools expend their resources in ways that promote quality teaching and learning conditions.

Many of California's more affluent parents, dissatisfied with the deterioration of public schools generally, elect to enroll their children in private schools, move to different neighborhoods with better quality schools, or push to create magnet or charter schools. Unfortunately, these choices deprive less affluent children of the opportunity to interact with their more advantaged peers and reduce voter support for increased investment to improve the quality of neighborhood schools in urban and rural locales. With the absence of adequate funding, many public schools have struggled to attract and retain qualified teachers and administrators, to provide the learning support needed by students, and to successfully engage parents and employers as partners in the education process. Given the fact that these difficulties are being experienced concurrently with growth in the numbers of students of color, some have chosen to characterize the resulting tensions as the politics of race. An equally persuasive case can be made that it reflects a politics of scarcity, with parents and voters willing to embrace reduced opportunities for some if it preserves opportunities for their own children.

## THE INFLUENCE OF COURT DECISIONS

Historically, traditional public school districts controlled both their expenditures and the revenues that supported expenditure decisions. Up until the 1970s districts had the ability to raise additional revenue by raising property taxes to pay for school operations and facilities. This led to substantial inequity in the amount of money available to districts, largely due to huge variation in property valuation throughout the state and to subsequent court challenges beginning in 1968. In the *Serrano v. Priest*[2] lawsuit, finalized in 1976, the courts ruled that California must take steps to reduce revenue disparity among schools to within an acceptable "band" of difference. In response to this ruling lawmakers took steps to devise a new method of financing public schools that was more equitable. They adopted revenue limits for all schools and sought to equalize funding between districts by limiting increases to high revenue districts and providing substantial increases to low revenue districts (EdSource, 2004).

The *Serrano v. Priest* decision, however, did not address the revenue-raising ability of different districts. California voters addressed this issue in more dramatic fashion in 1978 when they approved Proposition 13. It is important to note that as this radical change in school funding was occurring, the state and nation were also engaged in a series of actions to win the "War on Poverty" declared by President Lyndon Johnson. It is not surprising then, that California policy makers became increasingly involved in not only providing funding for public schools but also telling the schools how those funds should be used, a practice that has come to be known as categorical funding. The practice of categorical funding has now led to more than 100 categorical streams of funding, with class size reduction (CSR) being one of the more recent additions to this list, where schools receive these funds only if they agree to carry out a specific set of actions state leaders think will result in improved educational quality and learning outcomes and meet specified reporting requirements. The explosive growth of categorical funding has created an incredibly complex funding system for public schools. While categorical state and federal money has directed more funding to schools serving high concentrations of students from low-income families with English language learning needs or with special education needs, it has failed to promote efficient and effective use of these resources or provide a logical basis for assessing whether the state is providing adequate funding to meet state expectations of its public schools.

California's Master Plan for Education addressed these two issues by calling for the creation of a Quality Education Commission and limiting categorical funding to three broad areas. The Quality Education Commission (QEC), authorized by Assembly Bill 2217 in 2001, was charged with defining the educational components that the state should ensure are present in every public school and calculating the cost of each component. The aggregate costs represent the level of investment California would need to make to ensure that every public school has the capacity to provide quality teaching and learning opportunities and clarify what that investment is intended to support—a level of clarity not possible with the current funding system. The Master Plan also recognized that while the QEC product would represent an adequate and equitable investment in all public schools, meeting *Serrano-Priest* requirements, it would not recognize the differential needs and readiness of students to benefit from the educational opportunities to which they will be exposed. Consequently, the Master Plan also called for three broad categories for which supplemental or "weighted" funding is appropriated to schools:

1. Student Characteristics—where schools serve larger proportions of high need students (e.g., low-income, special education, disabled) than is assumed in the adequate funding model.
2. District Characteristics—where the geographical location of schools generates expenditure requirements that differ from the adequate funding model assumptions (e.g., rural transportation needs).

3. Initiatives—where promising practices for improving student achievement can be piloted and evaluated and the outcomes can be used to adjust the adequate funding model or rule out various practices from future funding.

California's Education Code (Section 51004, added by Statutes of 1976) states in part that every student "shall have the opportunity to be prepared to enter the world of work; . . . every student who graduates from any state-supported educational institution should have sufficient marketable skills for legitimate remunerative employment; . . . and . . . such opportunities are a right to be enjoyed without regard to race, creed, color, national origin, sex, or economic status." State leaders in recent years have tried to meet this responsibility by adopting ambitious academic standards for what every student should be taught at each level from kindergarten through 12th grade, an assessment system to measure the extent to which students have mastered the material and achievement/progress benchmarks that hold school site principals accountable for student performance. Review of these performance data by principals, districts, state leaders, and researchers has revealed that we have fallen far short of the goal expressed in the state education code.

There are inescapable fiscal requirements to successfully achieve the foregoing statutory goal for all students in the state. California has weathered two major recessions in each of the last two decades and a milder one in the mid-1980s. The most recent recession has strained the capacity of the state to provide the resources to schools that are needed to ensure that a steadily growing student body has their needs met as they struggle to meet the state's expectations for achievement. The cyclical pressure of recessions is not unique to California, but the size of the state and the growth of populist involvement in policymaking has magnified both the severity of the fiscal crises and the complexity of resolving them. The impact on public education at the state level has been to provide only the funding necessary to meet Proposition 98 guarantees and fund enrollment growth. Proposition 98[3] is a voter-approved initiative (1988) that attempts to smooth the "boom and bust" funding of public schools by guaranteeing roughly 40 percent of state general fund revenue every year will be allocated to public schools. This guarantee is keyed to state funding of public schools in 1989 as a proportion of total state appropriations rather than actual needs of schools and has frustrated efforts to increase state investment to meet documented capital and fiscal needs of schools during tough economic times.

At the local level, the minimum funding guarantee of Proposition 98 has served more as a ceiling than a floor of funding and has forced draconian decisions to preserve sufficient teachers to maintain a credible instructional program, even while ignoring the need for reasonably current instructional materials, adequate numbers of textbooks, counseling and healthcare services, and support for students in need of additional assistance. In some instances, conditions have been allowed to deteriorate to such an extent that it has prompted legal actions by students themselves. Such is the case in *Williams v. California*,[4] where a group of students claimed in a lawsuit that they were being denied opportunities to learn due to such factors as the unavailability of Advanced Placement courses, inadequate facilities, and unsanitary conditions. The courts have provided a preliminary decision that upholds the students' complaints, ruling that California failed to ensure that all students have access to quality learning opportunities and that the state Constitution does not permit the state to escape its responsibility to provide adequate school facilities. California's current governor, Arnold Schwarzenegger, agreed with the plaintiffs and negotiated a settlement of the lawsuit, committing an initial $1 billion to remedy the conditions cited in the lawsuit.

## UNEQUAL OPPORTUNITY—UNEQUAL ACCESS

Admission and enrollment in postsecondary education is often viewed as an indicator of the quality of educational preparation received by public school students. While any Californian who has attained the age of 18, earned a high school diploma or its equivalent, and who can benefit from instruction is entitled to enroll in a local community college, the state has limited eligibility for admission to the California State University and the University of California to the top one-third and top one-eighth of high school graduates, respectively. The California Postsecondary Education Commission has conducted five studies over the past two decades to estimate the proportion of high school graduates that qualify for admission to the state's two selective public universities. A fairly consistent relationship in eligibility between student groups is evident in each of these studies. Generally, White high school graduates qualified for CSU and UC admission at about twice the rate of their Black and Latino peers, and Asian graduates have qualified for admission at about twice the rate of their White counterparts. In the most recent of these studies on the class of 2003, 14.4 percent of all high school graduates met UC eligibility requirements, slightly higher than the recommended 12.5 percent, and 28.9 percent met CSU admissions requirements, below its 33.3 percent state guideline (California Postsecondary Education Commission, 2004). Black 2003 high school graduates doubled their eligibility rate (from 2.8 to 6.2 percent for UC) and Latino graduates also made impressive gains (from 3.8 to 6.5 percent for UC). However, they remain substantially behind their White and Asian peers in attaining eligibility and, therefore, access to CSU and UC campuses.

In examining the reasons why students from different racial/ethnic backgrounds achieved eligibility for admission to the University of California and the California State University at such different rates, several

*Charles A. Ratliff*

TABLE 5.3
Eligibility of California High School Graduates to CSU and UC, 1996 and 2003

|  | Eligibility Rates California State University | | Eligibility Rates University of California | |
| --- | --- | --- | --- | --- |
|  | 2003 | 1996 | 2003 | 1996 |
| State Guidelines | 33.3% | 33.3% | 12.5% | 12.5% |
| All Graduates, 2003 | 28.8% | 29.6% | 14.4% | 11.1% |
| African American | 18.6% | 13.2% | 6.2% | 2.8% |
| Asian | 47.5% | 54.4% | 31.4% | 30.0% |
| Latino | 16.0% | 13.4% | 6.5% | 3.8% |
| White | 34.3% | 36.3% | 16.2% | 12.7% |

*Source:* California Postsecondary Education Commission, 2004.

researchers (Allen, Bonous-Hammarth, & Teranishi, 2002; Oakes et al., this volume; Rumberger & Wilms, 1992) have concluded that there is considerable inequity in student K-12 educational experiences, opportunities for learning, educational settings where they are expected to learn, and resources available to support learning. The analyses offered in the Allen, Bonous-Hammarth, and Teranishi (2002) study reveal that students of all racial/ethnic backgrounds demonstrate higher levels of achievement when enrolled in schools where the student body is comprised of more than half Asian/Pacific Islander students. Similarly, when enrolled in schools where more than half of the students are from Black or Latino groups, students from all racial/ethnic groups demonstrated lower levels of achievement when compared to statewide averages. While there is a high correlation between the incidence of low-income families in a school service area and high concentrations of Black and Latino enrollment, these findings also raise serious questions about the expectations schools have of certain students and both the amount and use of resources to foster high student achievement in these schools.

California's Public Schools Accountability Act (PSAA), enacted in 1999, is aimed at dramatically reducing achievement gaps between different student groups and students attending different schools. Its major components include:

- Annual assessment of student achievement in English/Language Arts and mathematics to determine the level at which students are mastering the material specified in the state academic content standards;
- Adoption of a score of 800 on the Academic Performance Index (API) as the baseline for achievement of all students;

- Designation of annual performance goals to be achieved by students in all schools whose average student scores fall below the adopted baseline;
- Financial incentives to reward high performing schools and assist schools with student scores in the lowest deciles launch new initiatives to substantially improve student performance;
- Sanctions that can be levied against the leadership of schools whose student achievement scores consistently fall far below the adopted baseline over multiple years and that fail to demonstrate any annual improvement in scores. These sanctions can range up to removing the principal and state takeover.

To date, the PSAA has realized only marginal success. Three factors substantially explain this modest progress. First, the recessionary pressures faced by the state led to the elimination of financial rewards during the second year of implementation to schools making significant improvement. This factor assumes that financial rewards *cause* schools to improve, a proposition that is hotly debated. Moreover, the general lack of adequate resources overall is an equally big, if not bigger, problem. Second, while academic content standards are clear and challenging, teachers have not yet uniformly developed the skills needed to teach to these standards effectively. Finally, the annual performance goals emphasize year-to-year growth rather than achievement of the baseline performance standard. The API accountability system specifies a growth target of five percent of the difference between 800 and the school's most recent API score. Consequently, a school with an API score of 600 in year 1 would have a growth target of 10 points in year 2 (.05 x [800–600]). With the leniency of this formula, a school could meet annual growth targets for 20 years and never meet the 800 threshold for acceptable student achievement.

The federal No Child Left Behind (NCLB) Act reflects a similar focus by the federal government. It also places a heavy emphasis on assessment and measurable yearly progress in student achievement. Unlike California's PSAA, NCLB stipulates a goal of 100 percent proficiency by a certain time and requires that test results be reported for every major racial/ethnic group, economically disadvantaged, English-language learners, and students with disabilities. This is an important feature in that it precludes neglect or ignorance of under-achieving student groups due to the leveling up effect of a core of very high achieving students. A significant limitation of NCLB is that it cannot mandate or specify a set of academic content standards with which all states must comply but must permit variation among states. The sanctions included in NCLB do not permit federal takeover of schools but do include curtailing access to federal funding, which is a very significant sanction for many schools.

A major shortcoming of state and federal efforts to increase accountability for student outcomes is the absence of sufficient funding to support
necessary changes in practices. Indeed, a substantial part of the explanation
for why some schools serve students less well than others is the absence of
sufficient resources to provide rich teaching and learning environments that
support a culture of high expectations and the tools and support needed to
meet these expectations. Any sanction that results in further reduction in
resources available to low performing schools runs counter to the intent of the
various accountability programs. This mismatch between resources and needs
is exacerbated during times of economic recession.

## RECONCILING ACCESS TO QUALITY AND ACCOUNTABILITY

Defining quality education in a concise way has been extremely elusive in
California and elsewhere. A number of different measures have been introduced as indicators of quality, each with its advantages and limitations. Education is both a teaching and a learning process. Focusing on one and not the
other will not lead to quality. But education, particularly public education,
exists within a social, political, and economic environment in which negotia-
tion and compromise are often required. Addressing issues at one level of the
education continuum without considering the impacts, both short- and long-
term, generally results in unintended consequences.

Two examples of unintended consequences can be seen in California's
experiences in equalizing funding among schools and in reducing class sizes.
The primary intent of the *Serrano-Priest* decision was to reduce unequal
access to learning opportunities by equalizing funding for schools located in
both affluent and less affluent neighborhoods. This decision increased state
involvement in the allocation of funding to local school districts. The equalization funding mechanism devised by lawmakers at the time did not anticipate the drop in revenue collected by the state resulting from approval of
Proposition 13 (a voter-approved initiative to limit growth in property taxes)
or the shift in the proportion of school funding provided by local communities and the state. Nor did it anticipate the mild recession that the state faced
in 1984. It may not have been possible to anticipate these events at the time
lawmakers were required to respond to the court order. Nonetheless, two
notable consequences resulted from state efforts to equalize funding among
schools:

- Recessionary pressures coupled with growing demand for General
  Fund support inhibited state efforts to equalize school funding by
  investing substantial new funds in low-wealth schools until all
  schools had roughly the same dollars per student as the wealthiest

schools. Compromises in policy and fiscal decisionmaking ultimately resulted in average funding per student leveling at lower levels (Public Policy Institute of California, 2001).

• Schools located in wealthier school districts that lost ground in per-student funding under equalization formulas found themselves in the position of not being able to offer with state funding the array of courses and extracurricular activities that parents had come to expect. In response, school personnel became more entrepreneurial in their efforts to secure additional funding through such activities as pursuit of grants and categorical funding sources. Parents, too, have become more active in fundraising, ranging from traditional sales to creation of foundations dedicated to financial support of the schools.

Class size reduction provides a second illustration of unintended consequences. When California policy makers became sufficiently convinced of the potential qualitative benefits of smaller student-teacher ratios to act in 1996, they required class sizes in kindergarten through 3rd grades to be reduced to 20:1. The legislation limiting class sizes for the early grades was rigidly defined and was not permissive of average class size approaches. Technically, California's Class Size Reduction (CSR) program was not initially a mandate, but schools not electing to reduce class sizes were denied access to state funding set aside to support CSR. The decision to move forward with CSR failed to adequately consider the impact of collective bargaining and teacher preparation programs on efforts to ensure that qualitative benefits expected from CSR were distributed equally among all students. Unintended consequences resulting from implementation of CSR include the following:

1. Some of the first schools to elect to undertake class size reductions shared a commitment to provide the best possible learning opportunities for their students. Not all of these schools, however, had the facilities or resources to reduce class sizes successfully and state support for CSR efforts proved inadequate to cover the cost of actually doing so. Lounges, auditoriums, and portables were deployed to create new classrooms, with little priority assigned to compatibility of activities with the assigned classroom space.

2. The reduction in class size created a demand for hundreds of new teachers throughout the state. California's colleges and universities were ill equipped to ratchet up production of new teachers to meet the increased demand while adhering to traditional instructional practices. The result was a substantial increase in the numbers of teachers employed to teach in public schools with an emergency waiver, which provides temporary authorization for individuals to teach without having completed requirements for a clear teaching credential. This outcome could easily have been anticipated by policy makers and, if considered, may well have resulted in alteration of implementation steps and state investments.

3. California school districts are not uniform in the employee rights and responsibilities to which they agree to adhere. The state Superintendent of Public Instruction has little to no authority to influence the distribution of new or continuing teachers to schools throughout the state. Consequently, schools differ in their ability to attract and retain qualified and effective teachers. In most cases teachers with the greatest seniority have the option of choosing the school site at which they would most prefer to teach. One of the outcomes of embracing the state's commitment to smaller class sizes has been the migration of many of the state's most experienced teachers from schools serving students from moderate- to low-income backgrounds to schools serving students from more affluent families. Although experience is not a guarantee of effectiveness, schools serving students from poorer families have been forced to employ larger numbers of teachers who have not yet completed their professional training. Moreover, site administrators at less affluent schools frequently struggle with acquiring the resources needed to maintain good working conditions for teachers or provide the needed instructional materials. In a competitive environment, these factors inhibit the ability of schools to retain even the qualified teachers they do manage to attract.

Developing accountability programs is not something that can be done, nor should it even be attempted, without a clear sense of what goals are to be pursued. California has traditionally relied on what its universities have said is required for success in postsecondary education as an appropriate indicator of student motivation and the quality of their educational achievement. Unfortunately, this approach permits germination of lower assumptions about what students who don't choose to pursue the university-defined sequence of college preparatory courses are able and disposed to learn. The adoption of academic content standards is a positive step away from this reliance. It defines a specific set of academic content that should be taught to all students, regardless of where they happen to reside or what their personal backgrounds may be, providing both clarity of goals and a clear statement that all students should be held to the same expectations. Unfortunately, there is no formal linkage or alignment between the K-12 academic content standards and the competencies expected of entering freshmen at California's public postsecondary education institutions. Evidence of this absence of alignment can be found in data on demand for remedial instruction. Over the past two decades, roughly one-third of the top 12.5 percent of high school graduates who were admitted to the University of California required remedial instruction in English/Language Arts, while roughly 40 to 50 percent of the top one-third of high school graduates admitted to a California State University campus required remediation in English or math or both. As recommended in the Master Plan for Education, California's colleges and universities need to take at least two steps that will go a long way toward remedying the problem of unequal learning opportunities to which students are exposed. It would also contribute to breaking down historical practices of California's education sectors operating independent of each other, if not in competition with each other, and foster greater collaboration and less finger pointing:

1. Align expectations of freshmen and the accompanying freshman curriculum so that they match 12th-grade academic content standards. This step would reduce the need to rely on multiple proficiency exams as proxy measures of student readiness for success in college.
2. Modify teacher preparation programs to ensure that prospective teachers are required to demonstrate both content expertise and the pedagogical skills to effectively teach the content standards to diverse groups of students. California's Commission on Teacher Credentialing should monitor teacher preparation program standards to ensure that such modifications are made as a condition of re-accreditation of teacher education departments at public colleges and universities.

As previously mentioned, California initially took a misstep when then governor Wilson required the use of a commercially available norm-referenced test to measure growth in student achievement resulting from implementation of CSR. The fact that the Stanford Achievement Test, version 9, selected by the Superintendent of Public Instruction and State Board of Education was not aligned with California's academic content standards was not considered by the governor at the time and, in the opinion of many teacher representatives, pressured teachers to "teach to the test" in order to avoid negative labels or state sanctions. The incongruence between what was required to be taught and what was actually being measured was quickly recognized by the State Department of Education and efforts were undertaken to develop a criterion-referenced test that would actually measure what teachers were required to teach. While the California Standards Test (CST) is a better measure of how well schools are helping students meet or exceed state baseline standards, it has not reduced the concern among teachers that they are required to teach to the test. California's experience with its accountability program reveals the following observations: Adoption of standards by itself is not enough to improve quality, even with appropriately designed assessments to measure mastery of the standards; organizational capacity to achieve standards and consequences for poor judgment and absence of effort is also essential. Teachers who do not have the expertise or content knowledge to effectively teach the state's standards cannot fully contribute to student achievement or institutional performance. Even qualified, competent teachers are likely to be less effective in promoting student achievement if they lack appropriate or adequate instructional materials. Both the state and local districts must prioritize investment in building capacity within their professional staff to effectively teach state standards to all students and help them better understand how to apply the learned knowledge and skills to participate in civic affairs and secure satisfying career employment.

Education should always be thought of as a teaching and learning process. Accordingly, judgments about the quality of education should never be limited to measures of input, process, or credentials of teaching professionals. Measures of quality that do not include student learning are incomplete and misdirected. Too often, such measures provide only indicators of capacity or the consistency with which things "get done right." They fail to provide reliable indicators of the extent to which this capacity is actually used effectively to facilitate student achievement or to provide much insight into whether "the right things" get done. This is an important distinction in that measures of the teaching process or learning outcomes independently fail to make the connection between potential, behavior, and outcomes. Recent studies by Education Trust indicate that in classrooms where students achieve below desired levels, teachers often expect far less of students and use curricular materials that rarely challenge students to use or develop higher level cognitive skills. In contrast, in classrooms where students demonstrate achievement at or above desired levels, teachers frequently challenge the intellectual boundaries of students with rigorous curriculum and provide assistance to help students meet their expectations, when needed. High performing schools generally have sufficient numbers of experienced and effective teachers to expose students to three or more consecutive years of instruction by effective teachers (EdTrust 2004). Clearly what teachers do in the classroom matters a great deal as states pursue the twin goals of reducing achievement gaps among student groups and fostering student achievement at or above a standard of proficiency.

Money is an ever-present concern of California's education system. Annually, California invests more than $50 billion in support of its public schools. This is a substantial investment, yet it is subject to ongoing debate as to its adequacy in meeting the needs of today's students. The question of funding adequacy is an issue of increasing priority in California and other states. Studies comparing California's K-12 investment per student with other states places California in the lowest decile. Yet, when average teacher salaries are compared between California and other states, California average teacher salaries rank number one in the nation (EdSource, 2004). The cost of living in different states varies significantly, but the juxtaposition of these findings, coupled with measures of student achievement, suggest an important hypothetical assertion: What you do with what you have can be as important as what you have.

Examination of parochial and church-based schools has consistently revealed a capacity to produce students with higher achievement and educational aspirations than their public counterparts. And they are able to achieve these outcomes at a lower per-student expenditure despite emphasizing enrollment of students of color and from low-income backgrounds. Many would argue that this is an inappropriate comparison because public and non-public schools do not have the same set of requirements to meet with respect to employee qualifications or facilities, nor do they have to comply with the same set of state and federal requirements. This is an accurate observation. However, it does not reduce the value of understanding the ways in which resources are used by non-public schools to facilitate student achievement and college-going behavior. Similar examinations should be conducted to learn how resources are used in high performing public schools, particularly those successfully fostering high achievement among students from low-income families and from racial/ethnic groups that have been disproportionately represented among the lowest achieving students historically.

Creating an education system that is held publicly accountable for its performance in promoting student achievement is a desirable goal but one not easily attained in a segmented fashion. The absence of a coherent and comprehensive approach to providing access to quality education opportunities often results in unhealthy competition for limited resources. Each education segment seeks to develop its own standards and policies to accomplish its mission. Knowledge of the missions, goals, and practices of other segments of the education system are often not considered essential, except as possible explanations for undesirable educational outcomes (e.g., these students were not taught well before they were sent to us). A beneficial consequence of the current spotlight on accountability is the shift in focus from institutions and processes to students and outcomes. The interdependence of each sector of the education system has become increasingly apparent in public efforts to improve student achievement. This realization has softened some of the traditional resistance to collaborative efforts and evolving partnerships that pool resources to better meet a set of needs (both student and institutional). Many educational institutions have created partnerships, each with its own coordinating structure, to address educational needs from preschool through university levels. These P-18 approaches to education delivery foster ongoing communication among teachers, administrators, and research personnel alike as they seek ways to improve the learning opportunities available to all students within their region. Indeed, this comprehensive approach to education delivery was strongly embraced in the Master Plan for Education.

## WHAT LIES AHEAD?

California's Master Plan for Education offers a solid guide for California's education system, but its success is dependent on Californians—elected officials, educators, parents, students, and employers alike—finding the will to break away from old practices. Historically California's education community has relied on the strength of the state's economy to generate sufficient revenue to preserve historical practices as well as fund all new initiatives the state wished to pursue. This has been possible in large measure because of the benefits of strong state investment in the education of its citizens and in educational research that produced a burgeoning knowledge industry that has expanded the number of jobs available in the state, extended the average lifespan of individuals, and improved the quality of life in many ways. The public perception of the opportunities available in California has also proved to be a magnet to people from around the world, many seeking opportunities for education and employment not available to them in their own countries. But for these aspirations to be realized, California will be compelled to alter, if not abandon, some of its historical practices. Chief among these is the belief that enough money is the answer to all problems that confront the state and its public service programs, including education.

Even the strength of California's economy has been insufficient to meet all of the demands for public expenditure that are mandated by the state constitution, laws, and voter directives. This has been particularly true in public education. Population growth and diversity have generated new demands for construction of hundreds of new schools, renovation and expansion of hundreds of existing schools, hiring of thousands of teachers and other school personnel, and acquisition of new knowledge and skills to effectively teach English-language learners. Meeting these needs requires expenditures that exceed the capacity of policy makers without seriously reducing spending in other highly valued areas. California must find a way and muster the will to increase its investment in education to ensure that enriching experiences are available to all students regardless of personal circumstances or place of residence. At the same time, it must not retreat from current efforts to ensure that public education investments are used effectively to provide quality teaching and learning opportunities that promote the achievement of all students enrolled in a public school, college, or university.

The California Master Plan for Education encompasses its entire education system, preschool through university, and puts forward the vision of injecting coherence and seamlessness in public education by emphasizing the importance of meeting student needs at all levels of education. While numerous examples and recommendations for achieving desirable goals are provided, the plan stops short of providing a detailed plan to govern transition of the current segmented education system to a more coherent, collaborative system. Rather, it serves as a guide to reduce the likelihood that California will again permit concerns about process and the perquisites of education employees to supercede the importance of meeting the needs of students enrolled in public schools. Among the more critical issues to be addressed in transforming California's public schools are the following:

- *Injecting rigor and high expectations into every classroom at every school, not just in college prep courses.* Educators, parents, and policy makers must all fight the temptation to think about education as an either/or dichotomy; either students prepare themselves for further education or they prepare themselves for jobs. Educators should accept the responsibility to contribute to readying students for both options. Whether enrolled in courses traditionally called "college prep" or courses traditionally called "vocational," teachers of these courses should be teaching strands from the state-adopted academic content standards and both expect and assist students to master this content at or above the state benchmarks for the grade level.

- *Using periodic assessments to improve teaching and learning not just to meet state and federal reporting requirements.* The primary goal of all teachers should be to meet the learning needs of students. They should be encouraged to develop and use their own assessments, including old-fashioned quizzes, to measure student learning throughout the year and modify instructional practices as needed based on review of the assessment results. Teachers without the skills to design assessment instruments independently should receive training and/or assistance in acquiring such skills. High stakes tests designed and administered by the state seldom provide timely feedback about student achievement or sufficient detail to be useful to teachers in improving teaching and learning practices. Such test data can, however, provide policy makers with an empirical basis for annual policy and budget decisions that affect education.

- *Using competitive market forces to better match teaching expertise and effectiveness with student needs and abilities.* California has been handicapped in its ability to get qualified and effective teachers into the schools that have the greatest need for their talents. Provisions contained within many collective bargaining agreements have secured the right for the most senior teachers to choose the sites at which they would most prefer to teach. An assumption embedded in this right is that all teachers who have met credentialing requirements are equally qualified and should be equally compensated, given similar background and experience. But qualifications and effectiveness are not the same thing, a fact more readily acknowledged by the private sector. Not all teachers are equally effective, despite similar qualifications and experience. School site administrators at low performing schools should be equipped with the capacity and authority to offer differential compensation, within certain limits, to attract teachers with a demonstrated track record in promoting student achievement, particularly with students most like those enrolled at their school. State policy makers should also take steps to improve working conditions at low performing schools by placing a priority on remedying deferred plant maintenance and modernization needs at such schools—an action both consistent with the *Williams* settlement and teacher statements of what they value most.

- *Training site leadership and administrators for 21st-century schools and equipping them with the authority to both manage and lead them.* California is in the midst of a large turnover of public school administrators. Much of this turnover can be attributed to the decision of baby boomers to enter into retirement. But the decision of many has been hastened by the growth in responsibility and complexity of the job. California's colleges and universities must modify the core skill set considered essential in preparing the next generation of public school administrators to meet student and school needs in the 21st century. Policymakers and local school boards must also consider and grant the authority needed for school administrators to go beyond simply managing school sites. They also should be expected and empowered to provide schoolwide leadership.

- *Reducing prescriptive statutes and categorical funding balanced by stronger accountability.* A dynamic tension exists between educators and policy makers in California. Public school teachers and administrators are charged with providing quality teaching and learning opportunities for every student at every public school in the state. However, numerous anecdotes and calls from constituents about real or perceived inequities in public schools has fostered a climate of distrust among policy makers that schools will address the needs of disadvantaged students, often followed by legislation directing how public money must be used to serve particular needs (commonly known as "categorical funding"). At the same time, educators and school administrators frequently turn to legislators for legislation that gives them greater leverage to discourage or encourage certain local behavior (e.g., discourage academic fraud such as purchasing term papers over the internet; encourage better nutritional habits by banning soda machines on school campuses; etc.). The cumulative effect of these efforts is micromanagement by statute and regulations, which frustrates creativity and flexibility among school site leaders. Rectifying this condition will require an exchange wherein policy makers reduce the volume of legislative and regulatory mandates placed on schools but hold schools and their employees accountable for effective use of public resources to promote student achievement.

- *Promote fluency in multiple languages.* Available research indicates that young children are particularly disposed to learning as their brains are developing. With the large numbers of families that have immigrated to California, many young students enter public schools with knowledge of a language other than English. Their early experiences in public schools should treat this fact as an asset that can enrich the education of all students as these students are also taught English. Ultimately, all students will be competing for employment in a world economy and California should be preparing all of its students for effective competition in such a world. Fluency in a second language is a skill that will enhance the competitiveness of California's public school graduates. Such an approach may also open new vistas for professional educators seriously seeking effective ways to open access to the parents of English-language learning students to participate as partners in the education of their children.

There are no magic bullets as California attempts to restore the luster to its public school system. There are many lessons that can be learned from examining what other states have done to address similar challenges in their efforts to ensure quality learning opportunities for all students, just as others have frequently looked at California for guidance in the past. Similarly, there is no magic elixir contained within the pages of California's new Master Plan for Education. It provides a vision to guide multiple approaches to improving quality for all students, insists that student needs and achievement drive educational decisions at all levels, and strongly urges both a short- and long-term view. The decline of California's public school system did not occur overnight and its restoration to excellence will also require a commitment to holding the course over a sustained period of time. Nonetheless, it is important that California not be content with modest changes around the margins. It is the predisposition to tolerate tinkering around the edges of school reform that generates the crisis that we all lament. All available indicators of quality and achievement indicate that the groups of students that comprise the majority of the public school population have been least well served and exposed to fewer quality learning opportunities. State officials and local governing boards should take steps to ensure that these learning inequities do not continue to persist.

## CONCLUDING COMMENTS

California has recently settled the lawsuit *Williams v. California*, which reiterates to state policy makers that unequal access to educational opportunities cannot be due to race or income conditions of students and their families nor can the state escape responsibility for ensuring that all students have access to comparable teaching and learning opportunities. This is hauntingly reminiscent of the *Brown v. Board of Education* ruling of 50 years ago, which also ruled that educational opportunities could not be unequal due to race. It is indeed unfortunate that citizens, particularly students, have felt compelled to resort to lawsuits to assert their right to teaching and learning conditions that enable them and/or their children to meet or exceed the performance standards that California has set for all students. But such lawsuits have provided periodic booster shots to challenge states to conform their behavior to their public rhetoric in support of equity and equal opportunities. We are increasingly reminded that not all students arrive at the gates of our public schools equally prepared and ready to benefit from the experiences to which they will be exposed. Accordingly, we should not expect to observe similar achievement among them when they are all exposed to similar experiences. Some students will need more or more consistent exposure to quality teaching and learning opportunities to achieve at levels comparable to their more advantaged peers. It is neither fair nor ethical to expect less of some students simply because of where they happen to live or what their racial/ethnic heritage happens to be. Similarly, it is not ethical or even logical to assume that simply providing equal dollars to all schools will equalize learning opportunities for all students when they do not begin their education with equal readiness or equal needs for learning support.

As indicated earlier, policy makers and educators alike should base their decisions on a deliberative review of empirical data on teaching and learning outcomes. What is learned and used from this review to improve student achievement has major implications for postsecondary education institutions and the more mature sectors of the employer market. Which types of students, with what characteristics, are best prepared to be successful in postsecondary education? Better yet, how can colleges and universities best help all students to achieve their educational objectives? Becoming familiar with and understanding what strategies are most effective in promoting student achievement in public schools with what types of students offers both a challenge and an opportunity for postsecondary education institutions. With a growing pool of well qualified high school graduates, colleges and universities will be challenged to select from this talented pool, a diverse class of students who will continually stimulate each other's intellectual development and provide opportunities for respectful interaction with people from around the world.

California's much studied system of postsecondary education should be particularly challenged in this regard. Access to the state's public universities, the University of California and the California State University, have been guided since 1960 by a set of eligibility criteria designed to exclude students from consideration rather than define the knowledge and skills necessary to be successful at a UC or CSU campus. While this has contributed to efficiency in the university admissions process, it has an unfortunate and undesirable impact on the state effort to improve the quality of its public schools. As more and more high school students do what is expected to gain admission to UC and CSU, it prompts a reaction from the universities to modify eligibility criteria to reduce the numbers of students who are eligible. This action is frequently supported by the Department of Finance and the Legislative Analyst's Office, the state's fiscal watchdogs. The message that is sent to students from such actions is: *succeeding in completing a rigorous educational preparation with good grades will not necessarily lead to acceptance at your preferred, or even any, public university campus immediately after high school graduation.* Such a message provides little motivation to subsequent generations of students to apply themselves consistently in achieving a rigorous education. The message is even more insidious when the majority of students to whom it applies come from low-income families and from racial/ethnic groups that have not historically had high rates of college attendance. California policy makers should modify the state's policy guidelines to instruct its public universities to set eligibility criteria that define the knowledge and skills needed for college success and establish admission criteria that allow them to fairly select their freshman student body from among the entire pool of high school graduates demonstrating the requisite knowledge and skills. This will not be a popular or easy undertaking but in an environment in which California is seeking to provide access to a quality educational experience for all students and hold public schools accountable for student achievement, it cannot afford to arbitrarily restrict access to its colleges and universities based solely on historical practices.

## NOTES

1. The Master Plan for Education was not adopted in total, but aspects of it have continued to be debated up to the present.

2. In 1971 the California Supreme Court ruled education a fundamental constitutional right and remanded *Serrano v. Priest*, 487 P.2d 1241, for trial in what is generally regarded as the first of the modern-era education finance litigation decisions. In 1976, the same court, in *Serrano v. Priest (Serrano II)*, 557 P.2d 929, affirmed the lower court's finding that the wealth-related disparities in per-pupil spending generated by the state's education finance system violated the equal protection clause of the California constitution.

3. See EdFund Online (1996), "A Primer on Proposition 98," for summary of its provisions.

4. In May 1999, several California organizations brought an "adequacy" lawsuit, *Williams v. State of California*, in the Superior Court of San Francisco County. Filed as a class action, the complaint cites deplorable conditions in school districts across the state and asks the court to require the state to ensure the provision of certain educational basics, such as qualified teachers, safe facilities, and textbooks.

## REFERENCES

Allen, W., Bonous-Hammarth, A., & Teranishi, R. (2002). *Higher education in a global society: Achieving diversity, equity, and excellence.* Oxford, England: Elsevier Publishers.

California Department of Finance. (2004). *Population projections by race/ethnicity for California and its counties 2000–2050.* Sacramento, CA: Author.

California Department of Finance Demographic Research Unit. (2004). *California K-12 public school enrollment projections by ethnicity.* Sacramento, CA: Author.

California Postsecondary Education Commission. (May 2004). *University eligibility study for the class of 2003.* Sacramento, CA: Author.

California State Legislature. (1999). Public Schools Accountability Act (PSAA) of 1999, Education Code Chapter 3, Statutes of 1999, as amended by Chapter 695, Statutes of 2000.

California State Legislature. (2003). Education Code Section 48200.

California State Legislature. (2003). Education Code Section 51004, added by Statutes of 1976.

EdFund Online. (1996, October). A primer on Proposition 98. Retrieved on June 28, 2005, from http://www.edsource.org/pub_edfct_prop98.cfm

Ed Source. (2004, May). *Rethinking how California funds its schools.* CA: author.

Education Trust (Menlo Park). (2004, Spring). *The real value of teachers: Using new information about teacher effectiveness to close the achievement gap.* Washington, DC: author.

National Commission on Excellence in Education. (1983). *A nation at risk: The imperative for educational reform.* Washington, DC: U.S. Government Printing Office.

Public Policy Institute of California. (2001). *School finance and California's Master Plan for Education.* San Francisco, CA: Author.

Rumberger, R. W., & Wilms, J. D. (1992). The impact of racial and ethnic segregation on the achievement gap in California high schools. *Educational Evaluation and Policy Analysis, 14,* 377—396.

Part 2

# The Role of Higher Education
# in Creating Access and Opportunity

ESTELA MARA BENSIMON
LAN HAO
LETICIA TOMAS BUSTILLOS

Chapter Six

# *Measuring the State of Equity in Public Higher Education*

On June 4, 1965, President Lyndon B. Johnson delivered the commencement address at Howard University titled "To Fulfill These Rights."

> . . . freedom is not enough. You do not wipe away the scars of centuries by saying: Now you are free to go where you want, and do as you desire. . . . You do not take a person who, for years, has been hobbled by chains and liberate him, bring him up to the starting line of a race and then say, "you are free to compete with all the others," and still justly believe that you have been completely fair. Thus it is not enough just to open the gates of opportunity. All our citizens must have the ability to walk through those gates. This is the next and the more profound stage of the battle for civil rights. We seek not just freedom but opportunity. We seek not just legal equality but human ability. Not just equality as a right and a theory, but equality as a fact and equality as a result.

With these words, Lyndon B. Johnson rightfully pointed out that equity involves both opportunity as well as results. Yet, almost forty years later, on just about every indicator of educational outcome, from degrees earned to grade point average, Whites and Asians are proportionally overrepresented and Blacks, Hispanics, and Native Americans are proportionally underrepresented. This is true in institutions that are highly selective and predominantly White, are open-access with a diverse student population, or are classified as Hispanic serving. But the details of this stratification remain largely invisible to the higher education community.

College enrollments for Blacks and Hispanics have increased nationwide, and generally there is a perception that major strides have been made to meet the goals of equal educational opportunity. Even though the number of underrepresented students who go to college and earn a degree is an impressive accomplishment when compared to forty years ago, the gap between Blacks and Hispanics, on the one hand, and their White, non-Hispanic counterparts persists and continues to grow (Ruppert, 2003). Students of color lag well behind Whites in completing college. In 2001, of high school completers ages 25 to 29, about 37 percent of Whites, 21 percent of Blacks, and 16 percent of Hispanics had received a bachelor's degree. For every Black and Latino student who earns a degree Whites earn two and Asians earn three (Swail, Redd, & Perna, 2003).

Simply put, the assumption that progress has been made *beyond access* into higher education for African Americans and Latinos is not supported by the evidence (Swail et al., 2003). In fact, the achievement gap among these groups is substantial nationwide and has not diminished in the last fifteen years (Bok, 2003).

Notably, inequity in educational outcomes in higher education has not been as prominent an issue as the educational gaps between minority and nonminority K-12 students. Unlike the K-12 schools, which under the No Child Left Behind legislation are required to report all of their data disaggregated by race and ethnicity, comparable requirements for higher education at the national or state levels are lacking. In general, the mainstream discourse among higher education policy makers and practitioners with regard to educational opportunity for underrepresented groups has been framed much more by the standpoints of affirmative action and diversity than by the standpoint of accountability. We attribute the absence of equity as an indicator of institutional performance in higher education accountability systems as one of the major reasons for the invisibility of growing inequality in educational outcomes. The purpose of accountability systems is to monitor the performance of tax-supported institutions on measures that are considered important by policy makers and the public in general and to identify areas where improvements are needed. As a policy tool, accountability systems can be an effective way of judging whether institutions are promoting state priorities (Shulock, 2004). In a globalized economy, a state's well-being depends greatly on an educated workforce, and in many states this implies a substantial increase in the proportion of historically underrepresented minorities going to college and attaining the baccalaureate. Treating equity in educational outcomes as a matter of institutional accountability is in the public interest. Policy makers in majority/minority states will want to know whether the higher education outcomes for specific populations (e.g., Latinos/as) can effectively meet workforce needs. Even though the need for measures of equitable educational outcomes for racial and ethnic groups with a history of underrepresentation in higher education seems so obvious, the reality is that most states' higher education systems are rarely evaluated on the metric of equity. Indeed, when several observers of higher education and policy analysts were asked to comment on accountability in higher education, none of them spoke about the need for indicators of equitable educational outcomes for racial and ethnic minorities (How Can Colleges Prove They Are Doing Their Jobs?," 2004).

In order to address the lack of equity as an indicator of accountability in higher education we introduce a framework, the Academic Equity Scorecard, that can be useful to policy makers, institutional leaders, and the public to answer questions such as: How well is the public system of higher education preparing underrepresented students to participate in the knowledge economy? What are the outcomes of public higher education for underrepresented students? Do the higher education outcomes for underrepresented students represent access to equal educational opportunities?

## THE RATIONALE FOR MAKING EQUITY AN INDICATOR OF ACCOUNTABILITY IN HIGHER EDUCATION

Accountability systems represent a source of feedback for policy makers as well as institutional leaders and negative feedback is particularly effective in creating a sense of public crisis and the need for action (Birnbaum, 2002). However, if policy makers were asked to quantify the progress made by underrepresented groups across the United States with respect to retention and graduation rates, they would be unable to provide answers based on empirical evidence. Although intra-institutional stratification based on race and ethnicity is a reality at most of the nation's colleges and universities, explicit indicators are rarely used to measure an institution's effectiveness in decreasing educational inequities (Bensimon, 2004; Bensimon et al., 2004). Moreover, while the concept of equity is implicitly reflected in the standards of most accrediting agencies, none of them requires institutions to report statistics about students of color beyond numbers admitted or enrolled.

There are now 44 states that publish some type of performance report for higher education (Burke & Minassians, 2002). Of the few equity indicators that are in use by some states, most typically deal with inputs (e.g., enrollments) rather than outcomes (graduation rates). Burke and Minassians's analysis of 29 state accountability reports revealed 15 different equity measures that are specifically related to the status of minority students, faculty, and staff yet all but five consisted of input measures. While 21 states use enrollment by race and ethnicity as a performance indicator, the indicator for graduation and retention by race and ethnicity was used in only nine states. Moreover, student transfers by race from two-year community colleges (where the greatest numbers of African Americans and Latinos are concentrated) to four-year colleges or universities is a measure used by just one state. Significantly, the biennial national report card *Measuring Up* (The National Center for Public Policy in Higher Education, 2000 and 2002) that grades states on several indicators does not include a student enrollment indicator based on race and ethnicity. Commenting on this absence, Burke and Minassians say, "In an age when ethnic groups have already attained—or will soon attain—majority status in the population, an indicator comparing the racial composition of the state population and student enrollment seems desirable as a performance measure in the category of participation" (2002, p. 106). In sum, current accountability systems in higher education do not and can not provide data that are reflective of the status of African Americans and Latinos and thus prevent policy makers from considering equity as a policy goal or taking into account the potential effects of policymaking on the state of equity. To bring attention to this problem and offer a solution we created the Academic Equity Scorecard, which we describe in this chapter. We also demonstrate its usefulness by showing the results of its application to California's higher education enrollment data.

## THE ACADEMIC EQUITY SCORECARD

The Academic Equity Scorecard, which is a replica of the diversity scorecard (Bensimon 2004), is modeled after Kaplan and Norton's (1992) balanced scorecard for business. Like the diversity scorecard, the Academic Equity Scorecard consists of four concurrent perspectives on institutional performance in terms of equity in educational outcomes for students: access, retention, institutional receptivity, and excellence. Each of these perspectives includes no more than five measures. For example, an access measure could be the distribution of first-time college students in the two- and four-year public sector.

We chose California as the demonstration state for the Academic Equity Scorecard because as the most populous state in the nation, with an economy that rivals most countries, California will be carefully watched by the rest of the nation as it charts a course toward the future of a new multicultural society. As one of five states with the greatest influx of minority undergraduate enrollments, California acutely exemplifies the growing educational chasm between Latinos and African Americans on the one hand and Asian Americans and Whites on the other (see table 6.1 in the appendix). Projections estimate that California will have the largest minority and immigrant populations in the

United States (Vernez & Mizell, 2001). By 2015, two-thirds of all undergraduate enrollments in California will be comprised by African Americans, Asian Americans, and Latinos (Carnevale & Fry, 2000). However, data demonstrate the growing disparity between these groups. RAND projections estimate that approximately 75 percent of all high school dropouts will be Latino and African American students while 89 percent of state college and university graduates will be Asian and White students.

We were able to construct a prototype Academic Equity Scorecard from data that were downloadable from the California Postsecondary Education Commission (CPEC), the California State University system, and the California Community Colleges. The data collected for all indicators were already disaggregated by race and ethnicity, and, with a few exceptions, most were longitudinal and covered at least a ten-year time span. With the data available we developed twelve performance indicators, or fine-grained measures, under the four perspectives. We were constrained in the development of indicators by the availability of public data that was also disaggregated by race and ethnicity. For example, we had access to data on remediation for the California State University system but not for the University of California, and we had data on the racial and ethnic composition of the UC faculty but not for the CSU. Although the data available limited the number of indicators, our experience suggests that fewer indicators increase the scorecard's utility because it helps institutional actors to focus more intensely on more specific areas rather than be overwhelmed by a laundry list of indicators. Figure 6.1 demonstrates the Academic Equity Scorecard with the four perspectives and the equity indicators developed for California's higher education system.

The *access perspective* enables institutional leaders to be more fully informed about the extent to which underrepresented students have access to institutions, programs, and resources. It further informs leaders as to the extent this access improves the ability of traditionally disenfranchised students to compete for academic advancement. For California's prototype, we used four indicators that are indicative of equity in access to a four-year degree (see figure 6.1). The A-G requirements,[1] as evidenced by the first indicator, were a critical inclusion as completion of California's "college readiness" curriculum ensures that students are academically prepared for advanced coursework at the university level. We recognize that higher education has no control over student completion of the A-G curriculum; however, we decided to make it into an indicator because it is impossible to attain equitable educational outcomes in California if Latinos and African Americans fall below equity on this indicator. The rationale for the scorecard is to establish a sensor that detects inequalities and brings them to the attention of individuals and groups who have the power to mobilize resources to address them. We also view the scorecard as a powerful information tool for external community groups that advocate for the educational rights of minority groups.

FIGURE 6.1
The Academic Equity Scorecard Framework

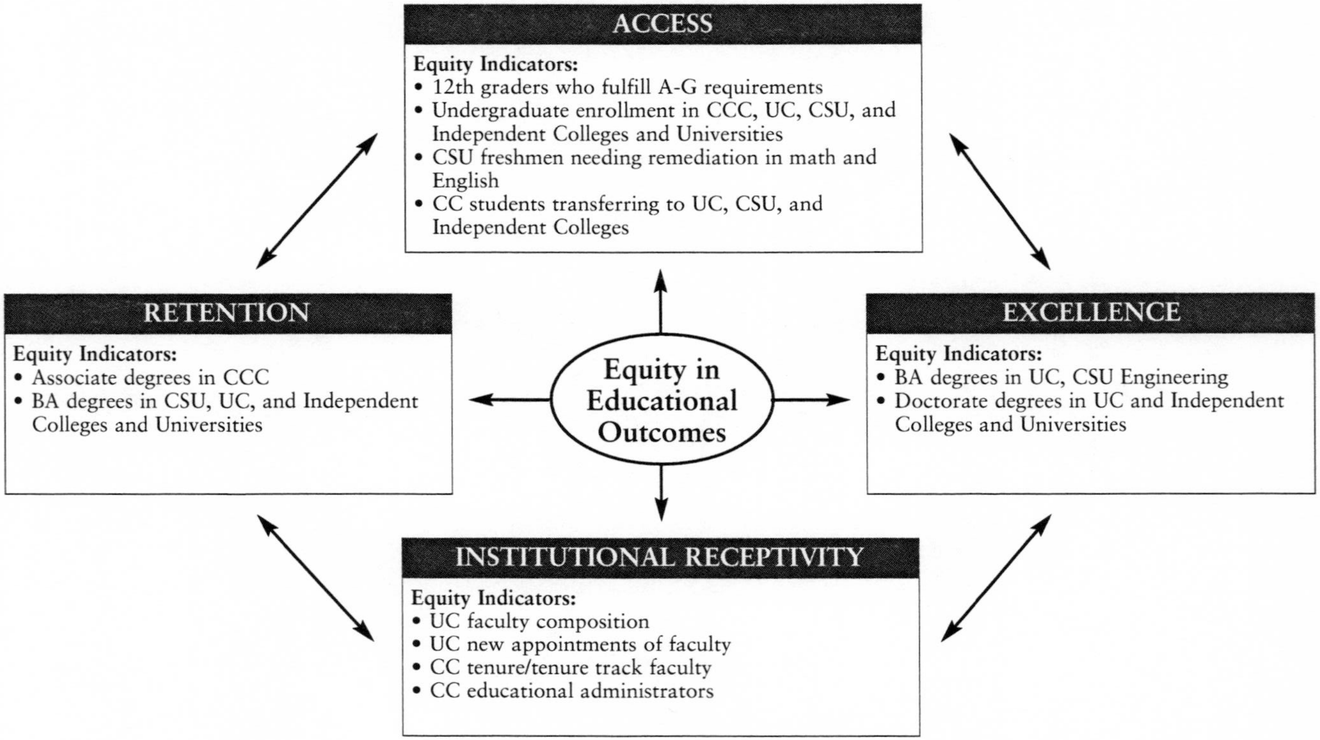

**ACCESS**

Equity Indicators:
• 12th graders who fulfill A-G requirements
• Undergraduate enrollment in CCC, UC, CSU, and Independent Colleges and Universities
• CSU freshmen needing remediation in math and English
• CC students transferring to UC, CSU, and Independent Colleges

**EXCELLENCE**

Equity Indicators:
• BA degrees in UC, CSU Engineering
• Doctorate degrees in UC and Independent Colleges and Universities

**Equity in Educational Outcomes**

**RETENTION**

Equity Indicators:
• Associate degrees in CCC
• BA degrees in CSU, UC, and Independent Colleges and Universities

**INSTITUTIONAL RECEPTIVITY**

Equity Indicators:
• UC faculty composition
• UC new appointments of faculty
• CC tenure/tenure track faculty
• CC educational administrators

Equally significant, the indicator for remediation was included in the scorecard because an exceedingly large proportion of California's African American and Latino students are found to need remedial courses. Moreover, new remedial policies in California[2] severely restrict the amount of time students have to master the coursework. The CSU remediation data provide a compelling picture of the large numbers of underrepresented students who are at risk of not completing the BA degree after having been admitted into a four-year college.

The *retention perspective* includes indicators that provide leaders with more concrete data on student outcomes. However, there were few outcome measures that are disaggregated by race and ethnicity, so it was only possible to develop indicators of AA or BA degree attainment. We could have included completion of occupational certificates but decided not to because the most urgent need, particularly for Latinos, is to double their rate of BA degree attainment (Fry, 2004; Swail, Cabrera, & Lee, 2004; Vernez & Mizell, 2001). The *excellence perspective* informs leaders about student outcomes associated with high achievement, such as providing access to competitive fields and leadership positions. This perspective answers such questions as: What are the comparative retention rates for underrepresented students by program? Do underrepresented students disproportionately withdraw from "hot" programs like engineering or computer science? The best indicator for this perspective would be GPA, but these data were not available to us. The final perspective, *institutional receptivity*, encompasses indicators of institutional support that create affirming campus environments for underrepresented students, such as faculty composition. Of the four perspectives, this one is the weakest in that it requires more qualitative measures that are difficult to obtain for an entire system. The use of disaggregated data in conjunction with the four perspectives yields a clear-cut measurement of institutional performance.

## THE ACADEMIC EQUITY INDEX: A FORMULA FOR EQUITY

The Academic Equity Index (AEI) is a measure of proportionality based on the population for each racial and ethnic group under analysis (Hao, 2002). The AEI is a ratio of two shares or percentages as expressed by the following formula:

$$
\text{Target Group's } \textit{Equity Index} \text{ for the educational outcome of interest} = \frac{\text{Target group with the educational outcome / Total students with the educational outcome}}{\text{Target group in the reference population / Total students in the reference population}}
$$

The numerator of the ratio is the share or percentage of the students from the target group (e.g., Latino students) among all students with a given academic feature, and the denominator is the corresponding reference measure. Different reference populations can be chosen as the denominator depending on the purpose of the data analysis. At its simplest level, it means that students in the K-12 system should be representative of the population demographics; college student enrollment should be representative of the K-12 students, the appropriate age cohort, or high school graduates; students who obtain post-secondary degrees should be representative of the college student body; students who successfully transfer from two-year community colleges to four-year colleges should be representative of the students in the community colleges; and the faculty composition should reflect the composition of the student body.

To illustrate how the AEI calculates equity, we will use a fictional high school's graduation numbers. The graduation class of this high school consists of 1000 students and 400, or 40 percent, are Latino students. From this graduation cohort a total of 450 students enroll in the state's flagship university, of whom 45, or 10 percent, are Latinos. These data, once placed in the formula for the AEI yield the following result:

$$
\begin{array}{c}
\text{Latino students' } Equity \\
Index \text{ for attending the} \\
\text{UC and CSU}
\end{array}
\quad
\dfrac{\begin{array}{c}\text{45 Latino students enrolled in college /}\\ \text{450 total cohort college enrollment}\end{array}}{\begin{array}{c}\text{400 Latino high school graduates /}\\ \text{1000 total high school graduates}\end{array}}
= \dfrac{10\%}{40\%} = 0.25
$$

## INTERPRETING THE ACADEMIC EQUITY INDEX SCORE

The Equity Index scores are easy to interpret. A score of 1.0 represents equity, a score less than 1.0 indicates below equity, and a score higher than 1.0 signifies above equity. Scores that are below or above 1.0 represent an equity gap that is reflective of an under-representation or overrepresentation in the specific indicator. In the fictional example just provided, the Academic Equity Index for Latino students attending the flagship public university is 0.25. Since the achievement of equity requires that each group's AEI result in 1.0, the result reveals a major gap in equity in the college-going rates for Latinos.

*Advantages of the Academic Equity Index*
*and Cautions for Interpretation*

Essentially, the Academic Equity Index is a standardized score that is indicator-specific, ethnic-specific, and year-specific that allows institutional leaders to make comparisons across groups based on their proportion of the population. It is also a simple, straightforward, and more accurate way of determining whether educational outcomes are improving or not.

The Academic Equity Index is a useful tool for quantifying the equity gap and can be useful for institutional researchers and policy analysts to analyze data already available to them. It also serves as a process of internal benchmarking or a point from which to judge improving performance standards. The choice of the denominator depends on whether the calculation of the index is driven by concerns for institutional improvement or external accountability of policy development. For example, if an institution wanted to calculate the AEI for Latino BA attainment to evaluate its own performance, it could choose as its reference population the group of people that represents the potential BA recipients such as Latino freshmen or the total undergraduate Latino population for the particular campus. Such an indicator would be institution-specific geared toward self-assessment and improvement. Applying the index to state-level equity analysis, there are similar considerations for the denominator. In this chapter the object of interest is the performance of California's higher education system in light of its changing demographic picture, thus the denominator for Latino BA attainment was based on California's 20–24 age group[3] from 1990 to 1999.

In absolute numbers, the condition of underrepresented students in California's postsecondary education system has been improving. More African Americans and Latinos are enrolled in college and more are transferring from the community colleges to the four-year institutions and attaining the BA degree. In California, the absolute numbers of Latino community college students who transferred to the UC system increased by a factor of 2.4 from 643 to 1,531 between 1988 and 2002. Yet increased headcounts can be deceptive because they do not reflect the gap in educational attainment with regard to trends in BA attainment in California over the past 20 years. Price and Wholford (2003) provide two reasons as to why the typical longitudinal analyses of the college participation of underrepresented students are inadequate measures. First, the statistics do not account for changes in the population growth over time, therefore overlooking the possibility that a group's larger percentage of, let's say, degrees earned could be a function of declining populations rather than increasing educational attainment. Second, a more useful measure from the perspective of equity is one that makes it possible to compare educational outcomes between different racial and ethnic groups. An important element of the Index is that it provides a natural benchmark. Given that equity is always designated as 1.0, it is fairly simple for policy makers and institutional leaders to interpret a group's status on a particular measure.

It is important to be cognizant of numerous factors that can contribute to an increase or decrease in the Equity Index number when interpreting the AEI for a particular group. Among them, an increase in the numerator that is faster than the increase in the denominator will result in an increase in the index that is representative of real progress. An increase in the numerator that is slower than an increase in the denominator will result in a decrease in the index, thus slowing improvement. A decrease in the numerator that is faster than a decrease in the denominator will result in a decrease in the index that is indicative of a real setback. Lastly, a decrease in the numerator that is slower than the decrease in the denominator will yield an increase in the index, which is not a true reflection of progress.

Because the index is sensitive to shifts in the population, Table 6.6 in the appendix provides a longitudinal overview of high school graduates and college enrollment trends in California by institutional sector for each racial/ethnic group from 1988 to 2001. These trends take into account the interpretation of changes in a group's Academic Equity Index, especially when the denominator of the index is based on high school graduates or college enrollments. For example, from 1988 to 2001, Latino enrollment at the UC system increased 60 percent, from 11,600 to 18,600, which represents significant progress in terms of access to educational opportunity. However, the Latino UC access equity index that uses high school graduates as the reference population shows a decrease along the timeline, due to the fact that Latino high school graduates increased at a much faster rate, from 49,000 to 104,000 (112 percent) in the same time period. This reflects the merits of the equity index in that educational data should not be interpreted without applying it to a meaningful context.

## CALIFORNIA'S ACADEMIC EQUITY SCORECARD

An Academic Equity Index was calculated for each indicator in the *access*, *retention*, *excellence*, and *institutional receptivity* perspectives. Data downloaded from the CPEC website are disaggregated into nine racial and ethnic categories. For this study we calculated the AEI for all of them, however, we only report the results for African Americans, Asian/Pacific Islanders,[4] Latinos,[5] and Whites. The calculation of the AEI involves turning headcount data (e.g., undergraduate enrollment, degree recipients) into percentages.

Table 6.1 provides an overview of the results on the Academic Equity Index for African Americans, Asians, Latinos, and Whites. For most of the indicators, the California Academic Equity Index (CAEI) represents a 15-year average unless indicated. We used three shades to indicate the state of equity for each group on each indicator as described as follows:

The use of shading makes two things eminently clear: African Americans and Latinos are below equity in the majority of indicators whereas Asians are above equity or at "almost-equity" in all but a few of the indicators. Whites are at or above equity in all indicators except in those few cases where they are in the "almost at equity" area. Although the column for African

Americans is primarily light gray, there are a few indicators in white suggesting that equity has been achieved in the transfer from community colleges to independent colleges and UC new faculty hires. Latinos exhibit the largest equity gap of all four groups; their column is primarily light gray with a smattering of medium gray. The most optimistic result for Latinos is having reached "almost at equity" in one indicator: community college transfers to the CSU system.

## THE RETENTION PERSPECTIVE: DEGREE ATTAINMENT

The retention perspective[6] consists of two degree attainment indicators, AA and BA, but we will address only the results for BA degree attainment in the University of California and California State University systems. The equity index for degree attainment for African Americans, Asians, Latinos, and Whites was calculated as follows:

$$\frac{\text{Target group degree recipients / all degree recipients}}{\text{Target group 20–24-year-olds / 20–24-year-olds in California}}$$

Table 6.2 provides the changes in the equity index for the University of California system from 1990 to 1999.

In 1999,[7] African Americans and Latinos had the lowest UC-BA attainment equity index of all groups. The share of UC-BA degree recipients among Asians was more than double their share in the 20–24 age group in California, resulting in an equity index of 2.3. The equity index trend for African Americans and Latinos shows almost no change in BA attainment from the UC system. In contrast, during the same period the AEI for Asians increased steadily, from 1.6 in 1990 to 2.3 in 1999. In contrast to African Americans and Latinos, more Asian Americans every year are concentrating in California's most elite higher education sector.

The results for the California State University System are provided in table 6.3. The average BA attainment AEI for Latinos graduating from the UC and CSU system was the same, 0.3. However, the trend for Latinos and Blacks in the CSU system shows a small but steady increase, which may be reason for cautious optimism. The CSU results for the Asian group are especially different from their UC results. First, their CSU index was more stable over the ten-year period and their outcomes are only slightly above equity. One interpretation for the marked overrepresentation of Asians in the UC system is that they have set their eyes on access to the more elite sector, and more of them are succeeding every year. Another interpretation is that Asians in the CSU system are more like African Americans and Latinos in terms of

**Color Codes for Three Levels of Equity**

| Level of Equity | Numerical Representation | Shade |
|---|---|---|
| Above Equity | > 1.0 | White |
| Below Equity | < 1.0 | Light Gray |
| Almost at Equity | 0.8–0.9 | Medium Gray |

TABLE 6.1
The California Academic Equity Scorecard

Equity Scorecard

| Perspectives | | Equity Indicators | White | Black | Asian | Latino/a |
|---|---|---|---|---|---|---|
| Access | 1 | 12th graders who fulfill **A-G requirements** vs. K-12 enrollment, 1988–2001 | 1.3 | 0.7 | 2.1 | 0.5 |
| | 2a | Undergraduate **enrollment in CCC** vs. high school graduates, 1988–2001 | 1.0 | 1.0 | 0.9 | 0.7 |
| | 2b | Undergraduate **enrollment in UC** vs. high school graduates, 1988–2001 | 0.9 | 0.5 | 2.4 | 0.4 |
| | 2c | Undergraduate **enrollment in CSU** vs. high school graduates, 1988–2001 | 0.9 | 0.8 | 1.2 | 0.6 |
| | 2d | Undergraduate **enrollment in independent colleges** vs. high school graduates, 1988–2001 | 1.2 | 0.8 | 1.1 | 0.4 |
| | 3a | Needing **remediation in math** upon entrance vs. number of freshmen in CSU, 2000–02* | 0.8 | 1.7 | 0.8 | 1.4 |
| | 3b | Needing **remediation in English** upon entrance vs. number of freshmen in CSU, 2000–02* | 0.6 | 1.4 | 1.4 | 1.3 |
| | 4a | CCC students **transferring to UC** vs. CCC enrollment, 1988–2002 | 1.0 | 0.4 | 1.9 | 0.6 |
| | 4b | CCC students **transferring to CSU** vs. CCC enrollment, 1988–2002 | 1.0 | 0.7 | 1.1 | 0.8 |
| | 4c | CCC students **transferring to independent colleges** vs. CCC enrollment, 1991–2000 | 1.2 | 1.1 | 1.0 | 0.7 |

TABLE 6.1 (*continued*)

*Equity Scorecard*

| Perspectives | | Equity Indicators | White | Black | Asian | Latino/a |
|---|---|---|---|---|---|---|
| Retention | 5a | AA degrees in CCC vs. 20–24 age group in CA, 1990–99 | 1.3 | 0.8 | 0.8 | 0.5 |
| | 5b | BA degrees in UC vs. 20–24 age group in CA, 1990–99 | 1.2 | 0.4 | 1.9 | 0.3 |
| | 5c | BA degrees in CSU vs. 20–24 age group in CA, 1990–99 | 1.3 | 0.5 | 1.0 | 0.3 |
| | 5d | BA degrees in independent vs. 20–24 age group in CA, 1990–99 | 1.5 | 0.6 | 1.0 | 0.3 |
| Excellence | 6a | BA degrees in UC Engineering vs. UC undergraduate enrollment, 1988–2001 | 0.9 | 0.4 | 1.2 | 0.4 |
| | 6b | BA degrees in CSU Engineering vs. CSU undergraduate enrollment, 1988–2001 | 0.9 | 0.4 | 1.8 | 0.5 |
| | 7a | Doctorate degrees in UC vs. UC undergraduate enrollment, 1988–2001 | 1.3 | 0.5 | 0.3 | 0.3 |
| | 7b | Doctorate degrees in independent vs. independent undergraduate enrollment, 1988–2001 | 1.0 | 0.6 | 0.6 | 0.3 |
| Institutional Receptivity | 8 | UC faculty composition vs. student enrollment, 2002 | 2.1 | 0.8 | 0.4 | 0.4 |
| | 9 | UC new appointments of faculty positions vs. student enrollment, 2002 | 2.0 | 1.0 | 0.5 | 0.5 |
| | 10 | CCC tenure/tenure track faculty vs. CC student enrollment, 2002 | 1.8 | 0.9 | 0.6 | 0.4 |
| | 11 | CCC educational administrators vs. CC student enrollment, 2002 | 1.6 | 1.4 | 0.4 | 0.5 |

TABLE 6.2

California Academic Equity Index Results for University of California
Based on BA Degrees Awarded by Race and Ethnicity for 1990–1999

| | California Academic Equity Index | | | |
| | White | Latino/a | African American | Asian |
|---|---|---|---|---|
| Year 1990 | 1.3 | 0.2 | 0.4 | 1.6 |
| Year 1991 | 1.3 | 0.3 | 0.4 | 1.6 |
| Year 1992 | 1.3 | 0.3 | 0.4 | 1.6 |
| Year 1993 | 1.3 | 0.3 | 0.4 | 1.5 |
| Year 1994 | 1.2 | 0.3 | 0.5 | 1.6 |
| Year 1995 | 1.2 | 0.3 | 0.4 | 1.8 |
| Year 1996 | 1.2 | 0.3 | 0.4 | 2.0 |
| Year 1997 | 1.1 | 0.3 | 0.4 | 2.2 |
| Year 1998 | 1.1 | 0.3 | 0.4 | 2.3 |
| Year 1999 | 1.0 | 0.3 | 0.4 | 2.3 |
| 10-year average | 1.2 | 0.3 | 0.4 | 1.9 |

TABLE 6.3

California Academic Equity Index Results for California State University System
Based on BA Degrees Awarded by Race and Ethnicity for 1990–1999

| | California Academic Equity Index | | | |
| | White | Latino/a | African American | Asian |
|---|---|---|---|---|
| Year 1990 | 1.4 | 0.3 | 0.4 | 1.0 |
| Year 1991 | 1.4 | 0.3 | 0.4 | 1.9 |
| Year 1992 | 1.4 | 0.3 | 0.4 | 1.9 |
| Year 1993 | 1.3 | 0.3 | 0.5 | 1.9 |
| Year 1994 | 1.4 | 0.3 | 0.5 | 1.9 |
| Year 1995 | 1.3 | 0.4 | 0.5 | 1.9 |
| Year 1996 | 1.3 | 0.4 | 0.6 | 1.0 |
| Year 1997 | 1.2 | 0.4 | 0.6 | 1.1 |
| Year 1998 | 1.1 | 0.4 | 0.6 | 1.2 |
| Year 1999 | 1.1 | 0.5 | 0.6 | 1.2 |
| 10-year average | 1.3 | 0.3 | 0.5 | 1.0 |

socioeconomic and educational background than the Asians who go to UC. It is possible that the Asians in the CSU system are recent or first-generation immigrants from less well-educated families. However, without more detailed data on the students' backgrounds we can only speculate. One thing that these results make clear is that identity labels such as Hispanic or Latino/a and Asian are inadequate for states like California where the flow of immigrants is constant. Right now we lack the information to determine whether the Asian students in the UC and CSU represent different generations, national origins, and economic background. It is possible that Asians in the UC system are middle- or upper-class Chinese, Korean, Japanese, or Indian and that Asians in the CSU system are recent arrivals from Vietnam. The same problem arises with the Latino/a category in that we have no way of knowing what background characteristics distinguish Latinos/as in the UC from those in the CSU and CCCs.

An alternative way of looking at the baccalaureate equity index for the UC and CSU systems is by comparing whether the gap between groups is growing or shrinking. In tables 6.4 and 6.5, we provide an analysis of the gaps between Whites, Asians, and Latinos/as and the gaps between Whites, Asians, and African Americans.

Briefly, the White-Latino/a and White-Black gaps in BA attainment are getting smaller in both the UC and CSU systems. However, in the UC system the narrowing of the White-Latino/a/Black gap appears to be more of a function of declining White enrollments and a very large increase in Asian enrollments. As can be seen in table 6.4 the gap between Asians and Latinos/as and Asians and Blacks has been growing rapidly since 1997. In 1990 the Asian-Latino/a gap was 1.4 and in 1999 it had increased to 2.0. In the CSU system, as shown in table 6.5, the trends in the White-Latino/a and White-African American gaps are also shrinking, making the ten-year average the same for the UC and CSU systems. The Asian-Latino/a and Asian-African American gaps in the CSU are notably smaller than in the UC system.

## CONCLUSIONS AND IMPLICATIONS

Nationally, there is an absence of baseline data and benchmarks that would make it possible to engage in a systematic and continuous self-appraisal at the state and institutional levels of the educational outcomes for underrepresented students. The reason for the absence of equity indicators is not lack of data, but that much of the available data are not disaggregated by race and ethnicity. Where the data are available, they are not reported in a manner that permits policy makers to make a quick assessment of the state of equity in higher education. The disaggregation of data by race and ethnicity, particularly in relation to outcomes, is not a routine practice with the exception of data on

### TABLE 6.4
California Academic Equity Index Gaps for University of
California BA Degrees Awarded by Race and Ethnicity for 1990–1999

| | California Academic Equity Index Gaps | | | |
| | White-Latino/a | White-African American | Asian-Latino/a | Asian-African American |
|---|---|---|---|---|
| Year 1990 | 1.1 | 0.9 | 1.4 | 1.2 |
| Year 1991 | 1.1 | 0.9 | 1.3 | 1.2 |
| Year 1992 | 1.0 | 0.8 | 1.3 | 1.2 |
| Year 1993 | 1.0 | 0.8 | 1.2 | 1.1 |
| Year 1994 | 0.9 | 0.8 | 1.3 | 1.2 |
| Year 1995 | 0.9 | 0.8 | 1.5 | 1.4 |
| Year 1996 | 0.9 | 0.8 | 1.7 | 1.6 |
| Year 1997 | 0.8 | 0.7 | 1.9 | 1.8 |
| Year 1998 | 0.7 | 0.7 | 2.0 | 1.9 |
| Year 1999 | 0.7 | 0.7 | 2.0 | 1.9 |
| 10-year average | 0.9 | 0.8 | 1.6 | 1.5 |

### TABLE 6.5
California Academic Equity Index Gaps for California State University
BA Degrees Awarded by Race and Ethnicity for 1990–1999

| | California Academic Equity Index Gaps | | | |
| | White-Latino/a | White-African American | Asian-Latino/a | Asian-African American |
|---|---|---|---|---|
| Year 1990 | 1.2 | 1.0 | 0.7 | 0.6 |
| Year 1991 | 1.1 | 0.9 | 0.6 | 0.5 |
| Year 1992 | 1.1 | 1.0 | 0.6 | 0.5 |
| Year 1993 | 1.1 | 0.9 | 0.6 | 0.4 |
| Year 1994 | 1.0 | 0.9 | 0.6 | 0.4 |
| Year 1995 | 1.0 | 0.8 | 0.6 | 0.4 |
| Year 1996 | 0.9 | 0.7 | 0.6 | 0.5 |
| Year 1997 | 0.8 | 0.6 | 0.7 | 0.5 |
| Year 1998 | 0.7 | 0.6 | 0.7 | 0.6 |
| Year 1999 | 0.7 | 0.5 | 0.7 | 0.6 |
| 10-year average | 0.9 | 0.8 | 0.7 | 0.5 |

college access. Thus, even though the values of diversity and equity are espoused in the mission statements of higher education institutions and in state level documents, progress toward their attainment is not something that is monitored because neither the institutions nor the states' higher education systems have adopted equity as a performance standard to judge their effectiveness in improving the educational outcomes of underrepresented students, including those from low-income backgrounds.

Without equity standards the performance of institutions or the states' higher education systems cannot be evaluated. Without performance measures, neither institutional leaders nor policy makers can learn about their systems' actual educational outcomes. Most importantly, if leaders and policy makers are not learning, changes in policies and practices are less likely.

Monitoring a state's progress toward the achievement of equity in postsecondary education outcomes is important for several reasons, among them:

1. In a global economy, employability is contingent on educational level. By 2006, one-third of all new job openings nationally will require at least some college education (Carnevale, 1999). The nation's economy will depend on the effectiveness of the higher education system to educate individuals from underrepresented groups, such as African Americans and Latinos/as, for the jobs of the future (Vernez & Mizell, 2001).

2. By 2015, 48 percent of Latinos and 18 percent of African Americans will enter a labor sector where job growth will primarily be concentrated among managerial, professional, technical, healthcare, and educational professions, all of which require postsecondary training (Carnevale, 1999). Indicators of educational status and attainment suggest that unless dramatic improvements take place, African Americans and Latinos/as will continue to be overrepresented in low-paying and service jobs and underrepresented in the higher paying jobs associated with the attainment of middle-class status (Myers, Parks, & Hacegaba, 2000).

3. Across the country, institutions of higher education suffer extraordinary periodic budget reductions that are resulting in the elimination of college classes and programs with a simultaneous increase in tuition costs. A consequence of these cuts and cost hikes is the turning away of thousands of students, many of whom are African Americans and Latinos/as, from four-year public institutions. In the community colleges, these students are being closed out of basic skills courses and denied special services because support centers have begun to fold as a result of lean budgets. While the impact of these cuts on historically underrepresented populations is not yet known, it is safe to say that marginalized students will be disproportionately disadvantaged by them. Budgetary cuts that result in reduced admissions for underrepresented students increases the imperative to monitor the educational outcomes for these students.

4. Performance indicators are particularly effective in service organizations like postsecondary education. Such organizations often exhibit information

asymmetries, that is, structures where campus-level staff possess much more information about outcomes than those to whom they are accountable. This unbalanced information structure can constrain or impede the development of policies to achieve desirable values (Gormley Jr. & Weimer, 1999).

It is said that what gets measured gets noticed. We are well aware that accountability systems in and of themselves will not solve the problem of inequality, but we believe that it is important to make visible the inequitable outcomes that are not currently addressed in accountability reports for the following reasons:

First, equity indicators call attention to differences in educational outcomes. Studies on the growing achievement gap for minority group students are published fairly regularly in journals and as special reports released by government agencies and education policy think tanks (see for example, Carnevale & Fry, 2000; Fry, 2002; Vernez & Mizell, 2001 ). These types of studies and reports, even though very important, are not useful for continuous monitoring of educational outcomes because they provide too many measures and they usually lack targets. In contrast, the Academic Equity Index provides a straightforward method of establishing the current condition of educational outcomes and the target for improvement (O'Day, 2004). Having a target for improvement enables policy makers, the public, advocacy groups, and institutional leaders to be cognizant of and continuously monitor progress toward equity, a practice that currently is not employed at the state or institutional level. Institutional leaders react to demands in their external environments (Birnbaum, 1996) thus the expectations of federal, state, and accrediting bodies, whether expressed in the form of accountability indicators, performance-based funding measures, or professional standards are likely to influence what gets attended to.

Second, concrete indicators can help mobilize action within the higher education community and they provide a better focus for applied policy than do more general directives (Ewell, 1994). Having indicators of equity increases the likelihood of continuous monitoring and feedback, which is important because "if interest in minority enrollments and degree achievement is uncoordinated and sporadic, administrative interest will likely follow suit" (Birnbaum, 2002, p. 457).

Third, if the feedback provided by equity indicators raises the specter of a crisis situation, it is also more likely to motivate the investment of resources. The initiatives that have had the greatest impact on higher education came about in response to events perceived to be national threats. The launching of Sputnik resulted in unprecedented amounts of federal aid to higher education; the racial disturbances that erupted in Watts, Newark, Detroit, and Washington DC in the 1960s led to the creation of special programs of financial aid and support services specifically targeted to increase access to higher education to low-income and minority students. Today demographers and others warn that if current patterns of educational outcomes continue there will be negative economic and social consequences for California (Lopez, Ramirez, & Rochin, 1999; Myers, Park, & Hacegaba, 2000). In several state and national reports policy analysts have emphasized the need to move more of the Latino/a population from the bottom of the economic and educational levels into the middle and upper levels (Myers, Park, & Hacegaba, 2000). The results of the California Academic Equity Index suggest that this is not happening and that educational outcomes for Blacks and Latinos/as have in fact worsened. Yet none of the current state-level reporting systems call attention to the growing inequity.

Fourth, indicators are useful in that they make intended outcomes more visible and concrete, and policy makers as well as institutional leaders can become more aware of what needs to be accomplished (Ewell, 1994). As Ewell points out, "Explicitly tracking degree-completion rates for minority students, for instance, sends a far more concrete signal about what needs to happen than does the more general goal of increasing access" (p. 8).

Equity represents an ideal state. In a situation that is marked by great inequalities, as is the case in California's higher education system, it is critically important to have a means of making these inequalities transparent in order to raise awareness of their existence. Without evidence, there is less urgency to act on the problem. Accordingly, we recommend:

1. Postsecondary education commissions across the United States, in consultation with representatives from the public and independent sectors, should incorporate equity performance indicators measured in terms of percentages shares, rate, and absolute numbers and report on them annually.
2. Institutions of higher education should incorporate equity performance indicators into their institutional studies, report on them annually to their boards of trustees, and post them on their websites for greater public dissemination.
3. Individual campuses should create their own equity performance measures and use them for decision making, resource allocation, strategic planning, program review, and the development of new initiatives.

In effect, if we do not become more intentional about the achievement of equity in educational outcomes, the combination of minority-majority states and their growing demand for a better-educated workforce portends a nation that will be polarized into two segments separated by a shrinking middle. As Myers, Parks, and Hacegaba suggest, an end result of this situation will be "an elite group of college educated workers [that] flourishes in the growing knowledge-based sector of the economy, while at the low end an even larger group of poorly educated workers—composed largely of immigrants and minorities—holds low-paying service and manual-labor jobs"

(2000, p. 2). Higher education plays a critical role in preparing individuals for participation in a knowledge-based economy. In view of the demographic changes in the student population, particularly among Latinos/as, to not be conscious of differences in educational outcomes is shortsighted; to not muster the political will to address the problem is irresponsible.


## NOTES

1. California's A-G curriculum consists of the minimum course requirements for admission into the California State University and University of California systems.

2. The new remedial policy for the California State University system (Executive Order 665, amended Title V of the California Code of Regulations) mandates that all incoming freshman complete any remedial coursework in English and mathematics within two semesters and the summer if they expect to enroll in the Fall semester of the second year. Those students who do not complete this requirement are given "stop-out" notices and are disenrolled from the university. These students are then required to complete coursework at the community colleges if they wish to re-enroll at CSU. The CSU website does not include data on the number of students who successfully complete the remedial coursework within the one-year time limit.

3. The California population data were downloaded from the RAND California's Population and Demographic Statistics (http://ca.rand.org/stats/popdemo/popdemo.html). This database consists of the U.S. Census data organized into five-year interval age groups, e.g., 15–19, 20–24, and 25–29. This chapter uses the 20–24 age group as the reference population.

4. Pacific Islanders do not include Filipinos because in the CPEC data they were reported as a separate category.

5. The Latino/a category includes everyone that was classified as Hispanic, as well as Mexican Americans.

6. Due to space limitations we only discuss in greater detail the results under the retention perspective; however, a detailed discussion of the results for all the indicators is available in a longer version of this chapter, which can be downloaded from http://www.usc.edu/dept/education/CUE/research.html.

7. For this indicator we downloaded the 20–24 age group for California from RAND's California Statistics website (http://ca.rand.org/stats/statistics.html), and 1999 was the most recent year for which data were available.


## REFERENCES

Bensimon, E. M. (2004). The diversity scorecard: A learning approach to institutional change. *Change, 36*(1), 45–52.

Bensimon, E. M., Polkinghorne, D. E., Bauman, G. L., & Vallejo, E. (2004). Doing research that makes a difference. *The Journal of Higher Education, 75*(1), 104–126.

Birnbaum, R. (1996). Administrative commitments and minority enrollments: College presidents' goals for quality and access. In C. Turner, M. Garcia, A. Nora, & L. I. Rendon (Eds.). *Racial and Ethnic Diversity in Higher Education* (ASHE Reader Series) (pp. 446–459). Needham Heights, MA: Simon & Schuster Custom Publishing.

Bok, D. (2003, October 14). Closing the nagging achievement gap in minority achievement. *Chronicle of Higher Education.*

Burke, J. C., & Minassians, H. P. (2002). Reporting higher education results: Missing links in the performance chain. *New Directions for Institutional Research* (p. 116). San Francisco: Jossey-Bass.

California State University. (1997). Executive Order 665: Determination of Competence in English and Mathematics. California State University: Office of the Chancellor, 1–4.

Carnevale, A. P. (1999). *Education = success: Empowering Hispanic youth and adults.* Washington, DC: ETS.

Carnevale, A. P. & Fry, R. A. (2000). *Crossing the great divide: Can we achieve equity when Generation Y goes to college?* Princeton Educational Testing Service.

Ewell, P. (1994). Developing statewide performance indicators for higher education: Policy themes and variations. In S. Ruppert (Ed.), *Charting Higher Education Accountability: A Source Book on State-level Performance Indicators* (pp. 147–166). Denver, CO: Education Commission of the States.

Fry, R. (2002). *Latinos in higher education: Many enroll, too few graduate.* Washington, DC: Pew Hispanic Center.

Gormley, W. T., & Weimer, D. L. (1999). *Organizational report cards.* Cambridge: Harvard University Press.

Hao, L. (2002). *The equity index: A method to measure equity in educational outcomes for minority students.* Poster session presented at the annual meeting of the Association for the Study of Higher Education in Sacramento, CA.

How can colleges prove they're doing their jobs? (2004, September 3). *The Chronicle of Higher Education, 51*(2), B6–B10.

Johnson, L. B. (1965, June 14). To fulfill these rights. Commencement address at Howard University.

Kaplan, R. S., & Norton, D. P. (1992). The balanced scorecard: Measures that drive performance. *Harvard Business Review, 70*(1), 71–79.

Lopez, E., Ramirez, E., & Rochin, R. I. (1999). *Latinos and economic development in California.* Sacramento: California Research Bureau.

Myers, D., Park, J., & Hacegaba, N. (2000). *Reversing the shrinking middle and polarization in California's labor force: Report of a pilot investigation.* Los Angeles: USC Center for Urban Education and Population Research Laboratory.

O'Day, J. A. (2004). Complexity, accountability, and school improvement. In S. H. Fuhrman & R. F. Elmore (Eds.), *Redesigning Accountability Systems for Education* (pp. 15–43). New York: Teachers College Press.

Price, D. V. & Wholford, J. K. (2003). *Race, ethnic and gender inequality in educational attainment: A fifty state analysis, 1960–2000.* Paper presented at The Harvard Color Lines Conference, The Civil Rights Project, Harvard University.

Ruppert, S. S. (2003). *Closing the college participation gap: A national summary.* Boulder, CO: Education Commission of the States.

Shulock, N. (2004, September 3). No less than a cultural shift. *The Chronicle of Higher Education, 51*(2), B6–B10.

Swail, W. S., Cabrera, A. F., & Lee, C. (2004). *Latino youth and the pathway to college.* Washington DC: Pew Hispanic Center.

Swail, W. S., Redd, K. E., & Perna, L. W. (2003). Retaining minority students in higher education: A framework for success. *ASHE-ERIC Higher Education Report, 30*(2).

The National Center for Public Policy and Higher Education. (2000). *Measuring up 2000: The state-by-state report card for higher education.* San Jose, CA: Author.

The National Center for Public Policy and Higher Education. (2002). *Measuring up 2002: The state-by-state report card for higher education.* San Jose, CA: Author.

Vernez, G., & Mizell, L. (2001). *Goal: To double the rate of Hispanics earning a bachelor's degree.* Prepared for The Hispanic Scholarship Fund. Santa Monica: RAND Education Center for Research on Immigration Policy.

# APPENDIX

## TABLE 6.6
High School Graduates and College Enrollment Trends
in California by Institutional Sector, from 1988 to 2001

Among public high school graduates, between the years 1988 and 2001:
- African Americans increased by 16%, from 19,000 to 22,000.
- Latinos increased by 112%, from 49,000 to 104,000.
- Asians increased by 61%, from 23,000 to 37,000.
- Whites decreased by 7%, from 150,000 to 139,000.

Among UC enrolled students, between the years 1988 and 2001:
- Black undergraduate enrollment decreased from 5,500 to 4,400.
- Latino undergraduate enrollment went up slightly from 11,600 to 18,600.
- Asian/Pacific Islander undergraduate enrollment doubled from 21,000 to 45,000.
- White undergraduate enrollment decreased from 70,000 to 55,000.

Among CSU's undergraduate students enrolled between the years 1988 and 2001:
- Black undergraduate enrollment increased slightly, from 15,000 to 18,000.
- Latino undergraduate enrollment has more than doubled from 30,000 to 64,000.
- Asian/Pacific Islander undergraduate enrollment increased from 33,000 to 45,500.
- White undergraduate enrollment has declined from 169,000 to 114,000.

Among independent institutions undergraduate students enrolled between the years 1988 and 2001:
- Black undergraduate enrollment increased from 5400 to 7200, which represents a growth of 33%.
- Latino undergraduate enrollment increased from 7,500 to 16,500, which represents a growth of 120%.
- Asian undergraduate enrollment increased from 10,000 to 16,000, which represents a growth of 60%.
- White undergraduate enrollment had a slight decrease, from 68,000 to 65,000, which represents a decrease of 4%.

Among community colleges:
- Black undergraduate enrollment had a slight increase from 85,000 to 114,000.
- Latino undergraduate enrollment has more than doubled from 178,000 to 415,000.
- Asian/Pacific Islander undergraduate enrollment almost doubled from 99,000 to 188,000.
- White undergraduate enrollment decreased from 735,000 to 647,000.

CATHERINE L. HORN
PATRICIA MARIN

Chapter Seven

# *Reaping the Benefits of* Grutter: *College Admissions and Racial/Ethnic Diversity*

The tool of affirmative action, while useful in its own right, has not succeeded in lifting the country's higher education system out of crisis. As outlined in the introductory chapter of this volume, even with the use of race-conscious admissions policies, there continues to be enormous disparity between college admission rates of students of color—particularly Blacks and Latinos—and Whites. Despite the gaps it has not been able to fill, however, affirmative action continues to be an important tool for the higher education community in working toward increasing access to college for traditionally underserved students.

In June 2003 the U.S. Supreme Court handed down two critically important decisions related to affirmative action and higher education and rekindled a broader discussion of how to work toward racial/ethnic diversity on college campuses. Specifically, the Supreme Court's *Grutter v. Bollinger* and *Gratz v. Bollinger* decisions confirmed both the compelling governmental interest of racially/ethnically diverse college campuses and the legality of narrowly tailored race-conscious means by which to achieve that diversity. As stated in the majority opinion in *Grutter*, "In summary, the Equal Protection

Clause does not prohibit the Law School's narrowly tailored use of race in admissions decisions to further a compelling interest in obtaining the educational benefits that flow from a diverse student body" (p. 32). Within this legal framework, postsecondary institutions (where state law does not prohibit it) are now empowered to (re)consider the ways in which students are assessed and admitted to their campuses. In particular, colleges and universities can think broadly about how admission procedures might work to enhance both the institutional and broader social justice agenda of expanding access and, from that, reaping the benefits of racial/ethnic diversity. Even for those states unaffected by *Grutter* because of overriding state law, such as California, with a non-White student body majority and a population increasing in its diversity, the challenge of expanding access nonetheless remains.

This chapter sets out to rethink how postsecondary institutions might consider proactively using their admission processes to promote racially/ethnically diverse campuses considering the broader goal of increasing access to higher education. It begins with a synopsis of the major historical, legal, and political events that have influenced access to higher education over the last half-century and led up to the University of Michigan affirmative action lawsuits. Within that context, the chapter next highlights the documented benefits of racial/ethnic diversity and discusses what the literature reveals about the effectiveness of various "race-neutral" admissions procedures at achieving such diversity on college campuses, particularly those tried within the last decade. Finally, it offers key considerations for reconceptualizing college admission procedures that might work toward achieving diverse student bodies rather than acting as additional barriers. This chapter will concentrate its discussion on the most selective campuses across the country because they are the institutions for which race-conscious admission policies are most relevant (Kane, 1998).

## HISTORICAL, LEGAL, AND POLITICAL BACKDROP

During the first forty years of the twentieth century, the majority of students on college campuses mirrored the dominant society—primarily wealthy, White males. Shortly after World War II, however, a sea change began to occur. The GI Bill, implemented in 1944, afforded hundreds of thousands of less affluent individuals an opportunity to attend college, and the country responded with a large expansion of its higher education infrastructure (Orfield, 1998). Further, the courts began to endorse the rights of minorities to an "equal" education comparable to that received by Whites (*Missouri ex Rel. Gaines v. Canada*; *Sweatt v. Painter*; *Brown v. Board of Education*). Serious interest in creating access to higher education did not begin in earnest, however, until the 1960s. The broader civil rights movement, coupled with increasing local, state, and federal attempts to end segregation and discrimination in the workplace, acted as the catalyst for such higher education efforts.

In particular, several executive orders and the enactment of the Civil Rights Act of 1964 reinforced a broad political desire to enhance minority opportunities in the United States. Title VI of the Civil Rights Act specifically furthered the desegregation of elementary, secondary, and postsecondary institutions by threatening to withhold federal funds from those programs that did not provide equal educational opportunity regardless of race/ethnicity. Interestingly, however, the numbers of Black students who were enrolled in the most selective colleges and universities across the country during the early- and mid-1960s did not increase significantly, in large part because of the admissions processes employed. As Bowen and Bok (1998) note, "although [selective schools] might recruit Black students vigorously, they did not seriously modify their regular standards for admission and financial aid. Their academic requirements were too demanding to accommodate more than a tiny number of African American students, and their tuition and fees were more than most of those who were admitted could afford" (p. 4). As the decade progressed, however, these institutions began to adopt more overtly race-conscious affirmative action admission policies in an effort to embrace strengthening civil rights efforts as well as to redress the historical and continued segregation and inequality that existed in the country's public elementary and secondary schools (Orfield, 1998).

Orfield (1998) argues that efforts to create a diverse college and university student body hit their peak in the mid- to late-1970s. The percentage of Black 18 to 24 year olds enrolled in college hit a high of 33 percent in 1976 (Pelavin & Kane, 1990). Further, the percentage of Blacks enrolled in Ivy League universities rose from 2.3 percent in 1967 to 6.3 percent in 1976 (Bowen & Bok, 1998). It was also during this decade that the U.S. Supreme Court issued its opinion in *Regents of the University of California v. Bakke* (1978), an example of how California has often been the site of controversy regarding race-conscious policies. Justice Powell, writing the controlling opinion of the Court, said that the educational benefits of diversity were a compelling governmental interest that justified using race as one "plus factor" among many in higher education admissions decisions. Despite the initial chilling effect the ruling had in California and the rest of the nation as higher education institutions struggled with interpreting the new law (Post, 1998), colleges and universities around the country eventually used this landmark decision as legal precedent for the consideration of race when developing their admissions policies.

The late 1970s into the 1980s, however, marked the beginning of two tumultuous decades for race-conscious affirmative action policies in higher education. As Sullivan (1998) notes, the broader political backlash against affirmative action policies flourished with the first Reagan administration.[1]

Further, the courts handed down a series of decisions that represented conflicting but generally increasingly conservative views as to the legality of such programs in the private employment sector.[2] This unrest set the stage that ultimately led to pivotal legal, legislative, and policy actions against higher education's race-conscious affirmative action in the decade to follow, the aftermath of which is still being felt.

In 1995 the University of California's Board of Regents approved SP-1, banning the use of race and ethnicity in admissions policies. Subsequently, in 1996, the voters passed the California Civil Rights Initiative (Proposition 209), amending the state's constitution to ban affirmative action not only in public higher education, but also in public employment and contracting. Although the Board of Regents repealed SP-1 in 2001, Proposition 209 still makes it illegal for higher education to consider race/ethnicity in admissions decisions (Horn & Flores, 2003). These efforts in California were the continuation of a trend toward states taking a narrow view of race/ethnicity and college admission.

In 1996, a decision from the United States Court of Appeals for the 5th Circuit in *Hopwood v. Texas* marked a critical point in the most recent series of court challenges against race-conscious admissions policies and ultimately generated significant influence over how universities admitted their students. Based on the court's interpretation of the strict scrutiny test of the Equal Protection law, *Hopwood* determined that diversity was not a compelling interest justifying the use of race and was interpreted in the 5th Circuit (Texas, Louisiana, and Mississippi) to mean that use of race/national origin in college admissions decisions could not be justified by the institution's interest in diversity. In response, many universities outside of the Court's jurisdiction also made the decision to eliminate racial/ethnic considerations from their admissions policies.[3]

In December 1998, Initiative 200 went into effect, banning the consideration of race in state decision making about employment, education, and contracting in Washington (Healy, 1998). Although the 9th Circuit (covering nine western states and two territories) ruled in *Smith v. the University of Washington Law School* that *Bakke* was still the law of the land (The Civil Rights Project, 2002), Initiative 200 prevents colleges and universities from implementing affirmative action in Washington. One year later, on November 9, 1999, Florida's Jeb Bush became the first governor to abolish affirmative action policies in higher education and other state agencies without a court ruling or citizen initiative when he announced the implementation of his One Florida Initiative (Executive Order No. 99–281). This initiative ended race-conscious decision making in public contracting, employment, and higher education (Marin & Lee, 2003). Although the NAACP filed a challenge against Governor Bush's initiative, an administrative law judge decided in favor of Governor Bush and the policy went into effect in July 2000 (Selingo, 2000).

Most recently, the Supreme Court ruled on two lawsuits originally filed in 1997 against the University of Michigan challenging the constitutionality of the law school and undergraduate admissions policies, each of which considered race/ethnicity as one among many components in the decision-making process. On June 23, 2003, the U.S. Supreme Court issued their opinions in *Grutter v. Bollinger* and *Gratz v. Bollinger* and, despite the anti-affirmative action legal and political backdrop in which the cases were heard, the decisions ultimately supported the compelling governmental interest of diversity and "upheld the constitutionality of race-conscious admissions policies designed to promote diversity in higher education" (Joint Statement of Constitutional Law Scholars, 2003, p. 1). In distinguishing such policies, however, the Court struck down Michigan's undergraduate admissions policy of giving a specific number of additional points to all underrepresented applicants but supported Michigan's law school policy of holistic review of applicants using race/ethnicity as a "plus" factor in that process. While this decision now represents the "law of the land," there are still states whose laws prohibit the use of race-conscious admissions policies (i.e., California, Washington, and Florida, as discussed previously).[4] In addition, state-level efforts and campaigns to end the use of such policies in higher education continue unabated. For example, in December 2003 shortly after the *Gratz* and *Grutter* rulings, Michigan's Board of State Canvassers approved a petition to gather voters' signatures for a ballot initiative similar to those that ended California's and Washington's affirmative action policies (Selingo, 2003).[5] It is clear that the struggle to maintain affirmative action in higher education is far from over.

Historically, legally, and politically, much of the struggle has been to create, and eventually defend, increased access to higher education through the use of affirmative action in admissions. Now, the fundamental assumption that a racially/ethnically diverse student body is critical to a successful learning environment is accompanying that effort. The next section of this chapter addresses those benefits of diversity that have now been well documented in research.

## RESEARCH ON BENEFITS OF RACIAL/ETHNIC DIVERSITY

Institutions have held as central the importance of diversity to their missions. Acknowledging this fact in her *Grutter* opinion, Justice O'Connor states, "Our conclusion that the Law School has a compelling interest in a diverse student body is informed by our view that attaining a diverse student body is at the heart of the Law School's proper institutional mission" (p. 3). While higher education officials have long made this assumption, the empirical basis for such assumptions was limited until recently. Specifically, much work has been done in the last decade to assess the extent to which racially and ethnically diverse college campuses result in both in- and out-of-school benefits to the student body as a whole.[6]

Although the scope of the chapter does not allow for a full treatment of the lines of research that have been developed,[7] there are three major emerging areas. First, several important studies have looked at various ways racial/ethnic diversity may enhance the learning opportunities students receive in college, and with much consistency, have found that a diverse student body does improve learning outcomes (e.g., Chang, Seltzer, & Kim, 2002; Maruyama & Moreno, 2000; Orfield & Whitla, 2001; Whitla, Orfield, Silen, Teperow, Howard, & Reede, 2003). As Chang, Seltzer, and Kim (2002) note, "Increasing the proportional representation of underrepresented students, in this case African American, Latino/a, and Native American students, contributes to establishing an entering class of students with a greater diversity of opinions . . . [and] can potentially contribute positively to students' learning and educational experiences" (pp. 31–32). In particular, several studies have shown benefits to the promotion of critical thinking skills specifically (e.g., Gurin, 1999; Marin, 2000).

Beyond the benefits of diversity in the classroom, research has been conducted to assess the extent to which democratic and civic values might be enhanced or affected by racially/ethnically diverse campuses. In a continued line of her work, for example, Gurin (1999) found that campus diversity leads to a stronger sense of commonality with other racial/ethnic groups. Further, such diversity has been shown to allow for increased opportunities for students to come in contact with and develop close friendships with peers from racial/ethnic groups different from their own (Antonio, 2001; Duncan, Boisjoly, Levy, Kremer, & Eccles, 2003), and to increase tolerance and cultural awareness (Hurtado, 2001). Work by Bowen and Bok (1998) found that students educated in diverse environments are also more likely to participate in civic activities such as voting.

Third, research has found that diverse learning environments better prepare students for entrance into a diverse society and workforce (e.g., Bowen & Bok, 1998; Orfield & Whitla, 2001; Whitla et al., 2003). As the country faces huge demographic shifts over the next several decades, the importance of being able to work and live effectively with peers of different racial/ethnic backgrounds will be paramount.

An emerging area deserving more study was raised in an amicus curiae brief submitted by a group of retired military officers on behalf of the University of Michigan in both *Gratz* and *Grutter* (Brief of the Retired Military Officers, 2003). They argue that fields like the military require diverse leadership, primarily trained through the higher education system and prepared to direct a diverse workforce.

> Based on decades of experience, amici have concluded that a highly qualified, racially diverse officer corps educated and trained to command our nation's racially diverse enlisted ranks is essential to the

military's ability to fulfill its principal mission to provide national security. . . . Today, almost 40% of servicemen and women are minorities; 61.7% are White, and the remaining almost 40% are minorities. . . . [I]ncreasing numbers of officer candidates are trained and educated in racially diverse educational settings, which provides them with invaluable experience for their future command of our nation's highly diverse enlisted ranks. (2003, pp. 5–7).

Such a rationale, coupled with the other benefits outlined in the aforementioned research, suggests that students trained in a diverse academic setting reap both in-class and long-term advantages that may enhance the civic and social infrastructure of our country. It is with this understanding, then, that the chapter now discusses how institutions have implemented various admission strategies that reflect legal mandates but still attempt to achieve institutional goals of creating racially/ethnically diverse campuses.

## RESEARCH ON ADMISSION PROCEDURES

While each college and university sets up its own unique admissions process, several prominent admission procedures have been adopted, in whole or in part, to create racially/ethnically diverse campuses. Those efforts, and the research assessing their effectiveness, are discussed in turn as follows, beginning first, however, with a description of the impacts of admissions policies that consider heavily or only the traditional measures of test scores and grades.

### Admission Based on Test Scores

In assessing the extent to which "traditional" approaches to admissions that heavily consider test scores affect racial/ethnic diversity, Cross's (1994) study highlights the potential impacts. This analysis found that the eleven most selective universities (as defined by *U.S. News and World Report*) have a median combined SAT of 1400. Blacks make up only 1.3 percent of all SAT test-takers who scored above 700 on the verbal SAT and fewer than 1.0 percent of all test-takers who scored above 700 on the math. If admissions policies were based solely on test scores, only 150 Blacks would be enrolled (rather than the 1,000 who are currently enrolled) in these selective schools.

While it is true that most selective institutions do not rely exclusively (or even heavily) on a test score in making a final admission determination, some large universities will use such performance as an initial screening mechanism, eliminating many students from consideration even before the full review process has been completed. Take, for example, the University of California's policy of determining eligibility based on a combination of SAT test scores and high school GPA using selected courses.

Based on the formula, students with the lowest GPAs must score extremely high on each of the exams in order to be eligible.[8] As such, the test score itself plays a critical role in determining who enters the pool of potentially admissible students (see table 7.1).

*Automatic Admission Policies*

During the mid- to late-1990s, percent plans guaranteeing admission to a fixed percent of the highest performing graduates of each high school to public universities in a state emerged as one response to the end of race-conscious affirmative action in Texas, California, and Florida. Several studies have been done to assess the potential effectiveness of such automatic admissions policies. In similar studies of California, Koretz, Russell, Shin, Horn, and Shasby (2001) and Geiser (1998) modeled the impacts of admitting the top 4 percent, 6 percent, and 12.5 percent of students from each high school and found that only the last of these would increase the racial/ethnic composition of admitted students relative to a baseline condition of accepting the top 12.5 percent statewide.[9] It is worth noting, however, that average

TABLE 7.1
University of California Eligibility Index

| GPA | Test Score Total* |
|---|---|
| 2.80–2.84 | 4640 |
| 2.85–2.89 | 4384 |
| 2.90–2.94 | 4160 |
| 2.95–2.99 | 3984 |
| 3.00–3.04 | 3840 |
| 3.05–3.09 | 3720 |
| 3.10–3.14 | 3616 |
| 3.15–3.19 | 3512 |
| 3.20–3.24 | 3408 |
| 3.25–3.29 | 3320 |
| 3.30–3.34 | 3248 |
| 3.35–3.39 | 3192 |
| 3.40–3.44 | 3152 |
| 3.45–3.49 | 3128 |
| > 3.50 | 3120 |

*Source:* University of California (n.d.)

*Test Score Total equals: [SAT I composite score] + [2 x (SAT II Writing score + SAT II mathematics score + third required SAT II score)]. SAT I composite is highest combined mathematics and verbal scores from a single sitting. Highest individual SAT II scores, from any sitting, will be considered (University of California, n.d.).

SAT scores and high school GPAs of admitted students dropped under the policy, highlighting the complexity of using any single factor to make admissions decisions (see table 7.2).

Looking specifically at the Texas 10 percent plan, simulations by Horn (2001) found that when a 10 percent rule was applied to the 1998 College Board data, the impacts on Blacks and Hispanics were marginal and directionally positive for Blacks and Hispanics "accepted" to only UT Austin, one of the two most selective universities in the state. At UT Austin, the proportion of Whites "admitted" dropped from 68.1 percent to 65.5 percent under a percent plan model (see table 7.3). Concurrently, Blacks and Hispanics saw a 0.2 and 1.4 percentage point increase, respectively, under the same rule (from 3.9 to 4.1 and from 15.2 percent to 16.6 percent, respectively); Asians also saw a 1.1 point increase. These boosts were not seen, however, at the remaining public institutions in the study. In fact, the 10 percent rule often had the effect of increasing the proportion of Whites at less selective public universities.

Tienda, Leicht, Sullivan, Maltese, and Lloyd's study (2003) examined how the end of race-conscious admissions considerations changed the probability of

TABLE 7.2

Simulating 12.5 Percent Automatic Admission Policy Compared to Current CA Policy

|  | *White* | *Asian**** | *Black* | *Latino* |
|---|---|---|---|---|
| % of Total Drawing from the top 12.5% 12.5% **from across the state** (current policy) | 49 | 29 | 2 | 10 |
| Mean SAT | 1211 | 1222 | 1136 | 1126 |
| Mean HS GPA | 3.87 | 3.89 | 3.90 | 3.93 |
| % of Total Drawing from the top 12.5% **from each school** | 42 | 27 | 4 | 18 |
| Mean SAT | 1198 | 1173 | 1001 | 999 |
| Mean HS GPA | 3.87 | 3.88 | 3.60 | 3.68 |

*Source:* Koretz et al. (2001).

*\*Note:* Row sums do not total to 100 percent because of rounding error and the exclusion of the "other" category in this table.

\*\*Data do not allow for the disaggregation into subgroups of the racial/ethnic category "Asian." This is important to note because certain Asian ethnic subgroups often face the same disparities in representation as other traditionally underrepresented minorities (U.S. Department of Commerce, Economics, and Statistics Administration, 1993).

TABLE 7.3

Simulation of Racial/Ethnic Composition of Admitted Students
under a 10 Percent Plan Compared with a Race-neutral
Admissions Policy at UT Austin and Texas A&M

|  | White | Black | Hispanic | Asian* | American Indian |
|---|---|---|---|---|---|
| "Admitted" to UT Austin by race neutral model, 1998* | 68.1 | 3.9 | 15.2 | 12.0 | 0.7 |
| Admitted Class under 10 Percent Plan | 65.5 | 4.1 | 16.6 | 13.1 | 0.6 |
| "Admitted" to Texas A&M by race neutral model, 1998* | 75.5 | 4.3 | 12.9 | 6.4 | 0.8 |
| Admitted Class under 10 Percent Plan | 76.6 | 3.6 | 12.5 | 6.6 | 0.7 |

*Source:* Horn (2001).

*Note*: Other numbers reflect actual percentages. Percentages may not sum to 100 because of rounding.

*Data do not allow for the disaggregation into subgroups of the racial/ethnic category "Asian." This is important to note because certain Asian ethnic subgroups often face the same disparities in representation as other traditionally underrepresented minorities (U.S. Department of Commerce, Economics, and Statistics Administration, 1993).

acceptance and enrollment at UT Austin and Texas A&M—the two most selective higher education institutions in the state. It further assessed what the net impact of the changed admissions criteria is on the likelihood an applicant would be admitted under the new policy. The authors found that, among the traditional "feeder" high schools to UT Austin and Texas A&M, their share of applications increased to both universities. Additionally, the share of Texas A&M enrollees from the major feeder schools remained unchanged pre- and post-*Hopwood* and the share of matriculants from these high schools went up at UT Austin. These findings suggest that the 10 percent plan has not hurt students from traditional feeder schools. The study also simulated the probability of admission to each campus. White students' probability of admission rose at UT Austin but not at Texas A&M post-*Hopwood*. Black applicants' probability fell from 75 to 58 percent at Texas A&M after the end of affirmative action, but less than 2 percentage points at UT Austin. Hispanic applicants at Texas A&M went from a likelihood of 80 to 68 percent during this shift in admissions policies. The findings of this study suggest that, because students in the top 10 percent of their graduating classes were admitted with near certainty well before the implementation of the 10 percent plan, applicants ranked in the second and third deciles were most affected by the end of affirmative action. The probability of admission to Texas A&M for African American applicants in the second decile, for example, fell from 85 to 72 percent after *Hopwood.*

Two companion studies released by The Civil Rights Project at Harvard University tracked the implementation policies and changes in enrollment over several years across all three states currently implementing automatic admission policies (Horn & Flores, 2003; Marin & Lee, 2003). The authors found that percent plans only set basic requirements for who can automatically be admitted to a campus or to a system, so the implementation of the plan at individual institutions varies dramatically. In Florida, for example, where the Talented 20 purports to admit the top 20 percent of students from each public high school into the State University System, students in the top 20 percent of their class must also complete nineteen required credits and submit an SAT or ACT score in order to be Talented 20 eligible. Research suggests, however, that such requirements have a significant dampening effect on admissions for underrepresented students (Marin & Lee, 2003).

To date there is insufficient evidence to suggest that the existing percent plans are effective alternatives to using race/ethnicity as a factor in admissions decisions. None of the most selective schools in California saw increases to pre-209 representation under the 4 percent plan. In Texas, only the University of Texas at Austin saw increases back to pre-*Hopwood* numbers using the 10 percent plan. In Florida, the Talented 20 plan led to the admission of very few students to the state university system who would not have been admitted under preexisting, non-race-conscious rules (Horn & Flores, 2003; Marin & Lee, 2003). The rapidly rising shares of Blacks and Hispanics among 15–19-year-olds in each of these states during the same time period meant that any gains were less than raw numbers suggested. Finally, all three states were consciously supplementing the percent plan policies with outreach, recruitment, and financial aid programs that race-attentively (in California and Texas) or race-consciously (in Florida) targeted underrepresented high school students.[10] In California it appears that the extra attention accorded to underrepresented students in implementing the percent plan accounted for most of the increases in applications noted (University of California Office of the President, Student Services, 2003).

*Whole File Review Policies*

In the *Grutter* decision, Justice O'Connor wrote the opinion supporting the Michigan law school's use of "a highly individualized, holistic review of each applicant's file, giving serious consideration to all the ways an applicant might contribute to a diverse educational environment" (p. 4). Similar whole file or comprehensive review policies, although not able to consider race/ethnicity, had already been adopted by the UC Board of Regents in November 2001 and applied for the first time in the Fall 2002 admissions cycle. Prior to the implementation of comprehensive review, University of California campuses were required to select 50 to 75 percent of their applicants based on a formula using ten "academic" criteria. The remainder could be selected using those plus four additional "supplemental" criteria.[11] Findings by the University of California (UC) Board of Admissions and Relations with Schools (BOARS) (2003) show that the academic quality of incoming UC freshman remained comparable to students admitted without comprehensive review. Further, the representation of low-income and rural students as well as students from families with no previous college experience or from low-performing schools was higher than prior to the implementation of comprehensive review. However, the study notes that these patterns do not hold true across all racial/ethnic groups. For example, they found an "erosion of UC's ability to enroll admitted underrepresented students in the top one-third of the applicant pool" (p. 10). Despite such disparities and the inability to fold race/ethnicity into the list of considerations, the committee endorsed the continued use of comprehensive review, writing, "In general, BOARS concludes that the greatest work involved in implementing comprehensive review is behind us and that, absent significant new external factors, modifications in future years would be the typical adjustments that any process undergoes with increased experience" (p. 20). Contradicting these findings, however, a report released by UC Regent Moores suggested that the whole file review process resulted in the admission of lower scoring minority students to the exclusion of applicants with higher SAT scores and high school GPAs (Hebel, 2003). The University of California system responded by conducting its own review of this admissions process, ultimately resulting in a resolution passed by the Regents supporting the policy in place (Selingo, 2004). Notwithstanding the limited impact on racial/ethnic diversity, the University of California regents reaffirmed their support for holistic review as a more fair approach to the admissions process.

*Policies That Add Weight to Non-racial Hardship Factors
(e.g., SES, Parental Education)*

Another policy aimed at increasing student diversity that has been considered is the placement of additional weight on hardship factors. Many researchers have studied the extent to which such policies might achieve this goal. For example, Kane (1998) assessed the impacts of alternative race/ethnicity neutral admissions criteria on campus diversity. In analyzing the potential effectiveness of a class-based admissions policy that maintained the diversity achieved through race-conscious affirmative action, Kane concludes, "the increasingly popular idea that nonracial criteria could substitute for race-based policies is simply an illusion. . . . There is an inescapable trade-off between race-blindness and diversity on elite campuses" (1998, p. 28).

A report by the Texas Higher Education Coordinating Board (THECB) (1998) looked at the effectiveness of alternative admissions criteria on racial/ethnic diversity of campus student bodies. Ten factors that might increase racial/ethnic diversity while remaining true to *Hopwood*'s race/ethnicity neutral mandate were considered, including: socioeconomic background; first-generation college status; bilingual proficiency (an indication of whether a language other than English is primarily spoken at home); financial status of student's school district; performance level of the students' school; student responsibilities; region of residence within the state of Texas; residence within rural or urban, central city or suburban areas of the state; effects of the use of alternative levels of ACT and SAT scores; and student ACT and SAT rankings within socioeconomic levels. The researchers found that four factors most affected the numbers of Blacks and Hispanics eligible for college admission: living in a home where a language other than English is spoken; living in a family below the poverty level (as indicated by socioeconomic background); having parents who did not graduate from college; and residing in South Texas or the Upper Rio Grand Valley (as indicated by region of residence). More importantly, the THECB found that no single criterion would result in a level of racial/ethnic inclusion that was achieved with policies in place prior to *Hopwood.*

When Koretz et al. (2001) modeled the effectiveness of giving additional preferences to students with disadvantaged backgrounds as defined by income, mother's education, high school graduation rate, percent of students on free/reduced lunch, and school location (up to the equivalent of a 200 point SAT increase) to function as a proxy for race/ethnicity, they found that even the largest effects of such efforts did not substantially increase Black or Hispanic representation among the admitted pool of applicants relative to a model that only considered SAT and GPA. Often, it was Whites that benefited most from such considerations.

Horn (2001) found that special consideration to parents' education, high school location, and parents' income individually gave rise to increased representation for Blacks and Hispanics at UT Austin and Texas A&M. For the most selective schools, then, providing an admissions "boost" to those from the disadvantaged backgrounds did statistically benefit Blacks and Hispanics. For neither flagship institution, however, did the use of alternative admissions criteria result in a return to pre-*Hopwood* representation for either Blacks and or Hispanics.

In sum, although many race-neutral approaches have been tried, none has successfully resulted in the production of a racially/ethnically diverse student body comparable to that achieved with the consideration of race/ethnicity. And despite the fact that affirmative action is far from a panacea and that much more is needed than simply old-style affirmative action, with the *Gratz* and *Grutter* decisions, most universities are now empowered to once again work toward serving their missions, expanding access to higher education, and reaping the benefits of racial/ethnic diversity through the consideration of race/ethnicity in their admission policies. The next section discusses possible ways for universities to proactively use this tool, often in combination with other efforts, to maximize those efforts to serve their missions.

## RETHINKING COLLEGE ADMISSIONS (AND BEYOND) TO WORK TOWARD A DIVERSE STUDENT BODY

Given the extremely limited impact of all alternative admissions strategies experimented with to date, universities that are now legally able ought to simply reinstate or continue to consider race/ethnicity as one factor among many in deciding whom to admit. As many have noted, however, race-conscious affirmative action used in isolation during the admission process has not necessarily resulted in the desired equitable outcomes (Orfield, 1998). With the *Gratz* and *Grutter* rulings, most colleges and universities can now consider how to best utilize race/ethnicity in combination with other policies, many of which may already be in place, to maximize the diversity achieved on campus. Texas provides an interesting example of such an integrated approach that should be monitored. As discussed previously, the state was the first to implement an automatic admission policy to mitigate the *Hopwood* decision eliminating race/ethnicity as a consideration. Now that that ruling has effectively been overturned, one of the flagships in the state—the University of Texas at Austin—has chosen to reinstate race/ethnicity as a factor in the admission process beginning with the incoming class of 2005–2006 (Office of Admissions, n.d.), but *also* keeping in place the percent plan, creating what might be described as an "affirmative action plus" policy.[12] Further, the University will continue to implement scholarship and retention programs (e.g., the Longhorn Opportunity Scholars Program) directly tied to admissions policies and intended to bolster gains made by such strategies alone (Horn & Flores, 2003). The extent to which an admission policy focused on enhancing diversity from multiple fronts will ultimately produce the desired effects remains to be seen, but it is certainly worth tracking as a possibility.

Similarly, the whole file review process, as it evolves, will be another important strategy to monitor. While some institutions are still bound by law that precludes them from considering race/ethnicity in such a process (e.g., institutions in The University of California system), most will now be able to fold race into a review process that attempts to assess the full set of qualifications, broadly defined, an applicant might bring to the university. The University of Michigan's revised undergraduate admission process is an example of such a whole file review.

During the evaluation process readers and admissions counselors will consider a broad range of criteria during their thorough, individualized review of every complete application. Factors that illustrate the student's academic achievements and potential—including high school grades, standardized test scores, the choice of curriculum, and the student's educational environment—will be given the most consideration. Other factors that will be considered by the readers and counselors will include, but not be limited to: geographic location, personal achievement, leadership, alumni connections, socioeconomic status, underrepresented minority identification, identification as a possible scholarship athlete, special skills or talents, unique experiences, the quality and content of the student's essay and short answers, and counselor and teacher recommendations. (University of Michigan, n.d.)

Such programs will need to be closely watched both for their potential successes as well as the limitations that may be set by the factors they include in their review. For example, preliminary data from the first year of the University of Michigan's new admissions policy that incorporates essay writing show a 23 percent drop in the number of minority applications and a 30 percent drop in minority admissions (Schmidt, 2004), which was reversed in fall 2005 (University of Michigan, October 26, 2005).

Although California remains unable to use race/ethnicity as a factor in admissions, other policies attempted in that state may be worth considering for implementation elsewhere. The Dual Admissions Program (DAP), in its original form implemented in the Fall of 2003, allowed students in the top 4 to 12.5 percent of their high school graduating class to be admitted to both a community college and a particular UC campus. Eligible students would complete their lower division coursework at the community college campus and then be guaranteed admission to a UC campus to finish classes toward a bachelor's degree. DAP students would also have access to transfer advising and monitoring and other UC resources such as libraries (Handel, Heisel, & Hoblitzell, this volume). More recently, however, serious financial, structural, and political setbacks led to cancellation of this program (see Handel, Heisel, & Hoblitzell, chapter 8 of this volume, for additional details).

Although the DAP no longer exists in its original form, the concept of more directly tying community and four-year college admissions processes together is an interesting one to track, particularly in states like California that rely heavily on two-year colleges. Important to watch, however, are the potential pitfalls that may arise, particularly given the lack of success community colleges have traditionally had in realizing the transfer function (Handel, Heisel, & Hoblitzell, chapter 8 of this volume). Additionally, the capacity issues that arise as a result of such a program would need to be reviewed, particularly as community colleges are asked to take on many more students to mitigate the shrinking number of spaces at four-year institutions. Moreover, to achieve success it may be important to implement additional components to the program, such as a cohort model that provides a supportive network within the community college campus (see Gándara & Chávez, 2003). As with other possibilities, a dual admissions program has promise but must be carefully monitored.

In addition to considering admissions policies that may have potential to increase campus diversity, it is simultaneously critical for institutions to evaluate what admission policies already in place may be working against this goal. For example, a large body of research documents differential test performance among Whites and Asians relative to Blacks and Latinos. Generally, studies have found that although differences in test scores have narrowed over time, substantial disparities still exist (e.g., Hedges & Nowell, 1998; Madaus & Clarke 2001; McNeil & Valenzuela, 2001).[13] Given the common practice of considering test performance as a predictor—and sometimes a primary predictor—of potential college success, colleges and universities may be unintentionally but effectively working counter to the goal of achieving a diverse student body when they rely heavily on test scores as key admissions criteria.[14]

More broadly, admissions officers must decide how to consider the current inequities in the K-12 system in their own selection process. Policies that give weight to facially neutral factors such as the prestige of an applicant's high school, Advanced Placement courses taken (Geiser & Santelices, chapter 4 of this volume), and participation in traditional extracurricular activities potentially undermine a university's diversity interests by biasing the admission process toward qualities more commonly held by White and Asian students, or more commonly available in schools that serve these students. Achievement of racial/ethnic diversity is, therefore, hampered by the extent to which traditional measures of merit continue to be the focus of attention in the design of admissions criteria. Intensified pressure on admissions officers to increase the selectivity of the student body based on test scores and GPA in order to improve a university's national or regional standing may exacerbate this problem.

Similarly, early-decision admissions policies may hinder campus diversity. In these programs predominantly employed at elite private colleges (Avery, Fairbanks, & Zeckhauser, 2003), a student applies earlier than the regular application deadline, receives early notification, and in doing so, promises to attend the institution if accepted (Fallows, 2001). A recent study by the *Journal of Blacks in Higher Education* ("Why the early decision," 2000–2001), for example, indicates that "[g]enerally speaking, Black students are far less likely to apply for early admission than are White students" (p. 50). An additional problem related to early-decision admissions is that of the financial aid cycle. Students in need of financial support are less likely to apply under an early-decision program because they must commit to attend an institution prior to receiving a financial aid package. This also makes it impossible for them to compare aid packages from various institutions (Hoover, 2002). Combined with the fact that early admission applications at many of the most selective institutions can make up more than half of the entering class, such a policy does not contribute to increasing the diversity of a campus.

Of course, there are state and federal influences far beyond the institutional-level decisions made during the admission process that also affect the diversity of the incoming class. For example, nationally, there was a 14.1 percent and 6.0 percent increase in average four-year public and private tuition and fees, respectively, from 2002–2003 to 2003–2004 ("Enrollment and Student Aid," 2004). Concurrently, states' 2003–2004 spending plans reduced aggregate appropriations for higher education by 2.1 percent (Arnone, 2004). Perhaps most troubling, the proposed Federal budget request for 2005 to 2007 asks for no increases to the maximum Pell Grant award (Burd, 2004; OMB, 2006) to offset the other potentially devastating trends emerging.[15] These influences require admission officers specifically, and the university broadly, to take a long-term approach toward the achievement of access and student diversity. It is to this issue that the chapter now turns.

## LOOKING BEYOND HIGHER EDUCATION

As O'Connor points out in her majority opinion in *Grutter*, access to higher education ultimately relies on a well-functioning K-12 system, which is not in place at present. "It remains the current reality that many minority students encounter markedly inadequate and unequal educational opportunities. . . . As lower school education in minority communities improves, an increase in the number of such students may be anticipated" (p. 3, 2003). Universities, therefore, must consider how directly, and in what ways, they want to be involved in the improvement of K-12 education and the K-16 pipeline if they are seriously committed to achieving a diverse student body. These efforts are especially important in light of O'Connor's admonition that affirmative action should no longer be necessary in 25 years. Among the many possibilities that ought to be considered, teacher training, formulation of strong university–school partnerships, and mentoring and outreach efforts are examples of ways in which postsecondary institutions can forge real bonds and potentially make serious inroads into improving the K-12 system and ending the need for affirmative action in 25 years. It is paramount, however, that universities begin actively engaging in, and budgeting for, such activities now rather than delaying; improving access, and ultimately campus diversity, through such means is a long-term endeavor.

## CONCLUSION

In a nearly united display, higher education came to the defense of the University of Michigan as its affirmative action admissions policies were challenged. Specifically, in 2003, 90 of the country's most selective colleges and universities, more than 50 higher education organizations, as well as various student groups submitted amicus briefs to the U.S. Supreme Court affirming the importance of diversity and recognizing the need to use race-conscious admissions policies in higher education. Now that this challenge has been won, higher education must actualize its commitment to achieving diversity by seeking out effective admissions policies, which can now legally consider race/ethnicity in most states, as well as by addressing existing policies that work against their stated desired outcome of achieving (and ultimately maintaining) a racially/ethnically diverse student body.

Similarly, states such as California and Washington that are unable to use race/ethnicity as a factor in admissions decisions nevertheless must also work to achieve a racially/ethnically diverse student body. Many of the options discussed in this chapter (e.g., reconsidering the use of early admissions in decision making and implementing dual admissions programs) can be attempted in such states, despite the inability to consider race/ethnicity. Additionally, improving the K-12 system to reduce the need for the consideration of race is an expensive but viable choice for them. Finally, if in the long term such states seek the capacity to reintroduce race into the admissions process because of the ineffectiveness of race-neutral policies, ballot initiatives amending the state constitution ought to be pursued.

The *Gratz* and *Grutter* decisions reversed the straitjacketing trend higher education faced of losing tools with which to make admissions decisions and, more broadly, helped reinforce the importance and the possibility of creating new ways of framing the issues of increasing access. An important opportunity to be more creative—to try to rethink the whole way the admissions problem has been approached—now exists, and institutions should use this opportunity to its fullest. In reconceptualizing how an admissions process might work to more effectively ensure a diverse student body, it is important for all states, whether or not they can use race/ethnicity in admissions decisions, to acknowledge that structural barriers will arise despite any college admission policy: reduction of higher education funding streams; a pipeline of students flowing through the K-12 system to college narrowed by differential preparation and completion rates; rapidly increasing tuition; and reductions in available financial aid assistance are just a few of such restrictions. In addition, procedural obstacles directly tied to the admissions process, such as large numbers of applications, may also feel burdensome.[16] While these challenges remain, the outpouring of support for the importance of racially/ethnically diverse campuses during the University of Michigan lawsuits demonstrates a deep commitment to the idea that a diverse student body is beneficial to all. In states like California and Washington where race/ethnicity cannot be considered in admissions, such support provides an opportunity for universities to continue to publicly engage in a discussion of the value of diversity and to think about ways within the bounds of the law to achieve that diversity. For the rest of the nation, universities have an obligation to take and use the tool that has been sustained through the *Grutter* and *Gratz* decisions and work toward making diverse campuses a reality, not only through their admission procedures, but ultimately through all their policies as well as the ways they educate and prepare their students to enter into society.

## NOTES

1. In particular, the Reagan administration cut funds for many of the programs dealing with education. "Student loan programs were cut back and administrative and financial restrictions relating to them were increased. As a result, access to higher education was diminished. Enforcement of anti-bias and affirmative action policies was significantly weakened" (Altbach, 1991, p. 8). For further discussion, see Belz (1991).

2. For example, the U.S. Supreme Court prohibited an affirmative action policy from overriding the seniority rights of non-minority workers in *Firefighters Local Union No. 1784 v. Stotts* (1984). In *Local 28, Sheet Metal Workers International Association v. EEOC* (1986), however, the Court, in a 5–4 decision, upheld a district court's use of statistical evidence to suggest a history of racial exclusion and its civil contempt power to impose fines on organizations not in compliance with Title VII of the Civil Rights Act of 1964. That same year, the Court invalidated Jackson, Michigan's affirmative action policy preserving the number of minority school teachers by protecting those teachers with limited seniority from layoff (*Wygant v. Jackson Board of Education*). Additionally, in 1989, the Court invalidated a minority set-aside program for contracts awarded to municipal contractors (*City of Richmond v. J. A. Croson Co.*).

3. At some institutions, such considerations also affected financial aid and scholarship decisions, as well as other race-conscious policies.

4. States such as Georgia, Texas, Louisiana, and Mississippi that had abandoned race-conscious admissions because of earlier legal rulings are now able to consider reinstating such policies.

5. The initiative did not appear on the 2004 ballot. However, as of this publication, the MCRI campaign has indicated that it will attempt to have it included on the 2006 ballot.

6. While acknowledging the potential importance of a broad spectrum of diversity characteristics (e.g., socioeconomic status) to the benefits students gain from their college experience, this chapter focuses exclusively on race/ethnicity.

7. For an in-depth review of these lines of research, see Chang, Witt, Jones, and Hakuta (2003).

8. See chapter 4 in this volume by Geiser and Santelices for an important discussion about the ways in which Advanced Placement factors into the admission process, both in screening and selection.

9. In California, under the Master Plan for Higher Education, the University of California is mandated to accept the top 12.5 percent of the state's high school graduates. Thus, the state already has a "percent plan" of sorts. However, the top 12.5 percent of students *at any given high school* may not be competitive with the top 12.5 percent of students statewide because there is enormous variability in the resources afforded to and the outcomes resulting in schools across the state. It is also important to note that automatic admissions policies assume sufficient capacity to absorb additional qualifying students. The current infrastructural reality in states where such policies are being implemented, particularly California, however, does not match such an assumption.

10. For an important discussion of which colleges and universities the most talented Black and Latino students are attending post-Proposition 209, see Geiser and Caspary (2005).

11. The full range of criteria upon which an applicant may be judged includes: academic grade-point average on all courses specified by the University's eligibility requirements; SAT I and SAT II scores; the number, content of, and performance in additional academic subjects beyond those required; the number and performance in university-approved honors, AP, and IB courses; identification as eligible in the local context; quality of senior year program; quality of academic performance relative to educational opportunities available; outstanding performance in one or more specific academic areas; outstanding work in any academic field; recent, marked improvement in academic performance; special talents, achievements, and awards in a particular field; completion of special school, community, or other projects; academic accomplishments in light of life experiences and special circumstances; and location of high school and residence (University of California Board of Admissions and Relations with Schools, 2003).

12. It is important to note that this is an institutional decision rather than a state one. For example, Texas A&M University, the other flagship, has not chosen to reinstate race-conscious admissions policies despite its option to do so.

13. These findings hold true across more traditional college entrance exams such as the SAT tests as well as those administered at the K-12 level, which are beginning to be considered by some universities in the admission process as well.

14. Moreover, the research on standardized test scores as predictors of college success relies on a static model of college conditions, which can never fully capture the dynamic nature of a first-year college experience.

15. See, also, Fitzgerald and Kane, chapter 3 of this volume, for a discussion of the complexities of the application and qualification process for financial aid.

16. The majority in *Gratz* has already reminded institutions, "the fact that the implementation of a program capable of providing individualized consideration might present administrative challenges does not render constitutional an otherwise problematic system" (p. 4).

## REFERENCES

Altbach, P. (1991). The racial dilemma in higher education. In P. Altbach & K. Lomotey (Eds.), *The Racial Crisis in American Higher Education* (pp. 3–18). New York: State University of New York Press.

Antonio, A. (2001). The role of interracial interaction in the development of leadership skills and cultural knowledge and understanding. *Research in Higher Education, 42*(5), 497–517.

Arnone, M. (2004, January 16). State spending on colleges drops for first time in 11 years. *Chronicle of Higher Education*, A24.

Avery, C., Fairbanks, A., & Zeckhauser, R. (2003). *The early admissions game.* Cambridge, MA: Harvard University Press.

Belz, H. (1991). *Equality transformed: A quarter-century of affirmative action.* London: Transaction Publishers.

Bowen, W., & Bok, D. (1998). *The shape of the river: Long-term consequences of considering race in college and university admissions.* Princeton, NJ: Princeton University Press.

Brief of the Retired Military Officers as Amici Curiae in Support of Respondents, *Grutter v. Bollinger*, 123 S. Ct. 2325 (2003) and *Gratz v. Bollinger*, 123 S. Ct. 2411 (2003).

*Brown v. Board of Education*, 347 U.S. 483 (1954).

Burd, S. (2004, February 13). In his 2005 budget, Bush proposes few increases in student aid. *The Chronicle of Higher Education*, A1.

California Civil Rights Initiative. (1996). American Civil Rights Institute: Text of the California Civil Rights Initiative. Retrieved on September 16, 2004, from http://www.acri.org/209/209text.html

Chang, M., Seltzer, M., & Kim, J. (2002). *Diversity of opinions among entering college students: Does race matter?* Paper presented at the National Academy of Education Meeting, Toronto, Canada. Retrieved on May 6, 2004, from http://www.gseis.ucla.edu/faculty/chang/viewpoints.pdf

Chang, M., Witt, D., Jones, J., & Hakuta, K. (Eds.). (2003). *A compelling interest: Examining the evidence on racial dynamics in colleges and universities.* Stanford, CA: Stanford University Press.

*City of Richmond v. J. A. Croson Co.*, 488 U.S. 469 (1989).

Civil Rights Act of 1964, U.S. Code, vol. 42, sec. 2004 (1994).

The Civil Rights Project. (2002, September 23). *Constitutional requirements for affirmative action in higher education admissions and financial aid.* Cambridge, MA: Author. Retrieved May 5, 2004, from http://www.civilrightsproject.harvard.edu/policy/legal_docs/legal_memos.php

Cross, T. (Autumn, 1994). What if there was no affirmative action in college admissions? A further refinement of our earlier calculations. *Journal of Blacks in Higher Education, 10*(5), 52–55.

Duncan, G., Boisjoly, J., Levy, D., Kremer, M., & Eccles, J. (2003). *Empathy or antipathy? The consequences of racially and socially diverse peers on attitudes and behaviors* (Working Paper 326). Chicago, IL: Joint Center for Poverty Research. Retrieved on May 10, 2004, from http://www.jcpr.org/wp/WPprofile.cfm?ID=384

Enrollment and student aid by the numbers. (2004, April 30). *The Chronicle of Higher Education.* Retrieved on May 21, 2004, from http://chronicle.com/prm/weekly/v50/i34/34b01701.htm

Executive Order No. 99–281. (1999, November 9). Retrieved on February 5, 2003, from http://sun6.dms.state.fl.us/eog_new/eog/orders/1999/november/eo99–281.html

Fallows, J. (2001, September). The early-decision racket. *The Atlantic Monthly, 288*(2). Retrieved on May 20, 2004, from http://www.theatlantic.com/issues/2001/09/fallows.htm

*Firefighters Local Union 1784 v. Stotts*, 467 U.S. 561 (1984).

Fitzgerald, B., & Kane, T. (2005). Lowering barriers to college access: Opportunities for more effective coordination of state and federal student aid policies. In P. Gándara, G. Orfield, & C. L. Horn (Eds.), *Expanding Opportunity in Higher Education: Leveraging Promise* (pp. ??). New York: State University of New York Press.

Gándara, P., & Chávez, L. (2003). Putting the cart before the horse: Latinos and higher education. In D. López & A. Jiménez (Eds.), *Latinos and Public Policy in California* (pp. 87–120). Berkeley: Regents of the University of California.

Geiser, S. (1998). *Redefining UC's eligibility pool to include a percentage of students from each high school.* Oakland, CA: University of California Regents.

Geiser, S., & Caspary, K. (2005). "No show" study: College destinations of University of California applicants and admits who did not enroll, 1997–2002. *Journal of Educational Policy, 19*(2), 396–417.

Geiser, S., & Santelices, V. (2005). The role of advanced placement and honors courses in college admissions. In P. Gándara, G. Orfield, & C. L. Horn (Eds.), *Expanding Opportunity in Higher Education: Leveraging Promise* (pp. ??). New York: State University of New York Press.

GI Bill Act (Servicemen's Readjustment Act). (1944). Unrestricted. (NWCTB–11–LAWS–PI159E6–PL78 (346)).

*Gratz v. Bollinger*, 123 S. Ct. 2411 (2003).

*Grutter v. Bollinger*, 123 S. Ct. 2325 (2003).

Gurin, P. (1999). Expert report of Patricia Gurin. In *The compelling need for diversity in higher education*, Gratz et al. v. Bollinger et al. No. 97–75231

(E.D. Mich.) and Grutter et al. v. Bollinger et al. No. 97–75928 (E.D. Mich.) (pp. 99–234). Ann Arbor, MI: The University of Michigan.

Handel, S., Heisel, M., & Hoblitzell, B. (2005). The effectiveness of the transfer path for educationally disadvantaged students: California as a case study in the development of a dual admissions program. In P. Gándara, G. Orfield, & C. L. Horn (Eds.), *Expanding Opportunity in Higher Education: Leveraging Promise* (pp. ??). New York: SUNY Press.

Healy, P. (1998, October 30). Foes of preferences try a referendum in Washington state. *The Chronicle of Higher Education*, A34.

Hebel, S. (2003, October 17). U. of California to review admissions in wake of critical report. *The Chronicle of Higher Education*, A29.

Hedges, L., & Nowell, A. (1998). Black-White test score convergence since 1965. In C. Jencks & M. Phillips (Eds.), *The Black-White Test Score Gap* (pp. 149–181). Washington, DC: The Brookings Institution.

Hoover, E. (2002, January 11). New attacks on early decision. *The Chronicle of Higher Education*, A45.

*Hopwood v. Texas*, 78 F. 3d 932 (5th Cir. 1996); cert. denied, 518 U.S. 1033 (1996).

Horn, C. L. (2001). Diversity in a race neutral setting: An empirical analysis of the potential effectiveness of alternative selection criteria in creating racially/ethnically diverse student bodies at Texas public universities. Unpublished doctoral dissertation, Boston College.

Horn, C. L., & Flores, S. M. (2003). *Percent plans in college admissions: A comparative analysis of three states' experiences.* Cambridge, MA: The Civil Rights Project at Harvard University.

Hurtado, S. (2001). Linking diversity and educational purpose: How diversity impacts the classroom environment and student development. In G. Orfield (with M. Kurlaender) (Eds.), *Diversity Challenged: Evidence on the Impact of Affirmative Action* (pp. 187–204). Cambridge, MA: Harvard Educational Press.

Initiative 200. (1998). 1998 Election: State ballot measures—Complete text of Initiative 200. Retrieved on September 16, 2004, from http://www.secstate.wa.gov/elections/1998/i200_text.aspx

Joint Statement of Constitutional Law Scholars. (2003). *Reaffirming diversity: A legal analysis of the University of Michigan affirmative action cases.* Cambridge, MA: The Civil Rights Project at Harvard University.

Kane, T. (1998). Racial and ethnic preferences in college admissions. In C. Jencks & M. Phillips (Eds.), *The Black-White Test Score Gap* (pp. 431–456). Washington, DC: The Brookings Institution.

Koretz, D., Russell, M., Shin, D., Horn, C. L., & Shasby, K. (2001). *Testing and diversity in postsecondary education: The case of California.* Boston College, Chestnut Hill, MA: National Board on Educational Testing and Public Policy.

*Local 28, Sheet Metal Workers International Association v. EEOC,* 478 U.S. 421 (1986).

Madaus, G., & Clarke, M. (2001). The impact of high-stakes testing on minority students. In G. Orfield & M. Kornhaber (Eds.), *Raising Standards or Raising Barriers: Inequality and High Stakes Testing in Public Education* (pp. 85–106). New York: Century Foundation.

McNeil, L., & Valenzuela, A. (2001). The harmful impacts of the TAAS system of testing in Texas: Beneath the accountability rhetoric. In G. Orfield & M. Kornhaber (Eds.), *Raising Standards or Raising Barriers: Inequality and High Stakes Testing in Public Education* (pp. 127–150). New York: Century Foundation.

Marin, P. (2000). The educational possibility of multi-racial/multi-ethnic college classrooms. In American Council on Education & American Association of University Professors (Eds.), *Does Diversity Make a Difference? Three Research Studies on Diversity in College Classrooms* (pp. 61–83). Washington, DC: American Council on Education & American Association of University Professors.

Marin, P., & Lee, E. K. (2003). *Appearance and reality in the sunshine state: The Talented 20 program in Florida.* Cambridge, MA: The Civil Rights Project at Harvard University.

Maruyama, G., & Moreno, J. (2000). University faculty views about the value of diversity on campus and in the classroom. In American Council on Education & American Association of University Professors (Eds.), *Does Diversity Make a Difference? Three Research Studies on Diversity in College Classrooms* (pp. 9–35). Washington, DC: American Council on Education & American Association of University Professors.

*Missouri ex. Rel. Gaines v. Canada,* 305 U.S. 337 (1938).

Office of Admissions. (n.d.). Addition of race and ethnicity to admission, scholarship, and fellowship policies for the academic year 2005–2006. Retrieved on May 12, 2004, from http://www.utexas.edu/student/admissions/

Orfield, G. (1998). Campus resegregation and its alternatives. In G. Orfield & E. Miller (Eds.), *Chilling Admissions: Affirmative Action Crisis and the Search for Alternatives* (pp. 1–16). Cambridge, MA: Harvard Education Publishing Group.

OMB (Office of Management and Budget), *Budget of the United States,* Fiscal Year 2007 (2006).

Orfield, G., & Whitla, D. (2001). Diversity and legal education: Student experiences in leading law schools. In G. Orfield (with M. Kurlaender) (Eds.), *Diversity Challenged: Evidence on the Impact of Affirmative Action* (pp. 143–174). Cambridge, MA: Harvard Educational Press.

Pelavin, S., & Kane, M. (1990). *Changing the odds: Factors increasing access to college.* New York: College Entrance Examination Board.

Post, R. (1998). Introduction: After *Bakke.* In R. Post & M. Rogin (Eds.), *Race and Representation: Affirmative Action* (pp. 13–27). New York: Zone Books.

Regents of the University of California. (1995). SP-1: Adoption of Resolution: Policy Ensuring Equal Treatment—Admissions. Retrieved on September 17, 2004, from http://www.ucop.edu/acadaff/otf/appen-a.html

*Regents of the University of California v. Bakke*, 438 U.S. 265 (1978).

Schmidt, P. (2004, March 5). Since court ruled, fewer students have applied to Michigan and Ohio State. *The Chronicle of Higher Education*, A22.

Selingo, J. (2000, July 21). Judge upholds Florida plan to end affirmative action. *The Chronicle of Higher Education*, A23.

Selingo, J. (2003, July 4). Decisions may prompt return of race-conscious admissions at some colleges. *The Chronicle of Higher Education*, S5.

Selingo, J. (2004, April 2). California Regents distance themselves from chairman's criticism of admission system. *The Chronicle of Higher Education*, A22.

*Smith v. the University of Washington Law School*, 233 F.3d 1547 (3d Cir. 1996), cert. denied, 121 S. Ct. 2192 (2001).

*Sweatt v. Painter*, 339 U.S. 629 (1950).

Sullivan, K. (1998). The future of affirmative action: After affirmative action. *Ohio State Law Journal, 59*(3), 1039–1054.

Texas Higher Education Coordinating Board. (1998). Report on the effects of the *Hopwood* decision on minority applications, offers, and enrollments at public institutions of higher education in Texas. Austin, TX: Author.

Tienda, M., Leicht, K., Sullivan, T., Maltese, M., & Lloyd, K. (2003). Closing the gap? Admissions and enrollments at the Texas public flagships before and after affirmative action. Princeton, NJ: Texas Top 10% Project.

University of California. (n.d.). Admission as a freshman. Retrieved on September 10, 2004, from http://www.ucop.edu/pathways/infoctr/introuc/fresh.html#elig

University of California Board of Admissions and Relations with Schools. (2003). *Comprehensive review in freshman admissions – Fall 2003*. Oakland, CA: University of California. Retrieved on May 24, 2004, from http://www.ucop.edu/news/comprev/welcome.html

University of California Office of the President, Student Services. (2003). Undergraduate access to the *University of California after the elimination of race-conscious policies*. Oakland, CA: Author. Retrieved November 17, 2004 from www.ucop.edu/outreach/aa_finalcx%202.pdf

University of Michigan. (n.d.). Undergraduate admissions 2003–2004: Overview. Retrieved on May 12, 2004, from http://www.admissions.umich.edu/process/overview/

U.S. Department of Commerce, Economics, and Statistics Administration. (1993). We the Americans: Asians. Washington, DC: Bureau of the Census.

Whitla, D., Orfield, G., Silen, W., Teperow, C., Howard, C., & Reede, J. (2003). Educational benefits of diversity in medical school: A survey of students. *Academic Medicine, 78*, 460–466.

Why the early decision application works against college-bound Blacks. (2000–2001, Winter). *Journal of Blacks in Higher Education, 30*, 50–51.

*Wygant v. Jackson Board of Education*, 476 U.S. 267 (1986).

STEPHEN J. HANDEL
MARGARET HEISEL
BARBARA A. HOBLITZELL

Chapter Eight

# The Effectiveness of the Transfer Path for Educationally Disadvantaged Students: California as a Case Study in the Development of a Dual Admissions Program

## INTRODUCTION

Low-income and ethnic minority students enroll in two-year and community colleges in much higher proportions than other students (see, for example, NCES, 2004). For this reason, the effectiveness of transfer policies in broadening access to higher education, particularly for students from underrepresented groups, has become increasingly important as state governments look for ways of accommodating significantly greater numbers of college-age students. Especially important is assessing the effectiveness of transfer policies among public two-year community colleges and highly selective colleges and universities. Community colleges have long served as an important point of higher education access for underrepresented ethnic minority students and other disenfranchised groups (e.g., students with disabilities, immigrant students, students living in rural regions, students from low-income families), especially given the low cost, geographic convenience, and open access of these institutions (Dougherty, 1994, 2002; Miller, 1995). Highly selective colleges and universities serve as a critical training ground for preparing individuals for leadership positions and the professional ranks within American society (Bowen & Bok, 1998). Despite the importance of this educational pathway, a low percentage of community college students successfully transfer and earn a baccalaureate degree. The initiative described here links community colleges and selective four-year institutions using a statewide dual admissions program, with a stated goal of increasing student access to the baccalaureate degree. The lessons learned in developing this model in California have implications for the rest of the nation.

## TRANSFER POLICY IN CALIFORNIA

The policy structure for California higher education, the 1960 California Master Plan for Higher Education (California State Department of Education, 1960), establishes transfer from California community colleges to the University of California (UC) and the California State University (CSU) as a central element in the state's educational system. Originating in an era of rapid growth in the number of students, California's higher education policy was intended to provide access, economy, efficiency, and quality in the state's higher educational programs.

Cost savings to the state were intended to be achieved through segmental division of responsibility and function. With enactment of the Master Plan, UC and CSU tightened their standards for freshman admission and California's community colleges agreed to take responsibility for accepting a significantly greater number of the students in lower division programs with the expectation that these students could complete baccalaureate degrees at UC or CSU.

A critical feature of the Master Plan was its commitment to access; that promise was to be achieved, in large part, through transfer. Implementing this notion, UC and CSU are required to maintain an upper-to-lower division ratio of 60/40 to assure that there are spaces available for all eligible transfer students. UC has generally not exceeded 60 percent at the upper division level because of the high degree of demand for freshman admission. Nonetheless, eligible California community college transfer students are, by statewide policy, to be given priority in the admission process over other categories of freshman and transfer students.

During the 1980s, the number of transfer students admitted into UC did not keep pace with growth at the freshman and sophomore levels. Thus, lower division enrollment at UC exceeded the 40 percent level. A review of the Master Plan at that time focused strongly on the community college and on transfer programs. Legislation was enacted in 1989 that placed provisions in the California Donahue Act (the legislation authorizing the Master Plan) calling for UC, CSU, and the California community colleges to make transfer a central institutional priority.[1] UC and CSU were called upon to develop transfer agreement programs that specified the curricular requirements and level of achievement to be attained in order for community college students to be guaranteed a transfer space at particular campuses and in particular majors.

The Master Plan also addressed the issue of access by committing to the principle of tuition-free education to residents of the state. In recent years, that principle has been seriously eroded as the state has reduced budgets in higher education to the point that student fees must be used for instructional costs. Fees at California community colleges, however, have remained the lowest in the nation among all community colleges. Nonetheless, the Master Plan also included a provision for student aid, which was intended to address the issue of choice.

Underrepresented minority students make up a larger percentage of community college enrollments than of any other educational segment in California (*Chronicle of Higher Education*, 2003). How well does the transfer function serve these students? At the University of California, throughout the 1980s, not only was the number of transfers low, but minority students were even more poorly represented among entering transfers than among entering freshmen (University of California, 2003b). Despite the large numbers of underrepresented students in community colleges, the number of underrepresented transfers attending UC was disproportionately low (California Department of Education, 2003).

A second problem characterizing California's transfer function is the disparity in performance among community colleges. Roughly two-thirds of all transfers to UC come from less than one-third of the community colleges in California (a list of institutions that has not changed appreciably in nearly a decade and a half).[2] Low-transfer colleges tend to be those located far from any UC campus, frequently in inner city and geographically remote regions. Clearly, the effect of this pattern is to disenfranchise large numbers of the students for whom transfer is their best, or perhaps only, chance for earning a baccalaureate degree.

A third important problem now facing transfer is the enormous enrollment demand California higher education must accommodate in the next decade. By 2010, UC expects to accommodate roughly 227,000 students, up from 201,297 now. A high percentage of these will be ethnic minority students—many of whom will also be from low-income and immigrant families.

With transfer identified as the key feature intended to address sharp increases in demand, we need to examine its record in achieving its goal and identify those weaknesses in the structure that hamper its performance.

### Barriers to Successful Transfer

Within the policymaking community, there is consensus on a number of the problems that depress transfer numbers. Bracco and Callan (2002), writing about California transfer, mention "deficiencies in curricula and instruction offered by some community colleges; poor counseling, articulation and financial aid policies; some community colleges' lack of proximity to four-year campuses; and deficiencies of public schooling" (p. 3).

Wellman (2002), another researcher who recently addressed this question, looked at policy structures nationally and found that "the structure of state policy can make a difference in the effectiveness of statewide 2/4 transfer performance. States that have a comprehensive integrated approach to transfer policy seem to do better than those that focus primarily on transfer as an academic and institutional matter" (p. 52).

In summing up a study of statewide transfer policies in six states, Wellman makes eight policy recommendations, which include:

- Clarifying state transfer policy, while creating new goals and measures of performance;
- Identifying and investing in core resources for transfer at the institutional level;
- Conducting transfer policy audits;
- Making sure that articulation and credit transfer agreements are in place;
- Focusing policy change on low-performing colleges; and
- Using financial aid as a tool to promote transfer.

### UC's Dual Admissions Program

Experience with transfer programs over time and across the United States confirms the importance of these elements for transfer success, as noted by Wellman. Over the course of the past six years, UC and California community colleges have endeavored to systematically address each of these recommendations; the effort on which we are reporting—the Dual Admissions Program—was intended to integrate action on these recommendations into a coherent policy structure with far-reaching potential to increase student access.

A first step on this path was taken in 1997, when the California community colleges and the university signed a Memorandum of Understanding (MOU) setting specific transfer goals (University of California, 1997). Via this agreement (and a subsequent revision in 2000) the university committed to increase the number of transfers by 6 percent annually, to 15,300 students in 2005–2006 (up from 10,150 students in 1998–1999). The MOU also required agreements between UC and community colleges regarding lower-division requirements for "high demand" majors, increased course articulation, and transfer agreements between individual UC campuses and all of their regional community colleges.

These conditions have largely been met and transfer has increased since 1998–1999 to meet the numerical and other goals set. Beyond that, underrepresented minority students, in particular Chicano/Latino students, have grown at a markedly higher rate than other students (University of California, 2003b).

In the Fall of 2003, the University and community colleges took a further policy step that was intended to bring to bear all of these recent steps into a coherent initiative termed the Dual Admissions Program (DAP). DAP was planned to develop cross-institutional transfer infrastructure in several specific ways by:

1. Providing a guarantee of admission to a discrete group of high school seniors, assuring them space at a specific UC campus, provided they successfully complete a lower-division, major-specific transfer program at a California community college.
2. Linking transfer students with UC advisers and providing access to UC campus resources such as libraries, lectures, and other campus events. Students will develop a curricular plan with an adviser who will monitor individual progress term-to-term.
3. Developing policies, programs, and initiatives that communicate more effectively specific expectations for students, develop collegial models, identify coursework and course availability, and provide resources to promote persistence and success.
4. Providing financial aid, with the greatest investment slated for roughly one-third of community colleges with low transfer-going rates (located mostly in urban or rural areas) and that enroll significant numbers of underrepresented and low-income students.

To implement this new DAP transfer infrastructure, the University submitted a budget proposal in 2001 and the state provided $2.5 million in 2002–2003.

The review that follows evaluates the DAP program's first year of operation, pre-staging some policy questions about the degree to which higher education institutions can employ transfer to promote access to the baccalaureate degree, especially among students from educationally disadvantaged backgrounds.

## DESCRIPTION OF PROGRAM IMPLEMENTATION

*Student Identification Process*

The University of California identified DAP-eligible students and invited them to participate using procedures previously established for UC's Eligibility-in-the-Local-Context (ELC) program. Under ELC, students in the top 4 percent of their high school class (as determined by UC based on the GPA[3] and the number and type of college-preparatory courses completed) are invited to apply to the University and are guaranteed a spot at one of UC's undergraduate campuses. Similarly, under DAP, students in the top 4 percent to 12.5 percent of their high school class were invited to apply to the University during the regular November filing period and were guaranteed a spot at one of UC's nine undergraduate campuses, provided that they first completed a specific course of study at a California community college.[4]

UC identified DAP- and ELC-eligible students based on the courses and grades completed by the end of their junior year. Each summer, California public and private high schools are invited to submit transcripts for all students in the top 12.5 percent of their high school class.[5] (Although participation was voluntary, over 90 percent of California's public high schools and about 80 percent of all private high schools participated during Summer 2003.) UC admissions evaluators analyzed all submitted transcripts to determine if students had earned the necessary GPA and completed the appropriate course pattern to be eligible for DAP.

To be minimally eligible for DAP, students needed to complete a specific pattern of college preparatory courses. Required courses for DAP represent a subset of the basic college preparatory courses that all California high school students must complete in order to be minimally eligible for entrance to a UC campus. These college prep courses for UC are called the "A-G" courses.[6] For students to be UC-eligible at the freshman level, they must complete a total of 15 A-G courses. To be eligible for ELC, students must complete a specified set of at least 11 of these 15 courses by the end of their junior year of high school. To become eligible for DAP, students must complete at least nine of the courses specified for ELC eligibility (see table 8.1). UC defined DAP eligibility in this way so that it could identify students demonstrating high academic potential, but who were not freshman eligible to attend UC and could benefit from completing their lower-division work at a community college.

At the time of admission selection, high school students must have earned at least a 2.80 GPA on A-G courses only. (A GPA of 2.80 is the absolute minimum that UC will accept for eligibility purposes.)

Students did not have to complete standardized examinations, such as the SAT and ACT tests, to be DAP-eligible. Nevertheless, students were

TABLE 8.1
University of California A-G Course Pattern*

| Category | Subject Disciplines | Required No. of Year-long Courses | Required for ELC & DAP Eligibility |
|---|---|---|---|
| A | History/Social Science | 2 | 1 |
| B | English | 4 | 3 |
| C | Mathematics | 3 | 3 |
| D | Lab Science | 2 | 1 |
| E | Language Other than English | 2 | 1 |
| F | Visual & Performing Arts | 1 | 0 |
| G | Electives | 1 | 2 |
| TOTAL | | 15 | 11/9** |

*Adapted from information provided by the University of California, Office of the President (available at: http://www.universityofcalifornia.edu/admissions/undergrad_adm/paths_to_adm/freshman/subject_reqs.html).

**To achieve DAP eligibility, students needed to complete 9 of the 11 courses required for ELC-eligibility (any combination of courses).

strongly encouraged to complete these examinations, especially if they planned to apply to a highly competitive major where the results of such an examination would inform the applicant selection process.

After UC evaluators reviewed all transcripts, the University sent notification letters to all students (for whom a transcript was received) at the beginning of their senior year of high school. The letter indicated whether the student had been identified as: 1) ELC-eligible; 2) DAP-eligible; 3) "on-track" for freshman admission (students who met the course and GPA requirements for ELC, but who were not in the top 4 percent of their high school class);[7] or 4) ineligible for ELC or DAP.

UC invited students who were identified as DAP-eligible to apply to the University during the regular November 1–30 filing period. Like any other applicant, DAP-identified students could apply to as many UC campuses as they wished, but were allowed to accept an admissions offer from only one campus. Applicants were notified of their admissions status during the regular admission cycle (approximately March 1). Applicants then had until May 1 to indicate whether they wished to participate in the program and to identify the community college that they were likely to attend in the Fall.

Applicants admitted to a campus under DAP and who accepted an offer of admission were contacted by a UC academic adviser who, in consultation with the student, developed an academic contract outlining the courses and grades that needed to be completed during the student's enrollment at a California community college. DAP students have up to four years to complete this contract, although it is recommended that students complete this work as soon as they are able. A four-year timetable was instituted to accommodate students who, through no fault of their own, are unable to obtain courses needed to complete their contract. Moreover, a four-year timetable reflects sensitivity to the needs of community college students who often attend college part-time because of family or work commitments. DAP students may attend any of California's 109 community colleges and may attend as many community colleges as they wish to complete their lower-division requirements before transferring to UC. These students will not need to declare a major until they have completed 30 units at the community college. Students may request that their academic contract be revised (for instance, if they change majors), but approval will be at the discretion of the UC campus to which they were admitted.

## RESULTS

### Characteristics of Participating Students and High Schools

Data provide a snapshot of students who have been identified as eligible for DAP (as a result of the transcript analysis process described in the previous section), as well as those students who actually applied to UC during the November 1–30, 2003 application period. It is important to note, however, that since the first cohort of DAP applicants enrolled in a community college in Fall 2004, there will be no data to report regarding the number of students successfully transferring from a community college to a UC campus until late 2006.[8]

### High School Participation in DAP

To assist in the identification of DAP-eligible students, California high schools were asked to submit the transcripts of students in the top 12.5 percent of their graduating class. The submission of transcripts to UC for analysis was voluntary. Nevertheless, over 90 percent of all California public high schools submitted transcripts (734 total schools). In addition, about 90 percent of Catholic high schools submitted transcripts for analysis, along with 80 percent of all other private California high schools (242 total private high schools).

UC placed particular importance on the participation of "target" high schools. These schools are defined as being "low performing" using an academic ranking assessed by the California Department of Education. That is, student performance on statewide, standardized examinations at these schools is significantly lower than the academic performance of students statewide.[9] Moreover, these schools are less likely to offer a complete range of UC's A-

G college preparatory courses. Students attending these high schools, therefore, may not be able to make themselves UC eligible since they do not have access to all A-G courses. UC anticipated that students attending these target high schools would especially benefit from DAP, since students are assured a place in the UC system even though they may have completed only 9 or 10 of the 15 required A-G courses. During the first year of DAP implementation, 100 percent of these target high schools provided transcripts to UC for analysis (265 total target high schools).

### Characteristics of Students Identified as DAP-Eligible

Reviewing first the characteristics of students identified as eligible for DAP provides insight into the extent to which a percent plan such as this one is able to successfully identify students in California high schools showing good potential for college, but not yet eligible to attend UC as freshmen. A total of 2,994 students were identified as DAP-eligible, representing about 9 percent of all transcripts submitted to UC for analysis by California high schools. A total of 28,230 students were identified as ELC-eligible (about 86 percent of all transcripts submitted), with the remaining 1,486 students classified as neither DAP- nor ELC-eligible (see table 8.2).[10] Since California public (non-target) high schools constitute about 60 percent of all schools participating, it is not surprising that nearly two-thirds of the students evaluated for DAP or ELC attend these schools (see table 8.3).

Among students eligible for DAP, the greatest number are enrolled at California target high schools. More than 50 percent of all students identified for DAP attended a target high school, compared to 43 percent in other public high schools and 5 percent in private high schools (see table 8.4). Thus, while target high school students in this population comprise only 29 percent of all students identified as DAP, ELC, or not-DAP-qualified (NDQ), they constitute over 50 percent of the students identified as DAP-eligible.

*Academic characteristics.* As measured by A-G course completion, students whose transcripts were evaluated performed well in high school. Over 95 percent

TABLE 8.2
Number of California High School Students Identified as DAP- or ELC-eligible

| Student Status | Frequency | Percent |
|---|---|---|
| DAP | 2,994 | 9.15 |
| Not DAP Qualified | 1,486 | 4.54 |
| ELC | 28,230 | 86.30 |
| TOTAL | 32,710 | 100.00 |

TABLE 8.3
Distribution of School Type*

| School Type | Frequency | Percent |
|---|---|---|
| Private (n = 242) | 3,132 | 9.58 |
| Public Non-target (n = 734) | 20,126 | 61.53 |
| Public Target (n = 265)** | 9,452 | 28.90 |
| TOTAL (n = 1,232) | 32,710 | 100.00 |

*One hundred percent of the "target" high schools submit transcripts for evaluation, as compared with about 95 percent of all public California high schools, 90 to 95 percent of Catholic private high schools, and 70 to 80 percent of other private high schools.

**For ELC, "target" high schools are those who have an API score of 1, 2, or 3; a historic UC admit rate of less than 4 percent (a 3-year average); or are among the 70 lowest performing high schools in the state.

completed at least nine A-G courses by the end of the 11th grade (see table 8.5). While this would be expected from high schools that have a history of sending large numbers of students to highly selective colleges and universities, the data here reveal high achievement by students from high schools of varying performance levels throughout the state of California. Among DAP-eligible students, 78 percent completed at least 10 A-G courses by the end of their junior year, although only nine courses are required in order to make them minimally DAP-eligible (see table 8.5). This means that these students were completing, on average, over four college-prep courses per semester in their high schools. Moreover, among students attending target high schools, A-G course completion also was high. Ninety-two percent of students attending target high schools completed at least nine A-G courses by the end of their junior year (see table 8.6).

DAP-identified students also earn good grades in the courses they complete in high school. Table 8.7 shows that the average GPA of DAP-identified students is 3.63. Over 50 percent have cumulative GPAs above 3.60. Nearly one-third of these students have GPAs in excess of 3.80. For DAP-eligible students attending targeted public high schools, 38 percent have GPAs greater than 3.60 and 19 percent have GPAs greater than 3.80.

As impressive as these results are for DAP-eligible students, it is instructive to compare their performance with that of ELC students identified within the same cohort of transcripts. The average GPA of these students is 3.97 (see table 8.7). Among ELC-identified students, over 84 percent have cumulative GPAs greater than 3.60 and over 70 percent have GPAs in excess of 3.80. For ELC-identified students in target high schools, 66 percent have GPAs greater than 3.60 and 46 percent have GPAs greater than 3.80.

TABLE 8.4
DAP and ELC Student Status by School Type

| School Type | DAP | | NDQ* | | ELC | | Total | |
|---|---|---|---|---|---|---|---|---|
| | Frequency | Percent | Frequency | Percent | Frequency | Percent | Frequency | Percent |
| Private | 143 | 4.78 | 26 | 1.75 | 2,963 | 10.50 | 3,132 | 9.58 |
| Public Non-target | 1,289 | 43.05 | 624 | 41.99 | 18,213 | 64.52 | 20,126 | 61.53 |
| Public Target | 1,562 | 52.17 | 836 | 56.26 | 7,054 | 24.99 | 9,452 | 28.90 |
| TOTAL | 2,994 | 100.00 | 1,486 | 100.00 | 28,230 | 100.00 | 32,710 | 100.00 |

*Not DAP Qualified

TABLE 8.5

Student A-G Course Completion at End of Junior Year by UC Admissions Status*

| A-G Courses | DAP | NDQ | ELC |
|---|---|---|---|
| less than 6.9 | 0 | 808 | 0 |
| 7–7.9 | 0 | 242 | 0 |
| 8–8.9 | 0 | 348 | 0 |
| 9–9.9 | 661 | 21 | 0 |
| 10–10.9 | 2,333 | 38 | 0 |
| 11+ | 0 | 29 | 23,230 |
| TOTAL | 2,994 | 1,486 | 23,230 |

*Student A-G course completion is limited to the 11 ELC courses. Therefore, a student may have completed more than the number of A-G courses listed, and may be more likely to become freshman-eligible in their senior year, than is evident from these data.

TABLE 8.6

Target School Students' A-G Course Completion at
End of Junior Year by UC Admissions Status

| A-G Courses | DAP | NDQ | ELC |
|---|---|---|---|
| less than 6.9 | 0 | 423 | 0 |
| 7–7.9 | 0 | 151 | 0 |
| 8–8.9 | 0 | 192 | 0 |
| 9–9.9 | 380 | 18 | 0 |
| 10–10.9 | 1,182 | 29 | 0 |
| 11+ | 0 | 23 | 7,054 |
| TOTAL | 1,562 | 836 | 7,054 |

TABLE 8.7

Mean and Median GPA, Standard Deviations, and GPA Range
of DAP-identified, ELC-identified, and NDQ Students

| | Mean | SD | GPA Range | Median |
|---|---|---|---|---|
| DAP | 3.63 | 0.37 | 2.80–4.82 | 3.63 |
| | Mean | SD | GPA Range | Median |
| ELC | 3.97 | 0.35 | 2.80–4.91 | 4.00 |
| | Mean | SD | GPA Range | Median |
| NDQ | 3.45 | 0.74 | 0.00–5.00 | 3.57 |

*Student racial and ethnic diversity.* One of the goals for the implementation of DAP was to provide greater access to a UC education for students who might not otherwise consider attending a UC campus. UC policy makers envisioned DAP as a race-neutral way of identifying students with potential for good college performance, but who were not eligible to attend the university directly from high school.

The university tracks the admission and enrollment of students from several ethnic/racial groups that have historically been underrepresented at the UC. These groups are American Indian students, African American students, and Chicano/Latino students. Although UC no longer provides admissions consideration or special outreach services to applicants based on race or ethnicity (as a result of the passage of California's Proposition 209), the university continues to monitor the degree to which these students have gained access to a UC education.

Following passage of SP-1[11] and Proposition 209, many fewer of these students from underrepresented racial/ethnic groups enrolled at UC, although system-wide growth in recent years has been somewhat encouraging (University of California, 2003a). With this said, however, the gap between the proportion of students from these groups in California high schools and community colleges and the number that actually transfer to UC is still wide. For example, in 2002–2003, nearly 43 percent of all students in California high schools and 27 percent of all students in California community colleges were Chicano/Latino. Yet only 17.5 percent of UC's transfer students were from this group (California Community College Chancellor's Office, 2003; California Department of Education, 2003). Similarly, in 2002–2003, the proportion of African American students in California high schools and community colleges was 8 percent and 7 percent respectively. But African American students comprised only 3.2 percent of UC's transfer enrollment during the same period (California Community College Chancellor's Office, 2003; California Department of Education, 2003).

It is important to stress that, while data on the ethnicity of DAP-identified students reveal a diversity of students who are eligible for the program (see table 8.8), only about one in ten of all transcripts submitted by California high schools provide information on a student's race or ethnicity. The limited number of transcripts that provide information about the race/ethnicity of DAP-identified students raises a major question about the degree to which these data accurately reflect the race/ethnicity of students whose transcripts did not include this information.[12]

Among those students who provided information about their race/ethnicity, students from underrepresented groups (i.e., Chicano/Mexican/Latino American, African American, and American Indian) represent 53.3 percent of all students identified for DAP. Chicano, Mexican American, and Latino American students represent the majority of DAP-eligible students from

TABLE 8.8
Students' Race/Ethnicity by UC Admissions Status

| Ethnicity* | DAP | | NDQ | | ELC | | Total | |
|---|---|---|---|---|---|---|---|---|
| | Frequency | Percent | Frequency | Percent | Frequency | Percent | Frequency | Percent |
| American Indian/Alaskan Native | 1 | 0.26 | 3 | 0.54 | 7 | 0.36 | 11 | 0.38 |
| Black/African American | 37 | 9.66 | 19 | 3.39 | 155 | 7.88 | 211 | 7.25 |
| Chicano/Mexican American | 158 | 41.25 | 238 | 42.50 | 640 | 32.55 | 1,036 | 35.61 |
| Chinese/Chinese American | 9 | 2.35 | 21 | 3.75 | 79 | 4.02 | 109 | 3.75 |
| East Indian/Pakistani | 5 | 1.31 | 7 | 1.25 | 19 | 0.97 | 31 | 1.07 |
| Japanese/Japanese American | 2 | 0.52 | 6 | 1.07 | 25 | 1.27 | 33 | 1.13 |
| Korean | 30 | 7.83 | 20 | 3.57 | 72 | 3.66 | 122 | 4.19 |
| Latino/Other Spanish American | 46 | 12.01 | 50 | 8.93 | 145 | 7.38 | 241 | 8.28 |
| Other | 4 | 1.04 | 2 | 0.36 | 15 | 0.76 | 21 | 0.72 |
| Pilipino/Filipino | 11 | 2.87 | 28 | 5.00 | 105 | 5.34 | 144 | 4.95 |
| Polynesian | 3 | 0.78 | 4 | 0.71 | 7 | 0.36 | 14 | 0.48 |
| Thai/Other Asian | 12 | 3.13 | 17 | 3.04 | 53 | 2.70 | 82 | 2.82 |
| Vietnamese | 3 | 0.78 | 7 | 1.25 | 22 | 1.12 | 32 | 1.10 |
| White/Caucasian | 62 | 16.19 | 138 | 24.64 | 622 | 31.64 | 822 | 28.26 |
| TOTAL | 383 | 100.00 | 560 | 100.00 | 1,966 | 100.00 | 2,909 | 100.00 |

*A total of 29,801 transcripts did not include ethnicity description data. Among private high schools, 99 percent did not include ethnicity data; 94 percent of public high schools did not include ethnicity data; and 83 percent of target high schools did not include ethnicity data.

underrepresented groups. White/Caucasian students comprise the second largest group of DAP-identified students (16.2 percent), followed by Asian American students (14.3 percent).[13] Black/African American students constitute nearly 10 percent of DAP-identified students, ranking as the fourth largest group. While the proportion of students from underrepresented groups that were identified as DAP-eligible is significantly greater than current UC enrollments for these groups, the absolute numbers are small.

*Geographic representation.* Data on the geographic representation of DAP-identified students indicate that most live in large cities or suburbs. About 73 percent of all DAP-identified students reside in cities larger than 250,000 people or in immediately adjacent communities.[14] An additional 20 percent live in mid-size cities, defined as having a population less than 250,000 people. About 8 percent live in small towns, defined as having more than 2,500 people but less than 25,000, or in rural areas (less than 2,500 people). These proportions also hold generally for students identified as ELC-eligible.

### Characteristics of DAP-eligible Students Who Applied to UC

Students identified as eligible for DAP were sent a letter at the beginning of their senior year inviting them to apply to UC during the November filing period. Of the 2,994 students who were identified as eligible for the program, a total of 514 (17 percent) actually submitted a UC application.[15] Of the 514 students that applied to UC, 287 (56.2 percent) fit the original definition of a DAP student (bona fide DAP students). The remaining applicants were either ELC students (65 total applicants, 12.7 percent) or on-track students (159 total, 31.2 percent).

A majority of the 514 students who submitted a UC application attended public high schools (57.5 percent), although over a third attended targeted public high schools (38.2 percent). The type of high school attended, however, varied by student eligibility category (i.e., bona fide DAP, ELC, or on-track). Table 8.9 shows the type of school attended by student subcategories. What is interesting to note is that bona fide DAP applicants are slightly more likely to attend targeted public high schools compared to ELC and on-track students, who were far more likely to attend non-targeted public high schools. (ELC and on-track students also are more likely to attend private high schools, but the numbers are too small to make substantive comparisons.) Data showing that bona fide DAP applicants are more likely to attend targeted high schools is consistent with the idea that DAP students are generally less qualified than their ELC and on-track peers, as measured by A-G course completion and GPA.

*Academic characteristics.* Although, by definition, bona fide DAP applicants are less accomplished academically than ELC or on-track students, analysis of A-G course completion rates and GPA reveal good college preparation

TABLE 8.9

Eligibility Status of Identified Students Who Applied by School Type

| School Type | DAP | | ELC | | QOT | | Total | |
|---|---|---|---|---|---|---|---|---|
| | Frequency | Percent | Frequency | Percent | Frequency | Percent | Frequency | Percent |
| Private | 8 | 2.76 | 3 | 4.62 | 11 | 6.92 | 22 | 4.28 |
| Public Non-target | 137 | 47.24 | 40 | 61.54 | 118 | 74.21 | 295 | 57.39 |
| Public Target | 145 | 50.00 | 22 | 33.85 | 30 | 18.87 | 197 | 38.33 |
| TOTAL | 290 | 100.00 | 65 | 100.00 | 159 | 100.00 | 514 | 100.00 |

overall. Table 8.10 shows that regardless of eligibility type (i.e., DAP, ELC, or on-track), 97 percent of the DAP applicants completed 15 or more A-G courses by the end of their junior year in high school. Moreover, this trend holds, albeit to a lesser degree, for students attending targeted high schools—71 percent completed 15 or more A-G courses (68 percent for bona fide DAP students, 68 percent for ELC students, and 86 percent for on-track students). Thus, before DAP applicants begin their last year in high school, they were virtually eligible to attend the University of California.[16]

Earned GPA also is high among all applicants to DAP, although there is greater variability among subcategories. Bona fide DAP applicants had the lowest average GPA (3.63), followed by on-track students (3.72) and ELC students (4.02) (see table 8.11). These relative differences are consistent for DAP applicants attending targeted high schools, although the overall GPAs are lower (see table 8.12).

TABLE 8.10

Total A-G Course Completion by End of Senior Year by UC Eligibility Status*

| A-G Courses | DAP | ELC | QOT | Total |
|---|---|---|---|---|
| less than 11.9 | 1 | 0 | 0 | 1 |
| 12–12.9 | 2 | 1 | 0 | 3 |
| 13–13.9 | 9 | 0 | 0 | 9 |
| 14–14.9 | 3 | 0 | 0 | 3 |
| 15+ | 272 | 64 | 159 | 498 |
| Total | 287 | 65 | 159 | 514 |

*These data are self-reported by the applicants. Course completion verification occurs following admission with the review of the students' final high school transcript.

TABLE 8.11

Mean and Median ELC GPA, Standard Deviations, and GPA Range by Eligibility Status (by End of Senior Year)

| | Mean | SD | GPA Range | Median |
|---|---|---|---|---|
| DAP | 3.63 | .327 | 2.83–4.57 | 3.66 |
| | Mean | SD | GPA Range | Median |
| ELC | 4.02 | .264 | 3.20–4.91 | 4.00 |
| | Mean | SD | GPA Range | Median |
| QOT | 3.72 | .330 | 2.80–4.33 | 3.77 |

TABLE 8.12
Target School Students' Mean and Median GPA,
Standard Deviations, and GPA Range by Eligibility Status

|  | *Mean* | *SD* | *GPA Range* | *Median* |
|---|---|---|---|---|
| DAP | 3.52 | .330 | 2.83–4.40 | 3.52 |
|  | *Mean* | *SD* | *GPA Range* | *Median* |
| ELC | 3.94 | .223 | 3.62–4.35 | 3.91 |
|  | *Mean* | *SD* | *GPA Range* | *Median* |
| QOT | 3.54 | .260 | 2.88–3.95 | 3.43 |

*DAP applicant racial/ethnic diversity.* The ethnic diversity of students who applied for admission to UC via DAP are presented in table 8.13. Chicano/Latino students constituted the largest number of underrepresented students (26 percent), followed by African American students (4.14 percent), and American Indian students (.34 percent). For each group, the proportion of students in the applicant pool was smaller than the proportion of students in the DAP-identified student pool. The proportion of White students in the applicant pool was 31.9 percent (up from 25.2 percent in the DAP-identified pool), and the proportion of Asian American students increased to 23.2 percent (compared to 14.3 percent in the DAP-identified pool).

*Geographic diversity.* The proportion of students who applied to UC via DAP from rural regions of California also declined. The proportion of DAP applicants from rural areas or small towns was 5.4 percent (compared to 8 percent in the pool of students identified as DAP eligible). The proportion of bona fide DAP applicants from rural areas or small towns was even lower at 3.8 percent, although this was somewhat higher than the proportion recorded for ELC students (3.08 percent).

## DISCUSSION

As described at the outset, DAP was designed to increase access to the University of California by creating an infrastructure comprising all the major elements determined to be necessary for successful transfer, including advising, financial aid, full articulation of coursework, fully implemented core transfer resources, and the incentive of guaranteed admission upon satisfactory completion of lower division coursework. The following section focuses on the extent to which the DAP student-identification process was successful in identifying high potential students who might not otherwise be able to

TABLE 8.13

Applicants' Race/Ethnicity by UC Eligibility Status

| Ethnicity* | DAP | | ELC | | QOT | | Total | |
|---|---|---|---|---|---|---|---|---|
| | Frequency | Percent | Frequency | Percent | Frequency | Percent | Frequency | Percent |
| American Indian/Alaskan Native | 1 | 0.34 | 1 | 1.54 | 0 | 0.00 | 2 | 0.39 |
| Black/African American | 12 | 4.14 | 0 | 0.00 | 3 | 1.89 | 15 | 2.92 |
| Chicano/Mexican American | **75** | **25.86** | **14** | **21.54** | **32** | **20.13** | **121** | **23.54** |
| Chinese/Chinese American | 22 | 7.59 | 2 | 3.08 | 7 | 4.40 | 31 | 6.03 |
| East Indian/Pakistani | 7 | 2.41 | 1 | 1.54 | 2 | 1.26 | 10 | 1.95 |
| Japanese/Japanese American | 3 | 1.03 | 1 | 1.54 | 5 | 3.14 | 9 | 1.75 |
| Korean | 12 | 4.14 | 2 | 3.08 | 0 | 0.00 | 14 | 2.72 |
| Latino/Other Spanish American | 24 | 8.28 | 4 | 6.15 | 10 | 6.29 | 38 | 7.39 |
| Other | 19 | 6.55 | 4 | 6.15 | 22 | 13.84 | 45 | 8.75 |
| Pilipino/Filipino | 17 | 5.86 | 5 | 7.69 | 6 | 3.77 | 28 | 5.45 |
| Polynesian (Pacific Islander, Fall 1988) | 0 | 0.00 | 0 | 0.00 | 0 | 0.00 | 0 | 0.00 |
| Thai/Other Asian | 10 | 3.45 | 1 | 1.54 | 4 | 2.52 | 15 | 2.92 |
| Vietnamese | 15 | 5.17 | 1 | 1.54 | 6 | 3.77 | 22 | 4.28 |
| White/Caucasian | **73** | **25.17** | **29** | **44.62** | **62** | **38.99** | **164** | **31.91** |
| TOTAL | 290 | 100.00 | 65 | 100.00 | 159 | 100.00 | 514 | 100.00 |

attend a UC campus; and the attractiveness of the program for students as measured by the number of students who submitted an application to UC after being identified as DAP-eligible. These data, in turn, inform a series of policy recommendations presented in the final section of this chapter.

Data from this report yield three central findings:

1. *The number of students identified as DAP-eligible fell below original estimates.* When DAP was first proposed, UC conducted a series of simulation studies to determine the number of students who were likely to meet the program's eligibility requirements. Since this student identification methodology had never been attempted before, projections varied greatly, resulting in estimates as low as 700 students and as high as 12,000. The number of students actually identified for DAP numbered about 3,000, representing approximately half the number of students that would be expected if we take an average of the estimates provided by the simulation studies. This must be seen as a disappointing total given the size of the high school college-going class in California and the resources required to implement this program statewide. Why was the number of students identified as DAP so low? Results indicate that UC set the bar too high. Most of the students identified for DAP were already eligible to enter UC as freshmen or could have easily done so by completing the remaining A-G courses in their senior year of high school. Recall that to achieve DAP-eligibility, a student needed to complete at least nine A-G courses by the end of the junior year of high school. Data presented here, however, indicate that almost all students were more likely to complete many more courses, often as many 15 total (see tables 8.5 and 8.6). Students performing at this level are generally eligible to enter UC (or other four-year institutions) as freshmen.

2. *The number of DAP-eligible students who chose to submit an application to UC was lower than anticipated.* A total of 514 students out of a pool of 2,994 students submitted an application to one or more UC campuses, an application rate of 17 percent. Since such a program had never been implemented before, it was difficult to predict how popular the program would be within the pool of identified students. Nevertheless, speculation centered on an application rate of about 22 percent to 33 percent, which would have produced a range of students from 659 to 988.[17] It could be argued that the actual number of students who applied was acceptable. In reality, however, given the expectations of DAP as a means of increasing access to UC for students throughout California, this result must be seen as insufficient.

Why did so few DAP-eligible students apply for UC admission? There are at least two reasons. First, as noted previously, most students completed many more than the nine A-G courses required for the program and, thus, were probably eligible for freshman admission. Even if they were not freshman eligible at the end of their junior year in high school, many could have made themselves eligible during their senior year. Moreover, since A-G courses are considered to be some of the most demanding within any high school curriculum, students completing nine of these courses are more likely to be preparing for a selective four-year institution rather than a community college. Thus, for these students, the option of attending a California community college for their first two years of college may not have been an attractive one. Again, by setting the bar too high, it is likely that many students who would have been good candidates did not apply.

The second reason for the low application rate is that the primary incentive of DAP was withdrawn between the time students were identified for the program and the UC application filing period. Recall that a major tenet of the program promised DAP-eligible students a guaranteed spot at one of UC's undergraduate campuses, so long as they submitted an on-time application and completed appropriate preparatory coursework at a California community college. Yet, late in the summer of 2003, when it appeared that the state might make significant cutbacks in funding for UC enrollment, this guarantee was retracted. Instead, DAP-eligible students were invited to apply to the program and advised that, *if selected for admission to one or more UC campuses*, they would then be guaranteed admission at the junior level (again, after successfully completing their lower-division major coursework at a California community college). This new "commitment" was no different from that offered to any UC-eligible transfer who entered into an academic contract as part of a campus-based transfer agreement guarantee (TAG) program.[18]

Without a sufficiently tangible incentive, *not* applying under DAP could be seen as a more instrumental way for students to gain admission to UC. To the extent that DAP offered no significant advantage over regularly admitted transfer students who participated in a TAG program, most DAP-identified students may have chosen to take their chances at freshman admission (especially given their high level of academic achievement as measured by completion of A-G coursework). If they were not accepted at the freshman level, they could attend a community college and apply to UC later as a regular transfer student or take advantage of a campus-specific transfer guarantee program.

3. *While the number of students from underrepresented groups identified as DAP-eligible was encouraging, the number who actually submitted an application was smaller than anticipated.* The identification process under DAP was seen as a way of reaching greater numbers of students from underrepresented ethnic/racial groups given that eligibility was determined by a student's performance in his/her high school rather than within a statewide context (i.e., students are compared with peers in their high school rather than with peers statewide). Initial data indicated that a sizeable proportion of underrepresented students were eligible for DAP, especially among Chicano/Latino students. This trend was not sustained, however, when it came time for students to submit a UC application. Given the intensity with which talented underrepresented students are recruited by private institutions, it seems fair to say that

a guarantee to the UC system via a community college was not an attractive offer for many of these students. A useful study would track the postsecondary paths these students took, rather than accept the DAP offer.

## IMPLICATIONS FOR HIGHER EDUCATION POLICY

The goal of DAP was to increase access to the University of California, especially for students who have been underrepresented in higher education, by increasing the efficiency of the transfer process and by creating a UC/community college infrastructure to help assure student transfer and completion of the baccalaureate degree. While UC designed DAP to meet specific institutional needs, the central elements of the program have policy implications for two- and four-year institutions nationwide. First, DAP constituted a significant extension of the higher education admission "percent plans" used in Florida, Texas, and California in that students' transfer eligibility was conferred both prior to their application for admission and at least two years prior to their anticipated transfer date. Second, in addition to an admission guarantee, students who participate in DAP are provided with ongoing counseling and advising to assure successful transfer and completion of the BA degree. Third, DAP incorporated a commitment to link more effectively the transfer missions of community colleges and four-year institutions.

The core of DAP and its enabling predecessors was to create a crosswalk between the university and individual community colleges, such that both institutions jointly support students throughout their undergraduate enrollment. The DAP model represents a potentially valuable strategy to increase student access to higher education, and available data suggest several important policy options for other higher education institutions. In assessing feasibility, other colleges and universities will need to keep at least the following issues in mind:

*Is community college transfer an appropriate and reasonable path to achieving the baccalaureate degree?* In California, there are several conditions that work in favor of using community colleges more effectively. First, California has a wide network of community colleges and geographic access to a college is relatively convenient (there is at least one community college in almost every county in the state). Second, the cost of attending a California community college is the lowest in the nation, making these institutions accessible to low- and middle-income students and families (Larose, 2003). Third, there are sizeable segments of the population in California whose experience with higher education is limited and who see community colleges as an appropriate first step to a college degree for their children. For example, surveys indicate that Chicano/Latino families are less likely to send their children away from home to attend college, preferring instead to keep them closer to home because of ongoing family responsibilities or economic reasons (Fry, 2004; Santiago & Brown, 2004). Clearly, the appeal of an initiative like DAP will be limited to those states that have invested in public community colleges and who believe that the current transfer pipeline could be more productive, especially for students from educationally disadvantaged backgrounds. Moreover, these institutions must be geographically accessible and inexpensive, at least relative to the cost of other four-year college/university alternatives.

*Does the DAP percent plan constitute an effective way of increasing access to higher education for students from educationally disadvantaged backgrounds?* Evaluations of programs in other states that offer admission to students based on their percentage standing in high school suggest that such initiatives have failed to meet enrollment expectations, especially with regard to increasing the number of ethnic minority students attending the most highly selective institutions (see Horn & Flores, 2003; Marin & Lee, 2003). Programs in Texas and Florida have been criticized because, while they may have increased the proportion of educationally disadvantaged students attending four-year institutions overall, they have failed to increase the proportion who attend the most selective institutions in those states. Under DAP, participation of all UC campuses was required—including the flagship campuses of UCLA and Berkeley, which also are the most highly selective for admission.

Data presented here are ambiguous. While on the one hand the proportion of students from underrepresented groups identified as DAP-eligible was higher than in the college-age population of California, the proportion who actually submitted an application under DAP was low. Yet these findings are confounded for at least two reasons: 1) most of these students were highly accomplished academically and probably had other four-year options to pursue; and 2) the one tangible advantage of DAP—a guarantee of admission to UC after being identified as DAP-eligible—was eliminated.

*Does the DAP advising infrastructure serve transfer students effectively?* The core element of DAP was to provide students with ongoing advising throughout their enrollment at a community college. The assumption was (and remains) that a sustained commitment to students and a guarantee of admission will provide sufficient incentive to increase transfer rates from community colleges to four-year institutions, especially for students from educationally disadvantaged backgrounds. This incentive is also to be linked to improvements in transfer infrastructure at both the two-year and four-year institutions. One of the persistent criticisms of community colleges is that students who enter these institutions are less likely to successfully transfer and earn a degree (Dougherty, 1994, 2002). For example, while over 80 percent of students attending California community colleges have aspirations for completing a four-year degree, most never transfer (Egorin & Handel, 2001). The reasons for this are numerous, but one notable element is the type and extent of counseling that students receive at two- and four-year institutions. Noted critics of community colleges (see, for example, Brint & Karabel, 1989) often cite Burton Clark's (1960) now classic analysis of community colleges that documents the systematic tracking of students (especially less prepared students) to vocational certificates or other terminal degree programs rather than transfer. For students who come from families that have little college-going experience, the complexity of the transfer process is bound to work against timely transfer to a four-year institution. Clearly, there is a need for sustained and ongoing advising to ensure higher education access so that students may complete the baccalaureate degree.

*Budget Cuts and Retrenchment*

Since July 2001, when the UC Board of Regents adopted DAP, subsequent events in California altered significantly the higher education landscape. The University of California suffered deep cuts to its budget because of a severe state budget deficit. These reductions decreased the university's ability to enroll an ever-increasing number of college-age students and provide services to assist retention and graduation. As a result, the budget for DAP was cut by 50 percent in the 2003–2004 state budget and the remaining 50 percent was eliminated in 2004–2005. UC has suspended DAP, and, while there has been no official announcement, it is very unlikely that the University will reestablish the program. Nevertheless, UC has pledged to maintain support of the 271 students enrolled in the first year of DAP.[19]

At the same time that state funds were eliminated for DAP, the Governor proposed a new dual admissions program as a way of dealing with the budget deficit (called the "Guaranteed Transfer Option" or GTO). Under this plan, 10 percent of *UC-eligible* freshman would be guaranteed a place at a UC campus at the junior level, provided they first attended a California community college for their freshman and sophomore years and completed an academic contract. The proposal also included $1.5 million to provide academic advising for students who agreed to participate in this program. The Governor's office claimed that this program was necessary because the state lacked the resources to fund enrollment growth at UC for all UC-eligible freshmen (as stipulated in the California Master Plan). Diverting 10 percent of the UC-eligible freshman applicants (who in any other year would have been admitted to a UC campus) would save the state money because it is (presumably) less costly to educate students attending a California community college than those attending a UC campus. That program was only offered on a temporary basis, however. It is not expected to be renewed in the near future.[20]

When the state budget was finalized in August 2004, enrollment funding for the university was restored. As a result, each of the 7,641 students initially offered admission to UC via the GTO program received an offer of freshman admission for a term during the 2004–2005 academic year. Because these offers came well after the timeframe during which most applicants receive offers of admission, the yield rates were low. However, 21 percent of those applicants accepted an offer of freshman admission from a UC campus. In addition, more than 300 of these students opted to remain in GTO, beginning their postsecondary education at a California community college with guaranteed transfer admission to a specific UC campus as juniors.

## A DAP POSTMORTEM AND A FEW LESSONS
## FOR HIGHER EDUCATION ADMINISTRATORS

When this report was initially drafted, it was not anticipated that DAP would be eliminated in its first year of implementation. The specific reasons for this are beyond the scope of this chapter, but we believe there are useful lessons for others considering the implementation of similar percentage programs for transfer students.

1. *The criteria for the identification of prospective students in any admissions "percent plan" must be easily communicated to the public.* The way in which students were defined under DAP proved difficult to communicate to prospective students, their families, and counselors. Unlike percent plans in other states, DAP did not identify the highest achieving students in each high school, but rather students in the top 4 percent to 12.5 percent who demonstrated "high potential"—an achievement level far less precise in the minds of the public (and difficult for UC to measure—see item 2). Moreover, DAP was just the latest in a series admissions plans that UC initiated within the last five years, such as ELC and "comprehensive admissions." Explaining the purpose of these initiatives and the administrative interrelationships of each proved far more difficult that initially imagined.

2. *Criteria must target precisely the students to be recruited.* The definition of a DAP student was not effective in identifying "high potential" students who could benefit from attending a community college prior to entry to UC. As noted earlier, most of the students in this program were eligible, or very nearly eligible, for admission as freshmen and were more than likely preparing for a four-year college experience rather than attending a community college.

3. *The student identification process must be accurate and cost-effective.* The transcript review process used to identify DAP students was labor intensive, requiring the work of over 80 evaluators analyzing thousands of high school transcripts over a relatively short timeframe (June through August). This process itself was often unwieldy and occasionally unreliable. Variations in transcript data provided by high schools, difficulties in obtaining some data in a timely manner, and the lack of information about the courses completed by students in community college (prior to high school graduation) worked against effective assessment of student achievement for

DAP (although it should be stressed that this process was originally designed to identify ELC students and that the addition of DAP placed considerable strain on its overall effectiveness). Moreover, the DAP identification process cost over $500,000 to complete—an amount that could have been better spent on student support services.

4. *Partnerships with community colleges and high schools must be established at the outset to ensure effective implementation.* As noted earlier, changes in implementation goals and strategies and uncertainty regarding program budget worked against effective implementation of DAP. However, a tepid (sometimes hostile) response from constituencies that would be called upon to execute and maintain the program proved to be the tipping point in depressing statewide support for DAP. Although state legislators and educational system leaders praised UC's efforts to increase access through the California community colleges, when DAP was proposed in September 2000, high school, community college, and UC campus staff were wary. High school counselors worried that sending additional transcripts to UC for analysis would increase their workload significantly. Moreover, they questioned whether many of their students would be interested in attending a community college, even with a guarantee to UC, since they were likely to have other four-year options available to them.[21] Community college staff complained that the influx of new DAP students would overwhelm their already resource-starved student services and would create two classes of transfer students on their campuses: a "privileged" class holding a DAP transfer guarantee and students without a guarantee. Moreover, community college staff worried that encouraging greater numbers of students from high schools to attend a community college did not serve their primary constituencies, such as older, re-entry students.

Negative reaction to DAP also came from UC campus staff, who feared that DAP would create a new admissions mandate that was not coupled with appropriate resources. In particular, they were concerned that the advising commitment required under DAP would overwhelm their transfer outreach operations, especially since they would be required to track DAP students for 2 to 4 years while they attended a community college.

The concerns of these constituencies had merit. The addition of a new admission path was a significant administrative burden that was not offset—at least in the minds of campus administrators charged with implementing DAP—by the predicted gains in access to UC by students from educationally disadvantaged backgrounds. Beyond this reason, however, lies a different and subtler concern, one that relates to the perspective that many people hold regarding community colleges and the students that attend these institutions. While transfer is a primary element of California's Master Plan for Higher Education, it is often viewed as a secondary pathway to college (although such status is not conferred in the Master Plan). Moreover, the California Education Code requires public postsecondary education institutions, such as the California State University and UC, to provide students from California community colleges first priority in admissions consideration over all other applicants, except continuing students. Nevertheless, the four-year, residential model to the baccalaureate degree is often seen as preferable for college-age students, although research shows that earning a college degree via transfer—though imperfect in many ways—is perhaps the surest path for many students from educationally disadvantaged backgrounds to access a college education.

We are left, then, with a transfer admissions policy that was difficult to communicate to the public, employed a student identification process that was neither precise nor cost-effective, and presumed (inaccurately) the full cooperation of high schools and community colleges. Still, these implementation difficulties do not diminish the progressive vision of DAP to raise the profile and viability of the transfer path, increase access to higher education for students from educationally disadvantaged backgrounds, and provide ongoing counseling and advice for students who might not otherwise have considered entering a highly selective college or university. These remain central policy goals for the University of California and, one would hope, the rest of the nation. Given that America's community colleges remain the only substantive pathway of higher education access for less privileged students, programs like DAP—modified in ways that make implementation far less complicated and funded to assure sustained student advising and counseling—must be adopted if the nation is to fulfill its promise of universal educational opportunity.

## NOTES

This chapter was written while the first author was Director of Transfer Enrollment Planning and Undergraduate Outreach at the Office of the President for the University of California.

1. A number of follow-up evaluations of the Master Plan have been conducted since its 1960 implementation. Those emphasizing transfer education include reports by the Commission for the Study of the Master Plan for Higher Education in 1987 and the Joint Committee for the Review of the Master Plan in 1989. These and other reports have been compiled by the Center for Studies in Higher Education and are available at: http://sunsite.berkeley.edu/uchistory/archives_exhibits/masterplan/

2. It should be emphasized that many community colleges that do not send many students to UC campuses nonetheless are strong feeders to California State University campuses. The fact remains, however, that the students with the least resources are less likely to transfer to a UC campus given the distances they must travel, among other issues.

3. GPA calculation is based on students' completion of UC A-G courses only.

4. During the first year of implementation, this guarantee to students was significantly curtailed. Instead of guaranteeing all DAP-eligible students who applied a place at a specific UC campus, they were advised that admission was not guaranteed, but rather, if *selected* among all DAP-eligible applicants to a campus, they would have a guaranteed place at that specific UC campus. The reason for this policy change and its impact are discussed in the final section of this chapter.

5. High schools are required to secure parental authorization before they can release transcripts to the University for analysis.

6. Each letter represents a specific disciplinary area: (a) history/social science, (b) English, (c) mathematics, (d) laboratory science, (e) language other than English, (f) visual and performing arts, (g) electives.

7. These students are referred to as "on-track" because they will likely make themselves UC-eligible in their senior year of high school. Recall that DAP eligibility and ELC eligibility are determined by what courses and grades students earned in the 10th and 11th grades. The analysis does not include 12th-grade courses. Thus, it is possible that many of these students, who have completed at least 11 of the required 15 A-G courses by the end of the 11th grade, would become eligible by completing the remaining required courses in the 12th grade (senior year).

8. This is the only cohort of DAP students currently in the pipeline for reasons discussed in the next section.

9. "Target" high schools are those who have an Academic Performance Index (API) score of 1, 2, or 3 (on a scale of 10, with 10 being "highest performing"); a UC admit rate of less than 4 percent (based on a 3-year average); or are among the 70 lowest-performing high schools in the state using other measures of educational disadvantage.

10. The ELC category also includes students classified as "on-track" for freshman admission. These are students who are neither ELC- nor DAP-eligible (i.e., they are not in the top 12.5 percent of their specific high school class). Nonetheless, these students are likely to become freshman eligible if they complete appropriate courses in their senior year of high school.

11. In July 1995, the University of California Board of Regents adopted two resolutions, called SP-1 and SP-2, that changed the university's admissions, hiring, and contracting practices. SP-1 eliminated consideration of race and gender in the admission of students to the University. SP-2 eliminated race and gender as considerations in UC's hiring and contracting practices, except where such action would result in the University's loss of federal or state funds. The first full entering freshman class admitted under SP-1 enrolled at UC in Fall 1998.

12. In addition to the limited number of transcripts providing data on student race/ethnicity, data also indicate that the inclusion of race/ethnicity information was not evenly distributed across public, public-target, and private high schools that participated in the transcript submission process. Although 17 percent of target high schools provided data regarding the ethnicity or race of their students, only 5 percent of public high schools and 1 percent of private high schools provided this information.

13. For these data, Asian American includes students identifying themselves as Chinese/Chinese American, Japanese/Japanese American, Korean, Polynesian, Thai/Other Asian, and Vietnamese.

14. Geographic categories and definitions are based on U.S. Census Bureau classifications.

15. Changes to DAP student eligibility criteria instituted during the latter part of program implementation are one of several contributors to the relatively low application rate. This is addressed in greater detail in the final section.

16. Available data regarding A-G course completion are not sufficiently detailed to determine if students completed the required *pattern* of A-G courses; that is, courses clearing specific requirements in each A-G category. In addition, to be fully eligible, students must complete the appropriate standardized examinations and have earned at least a 2.80 GPA. However, this course completion pattern suggests that many DAP-eligible students may have been eligible to attend UC (or another four-year institution) at the freshman level.

17. This range was determined by calculating the average college-going rate of high school students enrolling at UC and then multiplying that figure by 3 to reach a sufficient number of applications that would likely meet the required enrollment threshold. The 10-year average college-going rate for UC was 7.5 percent (University of California, 2003b, p. 3), which, when multiplied by 3, produced an application rate of 22.5 percent. Given that UC campus enrollment rates vary greatly (some campuses are more popular than others are), the 22 percent to 33 percent range was calculated.

18. Eight of the ten undergraduate campuses of the University offer community college students the opportunity to enter into a contract after they complete approximately 30 units of lower-division work. This contract guarantees students' admission to the UC campus, provided that they complete all elements of the agreement at a California community college.

19. Ultimately, every DAP applicant was offered DAP admission to one or more UC campuses. Applicants who were not selected for admission to any of the campuses to which they applied were referred for admission to the new UC Merced campus, slated to open in Fall 2005. In addition, many DAP applicants were determined to be freshman-eligible and were offered a choice of freshman or DAP admission to one or more campuses. In the end, 271 DAP applicants accepted admission to a UC campus under the program.

20. The governor's proposal met with a generally negative response from a variety of constituencies. The university noted that by diverting eligible students to community colleges, the state was abrogating its pledge in the California Master Plan to secure a place at UC for all eligible high school students who applied. Freshman student applicants complained that they had worked throughout high school to earn entrance to a UC campus only to discover that the university's commitment was revoked at the last possible moment. Many families objected to the plan because, as taxpayers, they believed that their children were entitled to attend the University of California, not a community college—institutions that they contended were insuffi-

ciently challenging for their sons and daughters. Officials at the California community colleges objected to the $1.5 million appropriation for counseling given that no resources were provided in the budget for other students likely to be in greater need of such services.

21. This concern varied somewhat by region. Focus groups conducted prior to the implementation of DAP indicated that students attending high schools in parts of California that had low UC-college-going rates (such as the Central Valley) were more interested in attending UC via DAP than students in areas where admission to UC (at the freshman level) was higher, such as in the San Francisco Bay Area. This outcome confirmed one of the main goals of DAP, which was to increase college-going among students who might not otherwise consider attending a UC campus.

## REFERENCES

Bowen, W. G., & Bok, D. (1998). *The shape of the river: Long-term consequences of considering race in college and university admissions.* Princeton, NJ: Princeton University Press.

Bracco, K. R., & Callan, P. M. (2002). *Competition and collaboration in California higher education.* San Jose: National Center for Public Policy and Higher Education. http://www.highereducation.org/reports/calcomp/callen.shtml

Brint, S., & Karabel, J. (1989). *The diverted dream: Community colleges and the promise of educational opportunity in America, 1900–1985.* New York: Oxford University Press.

California Community College Chancellor's Office. (2003). Data accessed at http://www.cccco.edu/ Sacramento, CA.

California Department of Education. (2003). California Basic Education Data System. Sacramento, CA.

California State Department of Education. (1960). *A master plan for higher education: 1960–1975.* Sacramento, CA: State Department of Education, Master Plan Survey Team.

*Chronicle of Higher Education.* (2003, August 29). *Almanac Issue, 2003–04, 1*(1), 2.

Clark, B. (1960). *The open door college: A case study.* New York: McGraw Hill.

Commission for the Study of the Master Plan for Higher Education. (1987). *The master plan renewed: Unity, equity, quality, and efficiency in California postsecondary education.* Report available at: http://sunsite.berkeley.edu/uchistory/archives_exhibits/masterplan/ (The History of the Master Plan for Higher Education: A Project of the Center for Studies in Higher Education. University of California, Berkeley).

Dougherty, K. (1994). *The contradictory college: The conflicting origins, impacts, and futures of the community college.* Albany: State University of New York Press.

Dougherty, K. (2002). The evolving role of the community college: Policy issues and research questions. In J. C. Smart (Ed.), *Higher Education: Handbook of Theory and Research, 17* (pp. 295–348). New York: Agathon Press.

Egorin, M., & Handel, S. J. (2001). *Estimating the number of community college students preparing for UC Transfer: Results from an analysis of the California community college student database.* Oakland: University of California, Office of the President, Student Academic Services.

Fry, R. (2004). *Latino youth finishing college: The role of selective pathways.* Washington, DC: Pew Hispanic Center.

Horn, C. L., & Flores, S. M. (2003, February). *Percent plans in college admissions: A comparative analysis of three states' experiences.* Cambridge, MA: Harvard University, The Civil Rights Project (http://www.civilrightsproject.harvard.edu).

Joint Committee for the Review of the Master Plan. (1989). *California faces . . . California's future: Education for citizenship in a multicultural democracy.* Report available at: http://sunsite.berkeley.edu/uchistory/archives_exhibits/masterplan/ (The History of the Master Plan for Higher Education: A Project of the Center for Studies in Higher Education. University of California, Berkeley).

Larose, M. (2003, September 16). Tuitions increase as budgets wither. *Community College Times, 15*(18), 1, 7.

Marin, P., & Lee, E. K. (February 2003). *Appearance and reality in the sunshine state: The Talented 20 Program in Florida.* Cambridge, MA: Harvard University, The Civil Rights Project (http://www.civilrightsproject.harvard.edu).

Miller, L. S. (1995). *An American imperative: Accelerating minority educational advancement.* New Haven: Yale University Press.

National Center for Education Statistics. (2004). *The condition of education.* U.S. Department of Education, Washington DC (http://nces.ed.gov//programs/coe/).

Santiago, D. A. & Brown, S. (2004). *Federal policy and Latinos in higher education.* Washington DC: Pew Hispanic Center.

University of California. (1997). *Enhancing student transfer: A memorandum of understanding between the California community colleges and the University of California.* Oakland: Student Academic Services, Office of the President.

University of California. (2003a). *Undergraduate access to the University of California after the elimination of race-conscious policies.* Oakland: Student Academic Services, Office of the President.

University of California. (2003b). *UC Information Digest—2003: A reference guide on student access and performance at the University of California.* Oakland: Student Academic Services, Office of the President.

Wellman, J. (2002). *State policy and community college—Baccalaureate transfer.* San Jose: The National Center for Public Policy and Higher Education and The Institute for Higher Education Policy. (National Center Report #02–6).

NANCY SHULOCK
COLLEEN MOORE


Chapter Nine


# A Strengthened Community College Role in Teacher Preparation: Improving Outcomes for California's Minority Students


## INTRODUCTION

Effective, well-trained teachers are a critical component of a high quality K-12 education. For too many minority students in California, however, consistent access to a well-trained and experienced teacher is rare. With a persistent achievement gap between White students and underrepresented minority students, a shortage of qualified teachers for California schools hurts students, families, and the state's economy. If minority students are to gain access to higher education in California and succeed, they need committed, capable teachers in grades K-12 to help them become adequately prepared for college. This chapter describes some of the current recruitment and retention problems that California schools face and suggests some ways in which community colleges may be able to help alleviate California's teacher shortages in high need areas of the state and thus improve outcomes for minority students.

*California's Teacher Shortages: Focused in Critical Areas*

Growing school enrollments and a statewide class-size reduction initiative combined to create a severe shortage of fully credentialed and qualified teachers in the 1990s. Today, as a result of the economic downturn and state efforts to recruit new teachers, that general statewide demand for elementary school teachers has largely been met. However, teacher recruitment and retention remain serious problems for many California schools. California suffers from three primary needs in teacher preparation:

- To ease the shortage of qualified teachers in critical subject matter areas and in low-performing schools;
- To diversify the teaching workforce; and
- To improve teacher skills and effectiveness.

The need for qualified teachers is particularly acute in specialized subject areas such as math, science, and special education. Nearly half of high school math teachers in California do not have a major or minor in math (National Commission on Teaching and America's Future, 1997). Current research suggests that the strongest and most consistent predictor of a state's average student achievement level is the proportion of well-qualified teachers in the state, with "well-qualified" defined as teachers who are fully certified and hold the equivalent of a major in the subject taught (Darling-Hammond, 1999). Research also suggests that teachers' subject knowledge is particularly important in math and science as compared to other subject areas (Haycock, 1998).

Just as the shortage of teachers is not consistent across subjects, the shortage of qualified teachers is not uniform across districts. In 2001–2002, forty California districts had 20 percent or more of their teachers without full credentials (California Commission on Teacher Credentialing, 2003). The schools that suffer from general teacher shortages and hire large numbers of teachers without full credentials tend to be low-performing schools with high concentrations of poverty and underrepresented minority students (Shields et al., 2001). As shown in figure 9.1, California schools with large numbers of students receiving free or reduced price lunch have much higher shares of teachers without full credentials. Students who are taught year after year by inexperienced teachers are being denied an equal chance to reach high standards. Research has shown that teaching quality (linked often to years of experience) has a substantial impact on student achievement and that low-achieving students could benefit the most from capable teachers (Sanders & Rivers, 1996).

Many would argue that California needs a teaching workforce that better represents the diversity of its student population. Currently, while White students make up only 32 percent of California's K-12 students, almost 74 percent of California's teachers are White. Table 9.1 shows the racial compo-

FIGURE 9.1

Percentage of Teachers without Full Credentials by School Poverty Level

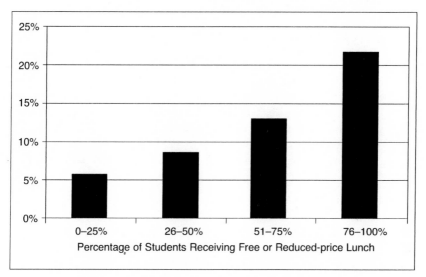

*Source:* Shields et al., *The Status of the Teaching Profession 2001*

TABLE 9.1

Racial Composition of California Teachers and Students, 2004/2005

|  | Non-Hispanic White | Hispanic or Latino | Black | Asian or Pacific Islander | Filipino | American Indian |
|---|---|---|---|---|---|---|
| Students | 31.9% | 47.7% | 8.1% | 8.9% | 2.6% | 0.8% |
| Teachers | 73.8% | 14.8% | 4.6% | 4.9% | 1.2% | 0.6% |

*Source:* California Department of Education, Educational Demographics Unit, online Dataquest available at http://data1.cde.ca.gov/dataquest.

sition of California's teachers and students. The disparity between the numbers of Latino students and teachers is most striking. While the percentage of students who are Hispanic or Latino in California has grown to almost 48 percent, the population of Latino teachers has not kept pace. In addition, research suggests that the percentage of teachers nationwide who are members of ethnic minority groups may have decreased in the past decade, even as the number of underrepresented minority students in both K-12 and higher education has increased. The National Education Association (2003) reported that the percentage of African American teachers declined nationwide from 8 percent in 1991 to 6 percent in 2001.

Researchers and advocates stress the importance of minority teachers for three main reasons (Clewell & Villegas, 1998):

- Teachers who share students' backgrounds may serve as models of academic success;
- Teachers' expectations for students can be important predictors of success, and teachers of color may have higher expectations for minority students than other teachers; and
- Teachers of color may be more likely to stay in schools serving high numbers of poor or minority youth, reducing high teacher turnover rates and increasing stability within schools.

Ultimately, most researchers agree that teaching quality, regardless of the teacher's race or ethnic background, is most critical to student achievement. But most researchers also maintain that diversity among our teachers can play an important role in raising student achievement among minority youth.

California also faces a growing need for teachers with new skills. In the 1990s California introduced rigorous new achievement standards for all students. In several years, all California students will have to pass a high school exit exam in order to earn a diploma. The federal No Child Left Behind legislation also places new requirements with regard to teacher training and effectiveness. In order for schools to qualify for federal funding, the legislation required that all teachers of core academic subjects be "highly qualified" by the 2005–2006 school year.[1] Researchers suggest that high standards for all students demand a different set of skills than teachers were trained to have in the past—when a much smaller percentage of students were expected to graduate from high school with a college preparatory curriculum.

*The Research Question: Can Community Colleges Play a Role?*

The traditional division of responsibility in California higher education placed teacher preparation under the auspices of the California State University (CSU) and, to a lesser extent, the University of California (UC). Despite playing a substantial role in California's higher education system as a whole, community colleges have played a more obscure role in the preparation of K-12 teachers. This report asks whether an increased role for California's community colleges in teacher preparation could help to improve the number of teacher candidates available for positions in low-performing schools, including teachers from minority backgrounds. Our analysis also examines the potential role for community colleges to increase teacher retention in high-poverty schools and improve the quality of training that teachers receive—all with the ultimate goal of improving academic achievement for minority students across California.

Research methods for this analysis included a review of the literature on teacher preparation, 23 interviews with program administrators at community colleges and other segments of California higher education,[2] and an analysis of pilot programs and recent legislation aimed at reforming teacher preparation in California. Specifically, we analyzed the two major statewide pilot programs[3] and interviewed officials involved in three local, department-based partnerships. There is no system-wide record of the number of local partnerships, however, so we were unable to account in any rigorous fashion for the outcomes of these local efforts.

Our methodology also included the development of a pipeline framework for evaluating the potential benefit of including community colleges in the teacher preparation system in a more systematic manner than has been done previously. Based on this framework and our analysis of qualitative interview data and the outcomes of the statewide pilot programs, we make recommendations for policies and practices that we believe could help to shore up the pipeline for new teachers in California.

## WHY TURN TO CALIFORNIA'S COMMUNITY COLLEGES?

With teacher shortages across the country in the late 1990s, researchers have suggested community colleges as a potential resource for new teacher candidates (Recruiting New Teachers, 2002). In California, where shortages have been especially pressing, where issues of equity are paramount, and where the community colleges play a larger role in higher education than in many other states, finding a new source of teacher candidates in the community colleges is a particularly compelling prospect.

*Community Colleges Serve Most Students, Especially Minority Students*

In California, community colleges were designed to be a more substantial part of the higher education system than in many other states, enrolling more than two-thirds of all students in public institutions. Nationally, community colleges enroll less than 40 percent of all college students (National Center for Education Statistics, 2003). Community colleges play an even greater role in the education of California's minority students, enrolling approximately 75 percent of African American and Latino freshmen.[4] Due to the sheer size of the community college segment in California (more than 1.7 million students), the community colleges are home to a much greater number of minority students than the other, smaller segments. Therefore, any effort to diversify the teaching workforce must consider students who begin in the community colleges.

Enrollments at California community colleges are expected to increase over the next decade, both in real numbers and as a percentage of all higher education enrollments, with the addition of as many as 500,000 students (California Postsecondary Education Commission, 2000). While all of California higher education is expected to experience substantial growth in enrollment, community colleges may see a disproportionately large increase due both to their greater capacity to admit new students and to the likely policy directives to guide lower division students to the community colleges in view of the cost savings to the state.[5]

*Community Colleges Hold Untapped Potential*

California's community colleges may be a source of untapped potential in terms of new candidates for teaching careers and new avenues for teacher preparation. We envision a framework for evaluating the potential for an efficient pipeline for teacher development in California that recognizes and includes community colleges as an important factor in the pipeline. The following is a description of how the pipeline to a teaching career through the community colleges can be understood as a series of four steps and an outline of how new efforts in community colleges could shore up the pipeline at each of these points.

1. *Recruitment of diverse teacher candidates into the community colleges.* A variety of factors have combined in California to deny community colleges an explicit role in teacher preparation and make it more difficult than in other states for community colleges to play a substantial role in the recruitment of new teacher candidates. The state's 1960 Master Plan for Higher Education assigned primary responsibility for teacher credentialing programs to the California State Colleges (later renamed the California State University). No role for community colleges in teacher preparation was authorized beyond the general education of any student interested in transfer. Moreover, with no baccalaureate-level education major in the state, community colleges have no formalized teacher education department into which faculty can work collectively to recruit students. Given a more formal role, such as designated "pre-teaching" faculty or departments, community colleges could produce many more students interested in a teaching career. If such faculty were explicitly charged with recruiting students from urban high schools into these "pre-teaching" departments, many of these students would likely be members of ethnic minority groups, math and science majors, or committed to teaching in low-performing urban schools.

2. *Support during the lower-division years.* Community colleges have long played a silent role in teacher preparation by providing the first two years of the baccalaureate to thousands who ultimately become teachers. While national studies show that 20 percent of teachers start their education in a community college (Recruiting New Teachers, 2002), that figure is surely higher in California with its extensive use of community colleges to educate undergraduates. Community college students in California, however, receive

little or no introduction to the classroom or instruction in pedagogy. If community colleges had a more defined role in teacher preparation, they could use the time they have with future teachers to formally start a teacher preparation curriculum, including exposure to the public school classroom. Research suggests that earlier exposure to the classroom can have a positive effect on teacher efficacy, particularly in the first few years of teaching (Darling-Hammond, Chung, & Frelow, 2002). An early introduction to teaching could solidify students' commitment to the teaching profession, ease the transition into teacher preparation programs, and improve learning and completion rates in baccalaureate and credentialing programs. In addition, a more formal structure for teacher preparation in community colleges, along with adequate counseling and support services, could keep students on the path to transfer and a credential. For example, community colleges could establish learning communities in which students interested in teaching could take a series of courses together, in conjunction with any needed remedial work.

3. *Success in transfer and completion of a baccalaureate and a teaching credential.* The process of obtaining a teaching credential is more complex in California than in many other states. There is no common transfer curriculum across community colleges, and transfer requirements differ among the senior institutions, increasing the complexity of articulation and impeding adequate counseling and advising for students.[6] A well-defined role in teacher preparation for community colleges could promote better articulation specific to teacher education and could encourage the segments to move toward a more standardized curriculum, contributing to better success in transfer and completion. While there are many other factors, such as academic preparation, financial need, and work and family commitments, that influence transfer outcomes, improved articulation could be expected to have a disproportionately positive impact on transfer outcomes for low-income students and students of color. Research and experience have demonstrated that students without much "educational capital" (i.e., students who lack a support system of persons knowledgeable about how to navigate the college environment) face many more obstacles to the successful movement through an academic course of study. A simplified structure of course and program articulation between and across community colleges and four-year universities could increase the numbers of educationally disadvantaged students who are able to complete a teacher preparation program.

4. *Placement and retention in the teaching workforce.* An efficient and effective teacher preparation pipeline must account for more than just increased numbers of new candidates. It must also consider the placement and retention of new teachers, their effectiveness in the classroom, and their development into future leaders in education and education reform (Clewell & Villegas, 1998). By recruiting new teacher candidates from among the large number of underrepresented minority students attending community colleges,

providing them with adequate counseling and advising needed for transfer to and success in universities and giving them an early introduction to the classroom, community colleges could greatly increase the chances of placement and retention in high-need positions and communities.

## CHALLENGES FACING COMMUNITY COLLEGES
## IN TEACHER PREPARATION

Drawing new teachers from the community colleges is a compelling prospect across the country, but especially in California, where students in the K-12 schools are so diverse and have needs that may best be served by a more diverse teaching workforce and where community colleges play a substantial role in higher education, particularly for minority college students. However, California's community colleges face substantial challenges if they are going to help the state alleviate serious shortages and provide adequate training for today's teachers.

### Unclear Role for the Lower Division in Teacher Preparation

Unlike most other states, California separates the four-year baccalaureate degree (meant to build subject matter competence) from the credentialing program, a fifth year of teacher preparation coursework designed to provide pedagogical instruction and student teaching experience. With the passage of the Ryan Act in 1970, the state prevented all California colleges from granting undergraduate degrees in education. By placing teacher preparation almost totally within postgraduate education, the Ryan Act denied community colleges any formal role in teacher preparation.

### Complexity of California Higher Education and Teacher Credentialing

In most other states, community colleges are able to offer coursework leading to degrees in education, and in many states students interested in teaching need only follow a common transfer curriculum. However, in California, there is no undergraduate education degree and no common transfer curriculum for prospective teachers. To ensure that community college students interested in transferring take courses that will be accepted for general education and major requirements, community colleges and four-year institutions develop articulation agreements on a course-by-course and campus-by-campus basis. Although the liberal studies major, the most common program followed by students interested in elementary teaching, is offered at every CSU campus, the requirements for the major differ across campuses, making planning for transfer more difficult for students and increasing the challenge for community colleges to prepare their students for transfer and teaching careers. In addition, there is no common major for students interested in secondary teaching, increasing the likelihood that students in critical fields such as math and science will get diverted from a teaching goal into the many other career choices available to them, including research and technical positions with health, biotechnology, and other high technology industries that may offer substantially higher salaries than those available in teaching.

*Low Transfer Rates*

Persistently low transfer rates in many of California's community colleges may serve as a barrier to increasing the number of teacher candidates they send on to four-year institutions. While some of the 109 community colleges transfer large numbers of students every year, other campuses have very low transfer rates. The National Center for Public Policy and Higher Education reported that only 39 of the community colleges supplied almost 65 percent of the transfers to CSU in 1999–2000 (Bracco & Callan, 2002). Possible problems that lead to low transfer rates as identified in the report include deficiencies in curricula and instruction in some community colleges, poor counseling, articulation or financial aid policies and deficiencies in K-12 preparation. Transfer agreements between community colleges and four-year institutions are also made individually, often requiring students to know not only which major they intend to pursue, but to which schools they intend to apply.

Transfer rates are particularly low among some groups of students that community colleges would be interested in tapping as future teachers. Our own research suggests that community colleges with large shares of African American and Latino students have significantly lower transfer rates than colleges with larger proportions of White and Asian students (Wassmer, Moore, & Shulock, 2002). The disparity is, in part, related to differences in average socioeconomic level and academic preparation in high school, but these factors do not entirely account for the racial/ethnic disparities. African American and Latino students may face greater work, family, and financial pressures that prevent them from transferring to four-year institutions, particularly when that involves leaving home, and may have unique obstacles to transfer related to being first-generation college students or encountering campus cultures that are not supportive of their educational goals.

*Poor Academic Preparation for*
*Postsecondary Education among Students*

Community colleges striving to produce more teacher candidates could face a particularly thorny obstacle in the poor academic preparation of many incoming students. Nearly 50 percent of entering students in the CSU system require remedial classes in order to prepare for college-level work. Because California community colleges have open enrollment and no admission requirements, the need for remedial education is likely to be much greater (the lack of a standard assessment policy across community colleges limits our understanding of remedial needs in this sector). Community colleges may face a particular obstacle in the preparation of more teacher candidates from underrepresented minority groups. Data from CSU indicate that African-American and Latino students are much more likely than White students to require remedial classes; similar patterns likely exist at the community college level. Poor academic preparation could slow the transfer process for many students as they complete remedial classes, decreasing the likelihood of retention and completion. Poor academic skills could also prevent students from becoming eligible for credentialing programs or passing licensure exams. Most importantly, however, poor academic preparation, especially if not corrected in the community colleges or four-year institutions, could prevent new teachers from being effective in the classroom and improving achievement among students.

## ANALYSIS OF RECENT DEVELOPMENTS

Recent developments, both nationally and in California, have started to better define the role that community colleges can and should play in teacher preparation.

### The National Context

The Carnegie Corporation is one supporter of new models of teacher preparation. In 2002, the Carnegie Corporation issued a "Carnegie Challenge" paper arguing that colleges of education should redesign teaching and teacher preparation as a clinical profession. In other words, teacher preparation should include much more supervised teaching in a classroom setting, with extensive mentoring, instruction, and support for beginning teachers. In this vein, the Carnegie Corporation has launched Teachers for a New Era, a major initiative to redesign teacher education and create "residencies" in education. The Carnegie Corporation believes that placing teacher candidates in the classroom earlier and providing them with mentoring and support will improve student achievement.

A number of states are designing and implementing new models of teacher preparation that incorporate ideas espoused by the Carnegie Corporation, and some are including community colleges in ways that go beyond traditional articulation efforts. The "university center" approach is particularly popular, in which baccalaureate teaching degrees are offered by universities on community college campuses. Examples of this approach are found in Illinois, Texas, Florida, and North Carolina. Other community colleges in Arizona, Texas, and Florida are working with universities to offer online certification programs for people who already hold a baccalaureate degree. In the most controversial model, some community colleges in Florida are being authorized by the state to offer baccalaureate degrees in teacher education.

## A Role for the Lower Division in California Teacher Preparation

Legislative efforts in California have sought to incorporate some aspects of the Carnegie Corporation ideas into efforts to reform teacher preparation. In 1998, the passage of Assembly Bill 2042 created a role for the lower division in teacher preparation by requiring universities to offer students earlier exposure to the classroom and to the pedagogical aspects of teaching. The legislation called on the California State University to begin developing "blended" programs that would combine the academic subject matter preparation for teachers of the undergraduate years with the credentialing program, effectively eliminating the separate admissions process after the baccalaureate and allowing students to begin their professional training as teachers while undergraduates. AB 2042 also encouraged the development of education minors, thereby calling on institutions to help students focusing on subject matter competency to learn about the profession and practice of teaching at the same time. The legislation also encouraged colleges to link teacher preparation with new state student achievement standards, which led the California Commission on Teacher Credentialing (CTC) to develop new requirements for many credentialing programs.

Almost every CSU campus now offers at least one blended program (alongside separate credential programs that will continue to operate as before). Also known as integrated teacher education programs, the programs allow students to engage in preservice fieldwork as undergraduates, some as early as freshman or sophomore year. Some blended programs enroll students as freshmen while others enroll students as juniors. With the recent passage of Senate Bill 81, all CSU campuses are required to enter into articulation agreements with community colleges in their regions to integrate transfer students into the blended programs by 2005.

The blended programs offer community colleges a tremendous opportunity and daunting challenges. By placing responsibility for teacher preparation in the undergraduate sphere, AB 2042 has opened the door for increased participation by community colleges. However, no additional resources have been provided to help community colleges deal with the challenges of preparing their students for these programs. Given the severe shortage of counselors, the colleges are struggling to provide students with the most up-to-date information about transfer requirements, to revise their curriculum to incorporate information on the practice of teaching, and to offer the early classroom experience that is a critical component of blended programs. Since there are no teacher education departments on community college campuses, the responsibility to teach education-related courses and to supervise fieldwork in K-12 classrooms falls to a collection of faculty and counselors—often to those assigned to a campus's learning resource center whose primary responsibility is to provide co-curricular support rather than direct instruction. There are very few faculty across the community college system whose primary teaching assignments are in the area of education.[7]

A recent evaluation of the new blended programs (SRI International, 2003) concluded that they could have a powerful impact on schools and students across California, in part by attracting new candidates who were put off by the complexities of a separate credentialing program. By eliminating the gap between the undergraduate degree and the credentialing program, blended programs may reduce the number of students choosing to enter the classroom with emergency credentials as soon as they receive a bachelor's degree. In addition, by offering students early experience in the classroom and combining academic subjects with coursework in pedagogy, the programs may produce more effective teachers.

### Other Efforts to Involve California's Community Colleges

Since 1995, California has funded the Paraprofessional Teacher Training Program (PTTP), designed to help paraprofessionals who are already working in schools to become fully credentialed teachers. The programs, operated through individual school districts, provide paraprofessionals (classroom aides) with academic and financial support, including tuition, money for books and other supplies, and counseling and tutoring services. The program has targeted paraprofessionals because they already have experience working in classrooms, tend to come from the same communities as their schools' students, and are often members of underrepresented minority groups. Since many paraprofessionals have less than an associate's degree, the program works with community colleges as well as CSU campuses. When the program was launched in 1995, it was designed as a pilot project with a maximum of 600 participants from 12 school districts. More districts have since joined, with a total of 2,266 participants to date, across more than 25 districts. The program has been a remarkable success as measured by placement and retention, allowing districts to focus on training teachers for specific local needs (e.g., bilingual teachers) and providing them with reliable candidates who are extremely likely to remain in the district (97 percent among the first program graduates).

In 1998, California passed legislation authorizing the Teacher and Reading Development Partnerships (TRDP) program, which provides community colleges with AmeriCorps funding to place students as tutors in low-performing elementary schools. Tutoring serves to expose students to the classroom and encourage them to pursue teaching careers. More than simply providing tutoring opportunities, many TRDP programs have also served to create a "home" for teacher preparation on campus. Many have drop-in centers where students can come for counseling and advising on teaching careers, transfer, and related topics. Most of the programs have strengthened the counseling and advising available for students interested in teaching careers, with a particular focus on helping students learn about financial aid for future teachers. Many TRDP programs have also focused on improving articulation of courses and credits with four-year institutions, developing additional courses in education, partnering with local school districts, and recruiting minority students into the program to increase diversity in the teaching workforce.

Partnerships have also developed in the past few years between departments at community colleges and four-year universities. These partnerships, designed to track students into single-subject credential programs, help students transfer quickly and complete the subject matter requirements for entry into a credential program. For example, Sacramento City College has developed a program linking its chemistry department with the chemistry department at UC Davis, in hopes of increasing the number of qualified chemistry teachers earning credentials. Whether there are several or dozens of similar programs remains unclear, but more institutional support would likely result in other programs developing across the state.

The efforts described here offer promising evidence for the value community colleges can add to teacher preparation in California at all points along the pipeline. Well-designed and targeted programs can produce more candidates for low-performing schools and increase teacher diversity. In the context of California's complex higher education system, more structured programs for community college students interested in teaching are needed. State efforts have begun to address the recruitment and support of students interested in teaching, but many of the efforts to date have been ad hoc and unsupported by data collection or analysis.

## CONCLUSIONS AND RECOMMENDATIONS

California higher education has made important strides in the last few years in its efforts to draw on a valuable resource for qualified teachers: the community colleges. It has started from a position of disadvantage compared to those states with undergraduate teaching majors, teaching minors, streamlined transfer processes, and less segmented higher education governance structures. In this final section, we offer several recommendations for policy makers and education administrators to shore up the pipeline for teacher development. The recommendations are structured around California's particular circumstances, but the overall focus on strengthening the role of community colleges all along the teacher preparation pipeline should be relevant to most other states. Our recommendations follow the four points on the pipeline as described earlier.

1. *Community colleges should focus on recruitment and early identification of prospective teachers—and the legislature should provide them with the support to do so effectively.* Community colleges are perfectly poised to

serve as a major recruitment arm for the teaching profession. With a better-defined role in teacher preparation, community colleges will be able to take on a greater role in the recruitment into a teaching pathway of high school students and newly enrolled community college students, particularly underrepresented minority students. Special efforts to identify and recruit potential teaching candidates are particularly important in California, where there is no education major and no "home" for students on community college campuses interested in teaching. Community colleges and universities in the state should support the concept of a minor in education to complement the subject matter preparation and engage students in the teaching profession. Colleges should try to match the requirements for a minor with many or all of the requirements needed to enter a credential program, allowing community college students to meet requirements in a streamlined way.

The paraprofessional programs have had significant success in preparing teachers that meet the particular needs of local school districts for bilingual and special education teachers and for teachers committed to serving the students of a particular community. Funding for this program should be continued and efforts made to expand the program to other districts, particularly those that have difficulty recruiting and retaining teachers.

States need to pinpoint where teachers are needed, and be strategic about what incentives to put in place to encourage people to enter the profession (Darling-Hammond as reported in Bradley, 1999). Appropriate strategies include increased outreach to students in math and science courses at community colleges (and in the other segments), tutoring opportunities for college students in math, science, and special education classrooms, and targeted recruitment of teaching candidates from low-income and underrepresented communities.

2. *Community colleges should enhance their support for students interested in teaching in order to keep them engaged, provide them with adequate preparation, and put them on a pathway to the profession.* All community colleges can learn some important lessons from California's TRDP programs. Many of the programs have become campus hubs of information about teacher preparation. The early classroom experience these programs provide is invaluable for nurturing the initial interest of students and solidifying their commitment to pursuing a teaching career. The enhanced advising services that have developed in a number of colleges with TRDP programs, along with selected improvements in articulation with teacher preparation programs, are helping to shore up the portion of the pipeline by which students position themselves for acceptance into a teacher preparation program. Other promising developments at community colleges that are worthy of replication include student teacher clubs, efforts to develop close connections with education departments at four-year institutions, and learning communities that allow students to complete remedial instruction and subject matter prepara-

tion with other students interested in teaching. In addition, every community college should designate at least one adviser on campus who can help students with course planning for transfer in light of the complexity of the teacher credentialing process.

3. *Community colleges, universities, and policy makers should work to enhance the prospects for students' successful transfer and eventual success at completing a baccalaureate and credentialing requirements.* The more seamless a state's transfer process, the greater the prospects for a strong community college role in teacher preparation. California's higher education segments should begin to standardize (or at least regionalize) transfer requirements for teacher preparation. As a long term goal, the segments should work toward a uniform teacher preparation curriculum for community colleges. Until then, regional efforts among community colleges and CSU campuses (like those prescribed under SB 81) should continue to promote articulation specific to teacher education. Without investing additional funds, the legislature has made it clear that articulation agreements are important. With the state's fiscal situation, the legislature should provide additional grants for regional groups to continue working on a teacher preparation curriculum that could be implemented statewide.

A reform with huge potential to increase the flow of community college students into teaching is the offering of teacher preparation programs on site at community college campuses, through cooperative agreements between community colleges and four-year institutions. The opportunity to complete a baccalaureate and a teaching credential on a community college campus removes the geographic barrier to transfer that particularly affects minority students who may have greater financial and family considerations.

4. *Policy makers and educators should increase their collective efforts to place and retain qualified teachers, particularly in high-need areas and fields, and should fully incorporate the community colleges in this effort.* Current teacher shortages in California and elsewhere are concentrated in certain subjects and schools, specifically, math, science, special education, and schools serving low-income populations. Although the community colleges in most states are not formally involved in the later stages of the pipeline (placement and retention of teachers), they can have a significant impact on teacher placement and retention. Many of the promising activities we identified have the potential to draw into the profession the kinds of people who will be more likely to serve in high-need areas and fields and to prepare these prospective teachers to succeed.

Community colleges and universities should actively promote department-to-department partnerships in science and math to identify students in these fields with an interest in teaching and support them through the process of transfer and completion of a single subject credential. Incentive funding could encourage these partnerships, which today rely on good will

and personal connections. Research demonstrates the importance of qualified teachers in these specialized fields, making it imprudent to rely on the
informal development of such collaborations (Darling-Hammond, 1999;
Haycock, 1998). All community college teacher preparation programs
should build links to local districts. Partnering with the school district
ensures that students will have an avenue for field experience in the first two
years of college and helps counselors and students to understand the
regional market for teachers.

Recruitment strategies that would yield more minority students, such as
those implemented so successfully in California's Paraprofessional Teacher
Training program, should be expanded. Most states, like California, need
more teachers of diverse ethnic backgrounds to ensure high expectations of
underrepresented minority students to serve as models of academic success
and to increase teacher retention in urban school districts. Achieving a more
diverse teaching workforce should follow from successful recruitment of
minority students in community colleges, adequate support to meet their educational needs, and early exposure to the classroom to encourage their commitment to the profession.

As a final recommendation, we suggest that states review and improve
as necessary their data collection systems to allow researchers to track students over time through the community colleges and the universities. It is only
through such efforts that we can understand better where the teacher development pipeline leaks and prospective teacher candidates are lost and how
strengthening the role of the community colleges can best help.

## NOTES

The authors acknowledge the substantial contributions to this research by Debra
Soloman, graduate student at the Richard and Rhoda Goldman School of Public Policy, University of California, Berkeley.

1. See *The No Child Left Behind Act of 2001: Reauthorization of the Elementary and Secondary Education Act*. Public Law 107–110. January 8, 2002.

2. Interviews included eight with representatives of the community college sector, six with representatives of the four-year universities, and nine with others, including legislative staff and representatives of the K-12 sector. Interviewees were selected
to cover the range of interests involved in the issue but should not be considered to
comprise a systematic or representative sample in a strict methodological sense.

3. See the following discussion of the Paraprofessional Teacher Training program and the Teaching and Reading Development Partnerships program.

4. Enrollment data available from the California Postsecondary Education Commission at http://www.cpec.ca.gov/OnLineData/FindRpt.asp

5. In his budget proposal for 2004–2005, Governor Schwarzenegger proposes reducing freshman enrollment in the state's public universities and redirecting those students to the community colleges with provisions to support their later transfer to UC or CSU. While the final California budget has not been passed as of this writing, UC and CSU are proceeding with the redirection proposal. UC and CSU both denied admission to some eligible freshman applicants (about 7,600 and 3,800, respectively), offering them deferred admission after two years of community college.

6. The CSU is working on a plan to streamline transfer for community college students into multiple-subject teacher preparation programs. The Statewide CSU Integrated Teacher Preparation program is developing 30 to 45 units of lower-division requirements that would be the same across all CSU campuses. The remaining 15 to 30 units needed to transfer (a total of 60) would continue to be negotiated between individual CSU and CCC campuses. This effort results from legislation (SB 81) requiring the CSU to ensure that community college transfer students can be accommodated in the "blended" programs.

7. Information on faculty teaching assignments for education-related courses is provided by Charlie Klein, Academic Planning Specialist in the Community Colleges Chancellor's Office.

## REFERENCES

Bracco, K. R., & Callan, P. M. (2002). *Competition and collaboration in California higher education.* San Jose, CA: National Center for Public Policy and Higher Education.

Bradley, A. (1999, March 10). States' uneven teacher supply complicates staffing of schools. *Education Week.*

California Commission on Teacher Credentialing. (2003). *Teacher supply in California 2001–2002: A report to the legislature.* Sacramento, CA: Author.

California Postsecondary Education Commission. (2000). *Providing for progress: California higher education enrollment demand and resources into the 21st century.* Sacramento, CA: Author.

Center for the Future of Teaching and Learning. (2002). *California's teaching force: Key issues and trends 2002.* Santa Cruz, CA: Author.

Clewell, B. C., & Villegas, A. M. (1998). Increasing the number of teachers of color for urban schools. *Education and Urban Society, 31*(1), 42–61.

Darling-Hammond, L. (December, 1999). State teaching policies and student achievement. *Teaching Quality Policy Briefs*, Number 2. Seattle, WA: Center for the Study of Teaching and Policy.

Darling-Hammond, L., Chung, R., & Frelow, F. (2002). Variation in teacher preparation: How well do different pathways prepare teachers to teach? *Journal of Teacher Education, 53*(4).

Haycock, K. (1998). Good teaching matters: How well-qualified teachers can close the gap. *Thinking K-16, 3*(2). Washington, DC: The Education Trust.

National Center for Education Statistics. (2003). *Digest of education statistics, 2002*. Washington, DC: US Department of Education.

National Commission on Teaching and America's Future. (1997). *Doing what matters most: Investing in quality education*. New York: Author.

National Education Association. (2003). *Status of the American public school teacher 2000–2001*. Washington, DC: Author.

Recruiting New Teachers, Inc. (2002). *Tapping potential: Community colleges and America's teacher recruitment challenge*. Belmont, MA: Author.

Sanders, W., & Rivers, J. (1996). *Cumulative and residual effects of teachers on future student academic achievement*. Knoxville, TN: University of Tennessee Value-Added Research and Assessment Center.

Shields, P. M., Humphrey, D. C., Wechsler, M. E., Riehl, L. M., Tiffany-Morales, J., Woodworth, K., Young, V. M., & Price, T. (2001). *The status of the teaching profession 2001*. Santa Cruz, CA: Center for the Future of Teaching and Learning.

SRI International. (2003). *Study of selected blended teacher education programs in California*. Menlo Park, CA: Author.

Wassmer, R., Moore, C., & Shulock, N. (2002). *A quantitative study of California community college transfer rates: Policy implications and a future research agenda*. Sacramento, CA: Institute for Higher Education Leadership & Policy.

JORGE CHAPA

Chapter Ten

# The Educational Pipeline and the Future Professorate: Who Will Teach California's and the Nation's Latino and African American College Students?

## LATINOS AND AFRICAN AMERICANS IN THE EDUCATION PIPELINE

The educational pipeline for Chicanos, Latinos, and African Americans is rife with massive leaks. The ultimate result of the extremely leaky pipeline is that faculty in the nation's colleges and universities do not reflect the racial and ethnic diversity of the population. California has the most racially and ethnically diverse population in the nation, and it is there that the disparity between the proportion of student-age African Americans and Latinos and the proportion of African American and Latino professors is the greatest. For example, in 2000 more than 42 percent of the college-age population in California were Chicanos or Latinos but only 7 percent of the California State University's (CSU) faculty and 4.6 percent of the University of California's (UC) faculty were members of these groups. Furthermore,

243

almost half, 49.5 percent, of California's college-age population in 2000 were underrepresented minorities (URMs); that is, Chicanos, Latinos, African Americans, and American Indians, compared to 7.2 percent of the ladder-rank faculty at all of the UC campuses and 10.5 percent of the ladder-rank faculty at the CSU campuses (tables 10.1 and 10.2). The gap between the large proportion of Latinos and African Americans among the student-age population and the small proportion among higher education faculty that currently exists in California is a pattern that will be found in a many other states in the near future.

The misleading nature of the term "pipeline" can be seen in the rapidly decreasing proportion of these three groups found at each successive educational level. In 2000, underrepresented groups were 40 percent of high school graduates; 32 percent of students enrolled in college (including community college); 17 percent of undergraduates enrolled in UC and approximately 12 percent of UC graduate students. A pipeline implies a smooth, steady flow along a fixed path over time, but this pipeline is full of massive holes. The demographic and educational trends discussed in this chapter suggest that the Chicano/Latino population will continue to grow very rapidly and their participation in higher education as students and faculty will not. In other words, these differences will likely grow larger with the passage of time.

It is easier to understand this disjuncture between Chicano and other underrepresented minority (URM) student populations and the successively higher steps of the educational pipeline after examining table 10.3, which presents some of the salient socioeconomic background characteristics of underrepresented minorities who apply for freshman admission to UC in comparison to those of the White applicants. White applicants to UC typically have parents with much higher educational levels and incomes than any other group shown. These differences in parental income and educational attainment are doubtless related to the differences in educational success and likelihood of even applying to college (Gándara, 1999a). The data in table 10.3 show that more Chicanos than any other group come from households with the lowest parental educational and income levels. Moreover, the differences between the parental backgrounds of Chicanos and Latinos illustrate why it is useful to present data about Chicanos and Latinos separately whenever possible.

## LATINO/A AND AFRICAN AMERICANS
## IN THE PROFESSORATE

While much research on the role that minority faculty can have in transforming higher education still needs to be done, there is evidence that a diverse fac-

TABLE 10.1

California Higher Education Pipeline for Underrepresented Minorities, 2000

|  | Percent of Total Population between ages 18–24* | Percent of All High School Graduates between ages 18–24* | Percent Enrolled in Higher Education* | University of California** | |
|---|---|---|---|---|---|
|  |  |  |  | Undergrads | Grad Students |
| Chicano | 34.1% | 25.8% | 17.6% | 10.0% | 4.7% |
| Latino | 8.4% | 7.1% | 6.5% | 3.6% | 3.6% |
| Black NL | 6.9% | 7.1% | 7.9% | 3.5% | 3.5% |
| Total URM | 49.5% | 40.0% | 32.0% | 17.1% | 11.8% |

*Source:* *2000 Census SF 4; **UC Office of the President, Student Academic Services, OA&SA, Student Ethnicity Report-CSS330, August 2001.

*Note:* Chicano refers to Mexican-origin Hispanics; Latino to all other Hispanic subgroups. Because some Latino subgroups have higher educational attainment levels than Chicanos, it is useful to present data for Chicanos separately whenever possible. Black NL refers to Blacks who are not Latinos.

TABLE 10.2

Minority Ladder-rank Faculty at the University of California in 2002 and California State University, 2001

|  | UC | CSU |
|---|---|---|
| Chicano & Latino | 4.8% | 6.6% |
| Black non-Latino | 2.4% | 3.9% |
| Total URMs | 7.2% | 10.5% |

*Source:* López and Reyes, 2004; Lopez and Rochin, 2003.

ulty that more closely represented the college-age population would attract and graduate more diverse students. From the standpoints of both intellectual understanding and community service, a more diverse faculty would almost certainly better reflect the perspectives, issues, and needs of the communities from which all students come. In addition to the personal interest that faculty of color often demonstrate in minority students (Gándara & Bial, 2001) and the more inclusive climate they can help provide, Gándara (1999b) suggests another often overlooked reason for creating a more diverse faculty:

> Of all the reasons given for diversifying the academy at the faculty level, one that is not often articulated is the need for a voice for

TABLE 10.3
UC Freshman Applicant Socioeconomic Background

|  | African American | Chicano | Latino | White |
|---|---|---|---|---|
| Median Parental Income | $45,000 | $36,000 | $43,500 | $85,000 |
| Father's Education: 4 yrs+ | 41% | 20% | 39% | 70% |
| Mother's Education: 4 yrs+ | 38% | 16% | 29% | 60% |
| Father's Education: HS or less | 25% | 59% | 37% | 9% |
| Mother's Education: HS or less | 22% | 60% | 41% | 10% |

*Source:* UCOP 2002a.

*Note:* African American excludes black Latinos.

> underrepresented minorities. . . . The few faculty of color are often
> overburdened with requests to serve on various committees and to be
> the experts on every issue dealing with racial/ethnic groups to the
> point that their research and teaching suffer and there are not enough
> faculty of color to form the critical mass necessary to have an audi-
> ble voice in the academy. (pp. 175–177, citations in the original not
> quoted here)

Those few institutions of higher education (IHEs) with high concentrations of African American and Latino faculty also tend to have higher proportions of underrepresented students. These institutions have numbers of
minority students that more closely reflect their proportion in their state's population in spite of the fact that across the nation, minority students are generally underrepresented in IHEs relative to their numbers in the general population. Table 10.4 shows that the proportion of faculty who are African
American, 32.2 percent, is ten times greater at IHEs where 25 percent or more
of the students are also African American than the 3.2 percent proportion of
African American faculty at IHEs in which African American student enrollment is less than 25 percent. Likewise, the proportion of Latino faculty is substantially higher at IHEs with high Latino enrollments than at those with low
enrollments. While correlation does not imply causation, faculty diversity and
student diversity tend to go hand in hand. A critical mass of students and faculty of similar background does help to create a more supportive environment
for students when they do not feel alone, or as if they are the "only" member
of their group in their classes (Moreno, 1999).

In addition to supporting the belief that diverse faculties attract and support student diversity, the research of Caroline Sotello Viernes Turner also
shows that minority faculty members play an important role in enhancing the
vitality and viability of institutions of higher education. The educational

TABLE 10.4

Percentage of African American and Latino Faculty at Campuses with
Low and High Concentrations of African American and Latino Students

|  | *Percentage African American* | *Percentage Latino* |
|---|---|---|
| Faculty percentage at All IHEs | 5.1 | 3.3 |
| African American Enrollment |  |  |
|     Less than 25% | 3.2 | 3.3 |
|     25% or greater | 32.2 | 2.8 |
| Latino Enrollment |  |  |
|     Less than 25% | 5.2 | 2.8 |
|     25% or greater | 3.9 | 13.7 |

*Source:* Analysis of NCES, 2001. National Study of Postsecondary Faculty, based on 1999 data collected from more than 18,000 faculty. See http://nces.ed.gov/surveys/nsopf/

importance of a diverse faculty is similar to the value of a diverse student body. They bring new ideas, new research paradigms, and new perspectives on issues (Turner, 2000). Robert Dynes, President of the University of California, made this point (cited in the introduction to this volume) by describing the value of diversity in the university: it stimulates innovation. Typically, African American and Chicano/Latino faculty members are also more likely to attend to issues of race and gender in their research (Milem, 2001), thereby adding important new knowledge that can result in significant breakthroughs and important benefits to society as a whole. Hayes-Bautista (2002) has demonstrated this point powerfully in his analysis of health research and minority populations. For example, he found that individuals of Mexican origin are significantly less likely to die of a heart attack than other ethnic groups. Thus, many lives could be saved annually if we were able to isolate the factors that are associated with such lowered risk in this population. However, this type of investigation would require ethnic-specific research that is rarely conducted by mainstream researchers.

Jeffrey Milem (2001) asked the questions: Do minority faculty have an educational benefit that only they can impart? Is there an empirical argument that increasing the number of minority faculty would enhance the education of all students? Milem did find that women and minority faculty are more likely than White and male faculty to use student-centered approaches and active learning methods in the classroom. Such methods have been shown to lead to better learning outcomes (National Research Council, 1999). African American and Chicano/Latino faculty members are also much more likely to include the perspectives of racial and ethnic minorities in the curriculum, which can lead to cognitive benefits for all students. Different perspectives on knowledge and its production can lead students to question old "truths" and investigate new ones.

## The Composition of Latino Faculty

National Census data provide an important perspective on the breakdown of Latino faculty. Not only are Latinos underrepresented as a whole, but Chicanos or Mexican origin Latinos, who are the overwhelming majority of California's Latino population, are dramatically underrepresented even among Latinos. The analysis of census data presented in Table 10.5 shows that Chicanos are only about a quarter of Latino faculty nationally despite the fact that they are two-thirds of the U.S. Latino population. Fully 37 percent of the Latino professorate is composed of South and Central Americans and other Spanish-speaking foreign born, often also foreign educated individuals—not members of the primary underrepresented groups in the United States. Furthermore, the huge differences found between the Latino proportions of the population and proportions of the professorate show that the connections between the Latino student body population and the professorate are tenuous. In other words, the Latino educational pipeline not only loses most Latino students long before they reach the professorate, it loses them in such a way that even the few Latinos and Latinas who are professors have a very different composition than the student body as a whole.

TABLE 10.5

Percent Distribution of National Origin Groups of U.S. Latino Professors
Compared to Percent Distribution of U.S. Latino Population, 2000

|  | *Population**  | *Professors*** |
|---|---|---|
| Mexican-origin/Chicano | 58.5% | 25.4% |
| Puerto Rican | 9.6% | 19.3% |
| Cuban | 3.5% | 16.1% |
| Dominican | 2.2% | 2.2% |
| Central American (excluding Mexican) | 4.8% | 4.4% |
| South American | 3.8% | 16.7% |
| Other Spanish, Hispanic or Latino | 17.3% | 15.9% |
| Total Percent | 100% | 100% |
| Total Number | 35,305,818 | 22,138 |

*Sources:* *U.S. Bureau of the Census, 2001. Census 2000 Summary File 1, Table PCT11; **U.S. Bureau of the Census, 2003. Analysis of Census 2000 1% PUMS (Public Use Microdata Samples) files.

Immigration may be one factor that can explain the difference in composition between the U.S. Latino population and U.S. Latino faculty. This hypothesis is supported by the data presented in table 10.6. The fact that just about half (49.2 percent) of Latino professors were immigrants suggests that the U.S. educational pipeline is producing an even smaller proportion of Latino professors than indicated by the fact that 4.6 percent of the University of California professors are Chicanos/Latinos (table 10.2). This is critically important because the argument is often advanced that universities are doing all they can to diversify their faculty and that they are hiring at rates that are commensurate with, or even higher than, the actual pool of appropriately trained PhDs from these groups. The data, however, suggest otherwise. It appears from the national data that the "pool" from which universities contend they are hiring is likely much larger than assumed, as it includes a substantial number of individuals who, in fact, are in the international PhD pool. The proportion of foreign born African American professors (20.4 percent) suggests that a similar, but much less pronounced phenomenon is occurring among African Americans.

*Rapidly Shifting Demographics*

Figures 10.1 and 10.2 illustrate that the same demographic patterns can also be found across the nation. Figure 10.1 shows the proportions of Latinos (including Chicanos) as a percent of the total national population in 1980, 1990, and 2000. Consistent with the concentration of Latinos in the younger age groups, the Latino proportion of the population between the ages of 18 to 24 grew even more rapidly than the rest of the population.

At each point in time, the proportion of college-age Latinos who finished high school, enrolled in college, earned a BA, and a PhD is sharply lower. Moreover, while the number of Latinos at each educational level is increasing over time, the population figure is increasing far more rapidly than educational attainment levels. This rapid population growth is outstripping the

TABLE 10.6
Percent Foreign Born Professors by Race/Ethnic Group in the United States, 2000

|  | Latinos | African American | Asian | White NL | All Faculty |
|---|---|---|---|---|---|
| % Foreign Born of Each Group | 49.2 | 20.4 | 88.5 | 12.0 | 19.5 |
| Total Number | 22,138 | 29,470 | 45,956 | 499,498 | 596,225 |

*Source:* U.S. Bureau of the Census, 2003. Analysis of Census 2000 1% PUMS (Public Use Microdata Samples) files.

FIGURE 10.1
National Latino Educational and Demographic Trends

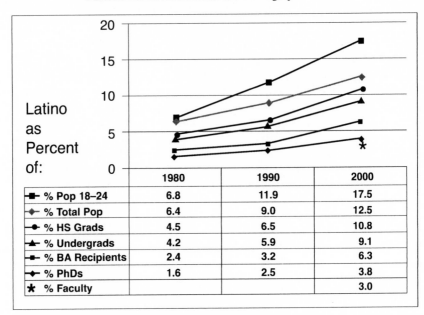

| | 1980 | 1990 | 2000 |
|---|---|---|---|
| ■ % Pop 18–24 | 6.8 | 11.9 | 17.5 |
| ◆ % Total Pop | 6.4 | 9.0 | 12.5 |
| ● % HS Grads | 4.5 | 6.5 | 10.8 |
| ▲ % Undergrads | 4.2 | 5.9 | 9.1 |
| ■ % BA Recipients | 2.4 | 3.2 | 6.3 |
| ◆ % PhDs | 1.6 | 2.5 | 3.8 |
| ✱ % Faculty | | | 3.0 |

*Source:* Various U.S. Bureau of the Census & NCES tables.

increase in educational attainment at all of the levels shown in figure 10.1, meaning that proportional representation is actually declining.

Figure 10.2 shows that the African American population has not grown as fast as the Latino population and participates at each level of education at a higher rate, but there is still a large disparity between the population proportions and the rates of participation in higher education. While there are many reasons for this, part of the explanation lies in the same socioeconomic differences shown in table 10.3.

Table 10.7 shows the proportion of African American and Latino tenure-tack professors at degree-granting institutions. For all ranks combined, 5 percent of all professors are African American and 3 percent are Latino. Both groups have similarly low representation among full professors, 2.9 percent and 2.7 percent respectively. It is interesting and possibly important to note that the proportion of African American associate professors is higher than the proportion of African American full professors and the proportion of African American assistant professors is higher than the proportion of African American associate professors. That is, at each successive step in the professoriate, the percentage increases. This pattern suggests that, if recruitment into the

FIGURE 10.2
National African American Demographic and Educational Trends

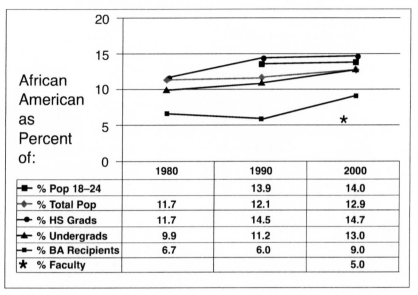

| African American as Percent of: | 1980 | 1990 | 2000 |
|---|---|---|---|
| **-■-** % Pop 18–24 | | 13.9 | 14.0 |
| **-◆-** % Total Pop | 11.7 | 12.1 | 12.9 |
| **-●-** % HS Grads | 11.7 | 14.5 | 14.7 |
| **-▲-** % Undergrads | 9.9 | 11.2 | 13.0 |
| **-■-** % BA Recipients | 6.7 | 6.0 | 9.0 |
| **★** % Faculty | | | 5.0 |

*Source:* Various U.S. Bureau of the Census & NCES tables.

TABLE 10.7
Full-time Minority Tenure-track Faculty in Degree-granting Institutions
by Academic Rank in the United States, 1998

| Academic Rank | % African American | % Latino |
|---|---|---|
| All Ranks | 5.0 | 3.0 |
| Full Professor | 2.9 | 2.7 |
| Associate Professor | 5.4 | 2.7 |
| Assistant Professor | 7.4 | 3.6 |

*Source:* Calculated with data from 2001 Digest of Educational Statistics, Table 231.

lower (beginning) levels does not decline, there should be an eventual increase in the proportion of African American full professors in the academy. The fact that there is no difference between Latino full professors and associate professors and less than a percentage point increase between the upper ranks and assistant professors shows that there is far less opportunity for increasing the proportion of Latino professors. Given the huge projected growth of Latino communities, without an immediate change in hiring practices, underrepresentation of Latino faculty will become more and more marked with time.

Most faculty enter academe at the assistant professor level and work their way up the promotion ladder. They typically spend six or more years at this level before becoming tenured and advancing to the next level—associate professor—where some will stay for the rest of their career. Most who receive tenure, however, will achieve full professorship. On the other hand, many assistant professors, especially in very selective institutions, do not achieve tenure and some of these will eventually leave academe altogether. For this reason we can expect a thinning of the ranks at each successive level, exactly as table 10.7 shows. In the hierarchical world of the academy, full professors hold the most power to affect hiring and other policies. If underrepresented groups do not reach this level, they remain in relatively powerless positions in the university, unable to advocate effectively for minority issues or for their own welfare. The problem of retention of ladder-rank faculty is especially acute for minority faculty. The literature suggests that this is probably related, at least in part, to the climate at many colleges and universities that may be inhospitable to minority faculty (Padilla & Chávez, 1995).

*Research on work climate for minority faculty.* Discrimination and negative campus climates are part of the problem of minority faculty retention. In surveys of Latino faculty, Verdugo (2003) finds that many Latino faculty believe that non-Latino professors hold racist beliefs about them and that they also have low opinions about the quality of their scholarship. According to Verdugo (2003), Latino faculty members believe that they are subject to discrimination because of their appearance, their accents, and their culture. Many Latino faculty also feel that opportunities within colleges and universities are constrained for them because of the institutional policies that are biased against them, double standards that exist in promotion and tenure, and institutional apathy/insensitivity to the chronic problems that plague these faculty. Padilla and Chávez (1995) have compiled personal accounts of the career pathways of Latino faculty in a variety of institutions. These individuals recount numerous incidences of discrimination and other barriers to achieving tenure in academe. The perceptions of these Latino faculty members are important because they function as barometers of overall job satisfaction and the likelihood of attrition. People who feel discriminated against and unwelcome are not likely to persist in the job. Thus, the problem of diversifying the professoriate becomes not simply one of a leaky pipeline and barriers to entry, but a fundamental problem with support and retention. If the hiring pool is shallow and the waters are poisoned, there are multiple threats to the goal of greater faculty diversity.

These considerations also apply to African American faculty. Substantially more African American and Latino than White professors disagree or strongly disagree with the statement in a federal government survey that "fac-

TABLE 10.8
Faculty Opinions about Treatment of Minority Faculty

Responses to: "Please indicate the extent to which you agree or disagree with the following statement. Faculty who are members of racial or ethnic minorities *are treated fairly at this institution.*"

|  | Percentage Strongly Disagree | Percentage Disagree | Percentage Agree | Percentage Strongly Agree |
|---|---|---|---|---|
| African American | 12.3 | 24.6 | 49.6 | 13.5 |
| Latino | 9.4 | 21.1 | 46.6 | 22.9 |
| White, non-Latino | 2.5 | 11.8 | 60.4 | 25.3 |

Source: Analysis of NCES National Study of Postsecondary Faculty, 2001, based on data collected in 1999 from more than 18,000 faculty. See http://nces.ed.gov/surveys/nsopf/

ulty who are members of racial or ethnic minorities are treated fairly at this institution" (table 10.8).

Feagin (2002) also reports the results of extensive interviews with African American faculty and finds that for 40 percent of these individuals racial barriers influenced employment patterns on their campuses. Feagin's interviewees further reported a full range of "subtle, covert, and blatant discrimination by White students, faculty, administrators as a number of chilling racial incidents and directed at Black faculty by White students, faculty, administrators, and other staff, as well as by some Whites in the surrounding community" (p. 21). After recounting a number of these incidents, Feagin (2002) concludes by pointing out that dealing with discrimination exacts a tremendous cost on the emotional well-being and academic productivity of Black faculty. Directly and indirectly, racial discrimination drives minority faculty away from academia and undermines their chances for success and diminishes the number of minorities at the professorate end of the pipeline (also see Turner & Myers, 2000). Even when universities do hire minority faculty, discrimination often results in their departure so that the hiring process becomes a revolving door (Feagin, 2002, p. 24).

*The Availability Pool of Potential*
*Latino and African American Professors*

Many people believe that because they are so scarce, minority PhDs would be barraged by job offers in fiercely competitive bidding wars. The research of Daryl Smith and her colleagues (1996) focusing on the employment patterns and prospects of minority PhDs, who were part of a competitive and prestigious fellowship program and had graduated from equally prestigious institutions, found that that there are few bidding wars for minorities with academically prestigious PhDs. Smith (1997) found that 89 percent did not have more than one offer. The bidding war is one of the myths used as an excuse to not even try to hire minorities (Turner and Myers, 2000).

Table 10.9 confirms that the annual production of African American and Latino PhDs is low. Latinos are 17.5 percent and African Americans 14.0 percent of the college-age population, 18 to 24 year olds.

The pool of qualified potential faculty members is far too small and must be expanded. However, the low numbers of PhDs is not uniform across fields. It varies greatly from discipline to discipline. This can be seen quite clearly in table 10.10, which presents the availability of underrepresented minority PhDs by field as calculated by the University of California. Availability is simply the proportion of URMs among PhD recipients in a given discipline. The proportion of African American and Latino PhDs is far lower than their proportions in the population. The procedure for calculating labor force availability used by UC for tenured faculty positions is the proportion of underrepresented minorities among all PhDs granted from 1981 through 1995 as indicated by the National Science Foundation's database of doctoral degree recipients. The current availability for assistant professors is the proportion of underrepresented minorities among all PhD recipients from 1996 to 2000. The NSF database covers all PhDs granted in the United States. Many calculations of availability are based on PhDs granted by a select set of top-ranked programs. Typically, the proportion of underrepresented minorities at these top-ranked programs is less than among all PhDs in any given discipline. The availability estimates presented in table 10.10 are an inclusive estimate and could be used as a starting point for the evaluation of hiring minority faculty at any U.S. university.

TABLE 10.9
Number and Percent of U.S. Citizen PhD Recipients, by Race/Ethnicity, 2000

| Race/Ethnicity | Number | Percent |
|----------------|--------|---------|
| Asian | 1,407 | 5.2 |
| Black | 1,656 | 6.1 |
| Hispanic | 1,157 | 4.2 |
| Native American | 169 | 0.6 |
| White | 22,911 | 83.9 |
| TOTAL | 27,300 | 100 |

*Source:* Hoffer et al. 2001. Table 9.

TABLE 10.10
Availability of Underrepresented Minorities
for Tenured and Untenured Faculty Positions

| | Availability of RMs for tenured faculty positions (1984 to 1998 NSF national doctoral degree recipients | Availability of RMs for faculty positions as assistant professors (1999 to 2003 NSF national doctoral degree recipients |
|---|---|---|
| **LIFE SCIENCES** | | |
| Agricultural Sciences | 6.7% | 8.8% |
| Biological Sciences | 5.0% | 7.5% |
| Other Life Sciences | 7.8% | 9.6% |
| LIFE SCIENCES TOTAL | 5.7% | 8.1% |
| **COMPUTER SCIENCE, MATH, ENGINEERING** | | |
| Engineering | 4.9% | 7.7% |
| Computer Science | 3.6% | 6.9% |
| Mathematics | 4.2% | 6.0% |
| CS, MATH, ENGINEERING TOTAL | 4.6% | 7.4% |
| **PHYSICAL SCIENCES** | | |
| Chemistry | 5.1% | 7.7% |
| Geological | 2.9% | 4.6% |
| Physics | 3.8% | 5.5% |
| Other Physical Science | 3.3% | 6.5% |
| PHYSICAL SCIENCES TOTAL | 4.3% | 6.6% |
| **HUMANITIES** | | |
| Psychology | 8.7% | 12.9% |
| Social Sciences | 9.5% | 12.2% |
| History | 6.9% | 9.3% |
| Letters | 5.8% | 8.8% |
| Foreign Language & Literature | 18.3% | 21.0% |
| Fine Arts | 5.0% | 6.4% |
| Other Humanities | 6.9% | 8.5% |
| HUMANITIES TOTAL | 8.4% | 11.3% |
| **EDUCATION** | 13.3% | 19.0% |
| **PROFESSIONAL FIELDS** | | |
| Business Management | 5.9% | 12.3% |
| Communications | 10.4% | 13.5% |
| Other Professional Fields | 10.5% | 15.6% |
| PROFESSIONAL FIELDS TOTAL | 8.4% | 13.7% |
| **GRAND TOTAL** | 6.9% | 10.0% |

*Source:* University of California Office of the President 2005a & 2005b.

The data show that law, foreign language and literature, and education all have relatively high proportions of minorities PhDs and computer science, the physical sciences, and mathematics have low proportions. However, even in the physical or life sciences where the availability of underrepresented minorities is low, approximately 4 percent, it is much higher than the proportion of minorities among actual hires. In the three-year period from academic year 1997–1998 through 2000–2001, not one minority assistant professor was hired in the physical sciences by any of the campuses in the entire University of California system (UCOP, 2003b).

## IS FACULTY AFFIRMATIVE ACTION LEGAL IN CALIFORNIA?

In spite of the devastatingly large under-representation of minorities among university faculty, the California electorate erected substantial barriers to addressing the problem by adopting Proposition 209, which went into effect in 1997. Proposition 209 stipulates that "the state shall not discriminate against, or grant preferential treatment to, any individual or group on the basis of race, sex, color, ethnicity, or national origin in the operation of public employment, public education, or public contracting" (http://vote96.ss.ca. gov/Vote96/html/BP/209text.htm). After the passage of this proposition, the number of women and minority faculty hired and the number of minority students admitted by the University of California decreased (Schneider, 1998). People may well believe that special outreach and recruitment programs are no longer permitted; however, the evidence does not support this assertion.

Despite Proposition 209, California universities are still subject to the federal regulations that require affirmative action to minimize any disparities between the availability of women and underrepresented minorities and in particular job categories. Under the supremacy clause of the U.S. Constitution, state law cannot supersede federal law. Therefore, Proposition 209 did not and does not negate the University of California's obligation to engage in affirmative action programs to hire underrepresented minorities for faculty positions. The following quote from the *University of California Affirmative Action Guidelines for the Recruitment and Retention of Faculty* are quite clear:

> However, Proposition 209 contains language stating that the prohibitions do not apply to actions which are necessary to establish or maintain eligibility for any Federal program, where ineligibility would result in a loss of Federal funds to the University. As a Federal contractor, the University of California has an obligation to comply with affirmative action regulations governing all levels of employment, including academic personnel practices. The University also has an obligation to comply with State and Federal laws that prohibit discrimination on the basis of race, sex, color, national origin, and other protected categories. Therefore, an effective affirmative action program for faculty remains a legal requirement for the University of California. (UCOP 2002, p.1)

As long as minorities are underrepresented in the UC faculty, federal guidelines require affirmative action regardless of Proposition 209. However, if minorities are represented among the faculty at their availability, then federal guidelines mandating affirmative action no longer apply. Thus it is critical to establish what the "real" hiring pool is and whether the U.S. pool of PhDs is a sufficient representation of the actual pool. Affirmative action does not mean hiring unqualified candidates. It simply means that among a pool of qualified applicants, being a member of an underrepresented race, ethnicity, or gender can be a consideration or a plus factor among all the factors considered in making a hire. Faculty affirmative action is legal in California and across the United States in departments and programs where minorities are underrepresented. In the disciplines where minorities are utilized at their availability, an increase in the pool would again permit the affirmative consideration of race or ethnicity in hiring.

## MODELS FOR "ACCULTURATING" NEW FACULTY

There are some areas in the United States where Latinos have long been a majority. The experience and successful practices of universities from such areas may provide useful guidance. In El Paso, Texas 76 percent of the population, 69 percent of the students, and 26 percent of the faculty at the University of Texas at El Paso (UTEP) are Latinos. Moreover, UTEP has a reputation and a record of engaging its students. It ranks second in the nation in the number of bachelor's degrees awarded to Latinos. The National Survey of Student Engagement (NSSE) has identified UTEP as a "high achieving" institution. The NSSE or other similar instruments could help measure academic expectations of students and student access to faculty, among other conditions (Andrade, personal communication, 2003; DEEP, 2003). UTEP is one of six universities nationally to be designated as a Model Institution for Excellence by the National Science Foundation (http://www.utep.edu/aboututep/index.html).

UTEP's success in engaging Latino students is likely due to the fact that there are strong and clear expectations on how faculty will relate to students. Note the following view of one professor:

> My view is that we do a great deal in communicating to new faculty our expectations with regard to their acculturation to the Border and UTEP. We make sure that interviewees are informed of our institutional priorities with respect to our academic and student development programs, and our obligations to the region. (Amastae, personal communication, March 2, 2003)

Another professor says, "From top down, and bottom up, most people get multiple cues about expectations like these" (Staudt, personal communication,

March 1, 2003). The communication and cues start with a short course in Spanish and an orientation to Latino and border culture for all new faculty and staff hired since the mid-1980s. The course materials include a guide to pronouncing Spanish names produced by the Language and Linguistics department entitled, *Como se Pronuncian* (Staudt, personal communication, March 1, 2003).

Most professors in the majority of selective universities do not have very much experience with Latino students. The example of UTEP indicates that developing programs and practices that would prepare faculty to effectively teach their Latino students could improve student outcomes. Similar lessons can be learned from successful HBCUs (historically black colleges and universities). Reddick (2003) makes a compelling case that "a dedicated faculty, devoted to the enterprise of teaching students, is essential" for student success at HBCUs. This finding may be generalizable to all colleges and universities.

## MODELS OF DEVELOPING MINORITY STUDENTS FOR THE PROFESSORATE

Many universities, including the University of California, offer programs that give underrepresented minority undergraduates the opportunity to work with faculty on research projects and in their laboratories. Faculty are provided a small stipend and offered other kinds of support, and students are selected competitively. Such programs have demonstrated that it is possible to stimulate the pool of minority graduate students across disciplines through the close mentoring of these students by faculty who take a personal interest in them (Gándara, 1999b; Martinez, 2000). Other programs, like the Meyerhoff Scholars at the University of Maryland or the McKnight Scholars in Florida, specifically target students of color for the next generation of professors, have shown extraordinary success in this endeavor by providing consistent financial support and acculturating experiences (Gándara, 1999b; Maton, Hrabowski, & Schmitt, 2000). In fact, there is a fair amount of knowledge about how to go about stimulating the pool of minority talent for the professoriate. Wise leaders would do well to take advantage of this knowledge.

## WHAT CAN BE DONE?

The minority population of the United States is increasing at a very rapid rate; the number of minority professors is not. Moreover, current numbers of doctoral degrees awarded to African Americans and Latinos do not indicate much potential for increasing the future number of minority professors. In addition, an unwelcoming campus climate increases attrition of the currently few underrepresented faculty in institutions of higher education. The facts presented in this chapter support three recommendations. The first is to do everything possible to increase faculty diversity. The second is to increase the faculty of any race or ethnicity who can effectively work with students of color and other faculty of color. The third recommendation is to assess and improve the campus climate so that it is more conducive to the retention and success of minority faculty and students. I have addressed several widely believed myths about hiring minority faculty. Here I will add that the biggest myth of all is that there is nothing anyone can do to increase the number of minority faculty. I close with the following suggestions for addressing the problem:

- Fund proven programs to stimulate and support a pool of underrepresented undergraduate and graduate students for the professorate pipeline;
- Compile and disseminate the growing literature on problems faced by minority faculty and effective ways to increase their numbers and success;
- Research the educational and intellectual impact of minority faculty on students and institutions;
- Clarify the legal status of programs to hire minority faculty and develop a strategy to promote these;
- Audit minority hiring and minority faculty retention;
- Develop a steadfast commitment throughout educational institutions to increase the participation of underrepresented minorities at all levels;
- Make the educational success of all Latino and African American students an expectation and obligation of all faculty members;
- Hire faculty who have knowledge of minority populations and an interest in relevant research issues; and
- Provide training for all professors on how to best teach students with a wide spectrum of learning styles and from all cultures.

These steps and strong leadership and accountability could begin to reverse the extreme severe underrepresentation of California's and the nation's growing non-White communities on campus. This in turn would help to recruit and educate the growing non-White population and to develop an understanding of a society in transformation.

## ACKNOWLEDGMENTS

I am deeply indebted to Patricia Gándara for her many contributions to this chapter. I must also thank Jon Amastae, Sally Andrade, Belinda De La Rosa, Phillip Garcia, Cathy Horn, Elias Lopez, Arturo Madrid, Gary Orfield, Richard Reddick, Refugio Rochin, Daryl G. Smith, Kathleen Staudt, Ellen Switkes, and Caroline Sotelo Viernes Turner for their comments, suggestions, and assistance.

## REFERENCES

Amastae, Jon. (2003, March 3). Professor of Linguistics & Director, Center for Inter-American and Border Studies, University of Texas at El Paso, personal communication.

Andrade, Sally J. (2003, March 3). Director, Center for Institutional Evaluation, Research and Planning, the University of Texas at El Paso, personal communication.

Armendáriz, E., & Hasty, L. (1997). Making mathematics instruction inclusive. In A. Morey & M. Kitano (Eds.), *Multicultural Course Transformation in Higher Education: A Broader Truth* (pp. 126–139). Boston: Allyn and Bacon.

Castellanos, J., & Jones, L. (Eds.). (2003). *The majority in the minority*. Sterling, VA: Stylus.

Chapa, J. (2000). *The pipeline is part of the problem: Understanding the low proportion of minority faculty at NASPAA schools*. Unpublished report for the National Association of Schools of Public Affairs and Administration, Washington, DC.

Chapa, J., & De La Rosa, B. (2004, February). Latino population growth, socioeconomic and demographic characteristics, and implications for educational attainment. *Education and Urban Society, 36*(2), 130–149.

DEEP (Documenting Effective Educational Practice). (2003). "Interim report: University of Texas at El Paso." NSSE Institute for Effective Educational Practice. Indiana University, Bloomington (http://cierp.utep.edu/presentations/main/DEEP_InterimRep.pdf)

Feagin, J. R. (2002). *The continuing significance of racism: U.S. colleges and universities*. Office of Minorities in Higher Education Occasional Paper: First in Series. Washington, DC: American Council on Education.

Gándara, P. (1999a). Staying in the race: The challenge for Chicanos/as in higher education. In J. Moreno (Ed.), *The Elusive Quest for Equality: 150 Years of Chicano/Chicana Education* (pp. 169—196). Cambridge: Harvard Educational Review.

Gándara, P. (with Maxwell-Jolly, J.). (1999b). *Priming the pump: Strategies for increasing the achievement of underrepresented minority undergraduates*. New York: The College Board.

Gándara, P., & Bial, D. (2001). *Paving the way to postsecondary education: K-12 interventions for underrepresented youth*. Washington, DC: National Center for Education Statistics.

Garcia, E. (2001). *Hispanic education in the United States. Raíces y alas*. New York: Rowman & Littlefield.

Geiogamah, H., Hunt, D., Nakanishi, D., & Noriega, C. (2003). UCLA Faculty Diversity Initiative. Retrieved on August 14, 2003 from http://www.sscnet.ucla.edu/aasc/fdi/index.html

*Grutter v. Bollinger*, 539 U. S. (2003).

Gurin, P., Dey, E., Hurtado, S., & Gurin, G. (2003). Diversity and Higher Education: Theory and Impact on Educational Outcomes. In A. Howell & F. Tuitt (Eds.), *Race and Higher Education: Rethinking Pedagogy in a Diverse College Classroom* (pp. 9–42). Cambridge: Harvard University Press.

Haro, R. (1995). Held to a higher standard: Latino executive selection in higher education. In R. V. Padilla & R. Chávez (Eds.), *The Leaning Ivory Tower: Latino Professors in American Universities* (pp. 189–207). Albany: State University of New York Press.

Hayes-Bautista, D. (2002). Health, families, languages, education, and politics: The Latino health research agenda for the 21st century. In Marcelo Suárez-Orozco and Mariela Páez (Eds.), *Latinos: Remaking America* (pp. 215–235). Berkeley: University of California Press.

Hayes-Bautista, D. (2004). *La nueva California: Latinos in the golden state.* Berkeley: University of California Press.

Hoffer, T., Dugoni, B., Sanderson, A., Sederstrom, S., Ghadialy, R., & Rocque, P. (2001). *Doctorate recipients from United States universities: Summary report 2000.* Chicago: National Opinion Research Center. Retrieved on February 10, 2003 from http://www.norc.uchicago.edu/issues/docdata.htm

Howell, A., & Tuitt, F. (Eds.). (2003). *Race and higher education: Rethinking pedagogy in a diverse college classroom.* Cambridge: Harvard University Press.

Ibarra, R. A. (1996). *Latino experiences in graduate education: Implications for change.* Enhancing the Minority Presence in Graduate Education VII. Washington, DC: The Council of Graduate Schools.

Ibarra, R. A. (2003). At the crossroads of cultural change in higher education. In R. Padilla (Ed.), *Strategic initiatives for Hispanics in higher education: Learning to change.* Washington, DC: Hispanic Caucus, American Association for Higher Education. This paper originally appeared in *NACME Journal 2001–2002* (Fall, pp. 58–66).

Knowles, M. F. (1997). *Achieving diversity in the professorate: Challenges and opportunities.* Washington, DC: American Council on Education.

Kuhn, T. S. (1970). *The structure of scientific revolutions.* Chicago: University of Chicago Press.

Light, P. (1994). "Not like us": Removing the barriers to recruiting minority faculty. *Journal of Policy Analysis & Management, 13*(1), 164–179.

Lipsky, M. (1994). Why we must increase diversity. *Journal of Policy Analysis & Management, 13*(1), 185–186.

Lopez, E. S., & Refugio, I. R. (2003). California State Faculty: 1985 to 2001. CRB 03-006. Sacramento: California Research Bureau.

Lopez, E. S., & Reyes, B. (2004). Faculty, managers, and administrators in the University of California, 1996 to 2002. CRB 04-009. Sacramento: California Research Bureau.

Martinez, G. (2000). The effects of an undergraduate mentoring project on the production of minority scholars. Unpublished Doctoral Dissertation, University of California, Davis.

Maton, K. I., Hrabowski, F. A., & Schmitt, C. L. (2000). African American college students excelling in the sciences: College and post-college outcomes in the Meyerhoff Scholars Program. *Journal of Research and Science Teaching, 37*, 629–654.

Merget, Astrid. (1994). The context of a search: The university's climate. *Journal of Policy Analysis & Management, 13*(1), 182–184.

Milem, J. (2001). Increasing diversity benefits: How campus climate and teaching methods affect student outcomes. In G. Orfield (Ed.) with M. Kurlaender, *Diversity Challenged* (pp. 233–250). Cambridge: Harvard Civil Rights Project.

Moreno, J. F. (Ed.). (1999). *The elusive quest for equality: 150 years of Chicano/Chicana education.* Cambridge: Harvard Educational Review.

Morey, A., & Kitano, M. (Eds.). (1997). *Multicultural course transformation in higher education: A broader truth.* Boston: Allyn and Bacon.

National Research Council. (1999). *How people learn: Brain, mind, experience, and school.* Washington, DC: National Research Council—National Academy of Sciences.

NCES. 2001. *CD-ROM: National Study of Postsecondary Faculty NSOPF:99 Public Access Data Analysis System (DAS).* NCES Number: 2001203. Release Date: September 12, 2001.

Nora, A. (2003). Access to higher education for Hispanic students: Real or illusory? In J. Castellanos & Lee Jones (Eds.), *The Majority in The Minority* (pp. 47–68). Sterling, VA: Stylus.

Orfield, G. (1999). Politics matters: Educational policy and Chicano students. In J. Moreno (Ed.), *The Elusive Quest for Equality: 150 Years of Chicano/Chicana Education* (pp. 111–121). Cambridge: Harvard Educational Review.

Padilla, R. V. (2003a). Reconstructing the Hispanic educational pipeline in the twenty-first century. In R. Padilla (Ed.), *Strategic Initiatives for Hispanics in Higher Education: Learning To Change.* Washington, DC: Hispanic Caucus, American Association for Higher Education.

Padilla, R. V. (2003b). Barriers to accessing the professoriate. In J. Castellanos & L. Jones (Eds.), *The Majority in the Minority.* Sterling, VA: Stylus.

Padilla, R. V., & Chávez, R. (Eds.). (1995). The leaning ivory tower: Latino professors in American universities. Albany: State University of New York Press.

Reddick, R. J. (October, 2003). The case for historically black collages and universities in the twenty-first century. Paper presented at ACE-Educating All of One Nation, Atlanta, GA.

Smith, D. G., Wolf, L. E., & Busenberg, B. & Associates. (1996). Achieving faculty diversity: Debunking the myths. Washington, DC: Association of American Colleges and Universities.

Schneider, A. (1998, November 20). What has happened to faculty diversity in California? *Chronicle of Higher Education*, A10.

Staudt, Kathleen (2003, March 1). Professor, Department of Political Science, the University of Texas at El Paso, personal communication.

Treisman, U. (1992, November). Studying students studying calculus: A look at the lives of minority mathematics students in college. *College Mathematics Journal, 23*(5), 362–372.

Turner, C. S. (2000, September–October). New faces, new knowledge. *Academe, 86*(5), 34–37.

Turner, C. S. V., & Meyers, S. L., Jr. (2000). *Faculty of color in academe: Bittersweet success.* Boston: Allyn and Bacon.

UCOP (University of California Office of the President). (2002a). *Information Digest 2002.* Retrieved on August 12, 2003 from http://www.ucop.edu/sas/infodigest02/pdf/id02swdp13.pdf.

UCOP (University of California Office of the President). (2002b). *University of California affirmative action guidelines for the recruitment and retention of faculty.* Retrieved on August 12, 2003 from http://www.ucop.edu/acadadv/fgsaa/affirmative.html.

UCOP (University of California Office of the President, Data Management and Analysis). (2005a). *UC tenured faculty, October 2002 & academic availabilities (1982 to 1996 selected national doctoral degree recipients) university wide.* Retrieved on June 23, 2005 from http://www.ucop.edu/acadadv/datamgmt/ avails-minorities-ten.pdf

UCOP (University of California Office of the President, Data Management and Analysis). (2005b). *UC non-tenured faculty, October 2002 & academic availabilities (1982 to 1996 selected national doctoral degree recipients) university wide.* Retrieved on June 23, 2005 from http://www.ucop.edu/acadadv/datamgmt/ avails-minorities-non-t.pdf

U.S. Bureau of the Census. (2001). Data Set: Census 2000 Summary File 1 (SF 1) 100-Percent Data. Washington, DC.

U.S. Bureau of the Census. (2003). Data Set: 1% Public Use Microdata Sample (PUMS) Files. Washington, DC.

UTEP (The University of Texas at El Paso, Office of University Communications). (2001). Addressing the challenge: UTEP's report to the 2001 commission. Retrieved on December 16, 2003 from http://2001commission.utep.edu/report.pdf

Valenzuela, A. (1999). *Subtractive schooling: U.S.-Mexican youth and the politics of caring*. Albany: State University of New York Press.

Verdugo, R. (2003). Discrimination and merit in higher education: The Hispanic professorate. In J. Castellanos & L. Jones (Eds.), *The Majority in the Minority* (pp. 241–254). Sterling, VA: Stylus.

BRUCE D. HAMLETT

Chapter Eleven

# Access to
# California Higher Education:
# The Promise and the Performance

California higher education has long been regarded as one of the best, if not *the* best, public systems of higher education in the country and in the world. The California Master Plan for Higher Education was developed in 1960 through the thoughtful work of several individuals and the leadership of Clark Kerr. In the four decades since the implementation of the Master Plan, California's colleges and universities have served the residents well, providing open access to higher education, affordability for students and families, quality in education and research, and a well-trained workforce to drive the state's economic growth. Unfortunately, the golden years have passed. California higher education is now suffering from severe multi-year budget reductions, a dramatic growth in student demand for enrollment, large increases in the price of attendance, and restrictions on student access for admission into the public universities. While the Master Plan policies continue to remain in place, several factors have caused the state to move away from the full implementation of these policies. The subject of this chapter is how and why California got to this state of affairs and what needs to be done to return to the commitments of the Master Plan.

## THE PROMISES OF THE CALIFORNIA MASTER PLAN

Access to higher education is the central theme of California's system of higher education. The Master Plan promises that every California public and private high school graduate can attend a public college or university to secure the opportunity for a college education. The 1960 Master Plan for Higher Education established, and the 2002 California Master Plan for Education reaffirmed, the State's commitment to four basic goals:

*Access for all eligible students.* The California State University (CSU) and University of California (UC) systems should adhere to the policy of guaranteeing that all students who apply for freshman admission and who are eligible to attend are offered admission to the system(s) for which they are eligible and have applied. Eligible students are those within the top one-third of high school graduates, in the case of California State University, and the top one-eighth of high school graduates, in the case of the University of California. Community colleges should continue to be open to all high school graduates and adults who can benefit from postsecondary instruction.

*Affordability for all.* The 1960 Master Plan strongly endorsed low student charges, prohibited tuition (direct payment for instruction), and assumed that fees were the most important factor in steering young adults toward or away from college. This promise was abandoned by the 1980s and replaced by the idea that any change in student fees should be complemented by a corresponding adjustment in financial aid that would recognize the overall costs of attending a public college or university in California and not exclude low-income students.

*Equal opportunity to prepare for college.* The state should provide the learning support necessary, including resources for career guidance and assistance, to enable students to successfully complete a college readiness curriculum. All students should receive an education, including intervention when necessary, that is sufficient to allow successful transition to the next levels of education and into the workforce.

*Quality instruction.* The state should provide adequate funding to the colleges and universities to ensure that the essential preconditions for quality teaching and learning would be provided for all students.

## THE TRIPARTITE STRUCTURE OF
## CALIFORNIA HIGHER EDUCATION

A fundamental component of California's system of higher education, compared with other states, is the tripartite structure of the public colleges and universities. Many states have several systems of higher education, but the functions and the hierarchy are much more sharply defined in California. The University of California is a semiautonomous, constitutionally protected "public trust" of research universities offering a broad range of undergraduate programs, as well as advanced graduate and professional degrees. The California State University is a set of regional universities offering education leading to the baccalaureate, as well as teacher training and other master's degrees; and the California Community Colleges offer "open door" access to serve the local community and provide lower division instruction and degrees, as well as vocational, adult, and workforce-related courses and certificate programs.

A major part of the rationale for this tripartite structure was to provide access to higher education for all Californians, while also creating efficiencies within the higher education system. The objective was to establish a high quality education system that was affordable for state and local governments. By directing the majority of the lower division students to the community colleges, this system helped to provide relatively low per student general fund costs. Similarly, by limiting state funded university research to a relatively small number of the public universities, the state has been able to achieve both excellence and efficiencies. This approach is fair because of the assumption that all students could obtain instruction at the lower division level, and then transfer to the upper division level at one of the public universities.

## THE CHALLENGES CURRENTLY FACING CALIFORNIA HIGHER EDUCATION

California's policy makers now face several significant challenges as they seek to maintain the promises of the Master Plan in the initial years of the 21st century. The most significant of these challenges include massive enrollment pressures, unpredictable state funding, uneven preparation of students including very high dropout rates, very large racial disparities in eligibility, serious affordability problems, and low levels of successful transfer and completion between levels. Looking just at the increasing number of high school graduates, the overall demand for higher education enrollment is expected to increase by more than 600,000 students in the current decade. The California Postsecondary Education Commission (CPEC) has projected that higher education undergraduate enrollments will grow from 2.11 million students in 2002 to more than 2.83 million students in 2012, about a third in just a decade, assuming that adequate funding is provided for this enrollment growth (CPEC, 2004, p. 5).

While this enrollment growth is a statewide issue, approximately 75 percent will occur in only 5 of the state's 58 counties. These 5 counties—Los Angeles, Orange, Riverside, San Diego, and San Bernardino—will experience the vast majority of the growth in the 18 to 24-year-old population during the next decade. The state level policy response must be sensitive to the regional imperative for dramatic increases in postsecondary education services in these 5 counties, which are the center of the largest Latino population in the country.

Approximately 30 percent of Californians aged 18 to 24 years old do not have a high school diploma. Of these, approximately half live in Los Angeles, Orange, San Diego, and San Bernardino counties, while more than one-third lives in Los Angeles County. As the National Center for Public Policy and Higher Education has reported, California "ranks 45th among the 50 states in the proportion of 18 to 24 year olds who have attained a high school diploma or the equivalent, and 49th among the states in redressing this problem through the use of the GED" (National Center, 2004, p. 13).

California higher education faces an extremely difficult challenge in the state budget. The state has a structural budget deficit of at least $6 billion after a quarter century of tax cuts. A recent study by Don Boyd of the Rockefeller Institute concluded that even after Califonia closes its current budget deficit, over the next eight years the state would face ongoing structural deficits equaling 2.5 percent of revenue (Boyd, 2002, p. 23). In short, California has both a short-term and a long-term structural budget deficit. At the same time, as indicated previously, higher education enrollments are expected to grow dramatically during the next decade.

In spite of clear statewide guidelines to determine eligibility for freshman admission to the UC and the CSU, in practice the eligibility rates vary substantially among racial and ethnic groups, who are concentrated in schools of very different quality according to state and No Child Left Behind statistics. A recent report from the California Postsecondary Education Commission (CPEC) indicates that "only 6.2 percent of African American graduates and 6.5 percent of Latino graduates were eligible for UC, compared with over 31 percent of Asian graduates and 16 percent of White graduates" (CPEC, 2004, p. 2). A similar pattern exists for CSU eligibility, with "only 19 percent of African Americans and 16 percent of Latino graduates eligible, compared to 48 percent of Asians and 34 percent of Whites" (CPEC, 2004, p. 2). Statewide, the fastest growing ethnic group in California K-12 schools is the Latino students. Beginning in 2008, and continuing thereafter, the number of Latino high school graduates each year is expected to exceed the number of White high school graduates in spite of a low graduation rate (Western Interstate Commission on Higher Education).

The system has not produced a high college graduation rate. Specifically, California now ranks 47th in the number of BAs awarded per 100 undergraduates enrolled in higher education. The baccalaureate completion rate for Latinos and African Americans is even lower, as California loses a large share of these students in the educational pipeline through high school and then through the community college system, before they have the opportunity to enroll in a university. The admissions standards guarantee that the vast majority of Black and Latino students must begin in community colleges. Given California's competitive position in the international economy, the state needs to place a higher priority of "access for success" in attaining the baccalaureate degree.

College costs change unpredictably and massively. California has no long-range policy to guide decisions about student fees. Yearly decisions about student fees are usually based upon the availability of state funds, rather than on a general policy about the appropriate share of the educational costs that a student should pay. In good fiscal years, student fees tend to remain constant or are reduced, and in bad fiscal years (such as 2004–2005) student fees are increased suddenly by a large percentage. As a result, in bad fiscal years student enrollments tend to decline and student access is restricted. Students deserve equitable treatment. However, the absence of a long-range policy to guide decisions about student fees has resulted in a practice whereby students who attend college in bad fiscal times pay more than those who attend college in good fiscal times. During 2003 and 2004, for example, undergraduate student fees at UC and CSU have increased by more than 30 percent and another 8 percent increase was implemented in Fall 2005.

The promise of affordability has guided California state-funded student financial aid programs serving all qualified students, using a balance of low fees and federal- and state-funded student financial aid for low-income students. Unfortunately, California's practice has moved away from this policy goal in recent years. Legislation enacted in 2000 modified the existing Cal Grant program into a two-tiered approach for Cal Grants. The first tier guaranteed an entitlement grant to graduating high school seniors and specified transfer students who meet the program eligibility requirements. The second tier provides 22,500 competitive Cal Grant awards to students who do not qualify for the entitlement grants. During the 2002–2003 fiscal year, only one out of six eligible applicants for the competitive grants (107,586 prospective students) received the award because of limited state funding. The typical competitively eligible nonrecipient in 2002–2003 had an average income of $17,586, average age of 27, and an average family size of 2.6. These families were without resources to pay for college costs. Clearly, California has moved away from the commitment of affordability for students who are older than 24 years of age. This is particularly significant because the average age of students enrolled in the CSU is 27.

## CAN THE PROMISES OF THE
## CALIFORNIA MASTER PLAN BE SUSTAINED?

During the first 30 years after the establishment of the California Higher Education Master Plan, California's system of higher education was seen as extremely effective in meeting the promises of this plan. This success must be attributed to several factors, above and beyond the logic and thoughtfulness of the plan. These factors include:

- Public K-12 education was reasonably effective in preparing high school graduates for success in college, with a consistently rigorous curriculum in most public schools across the state for those students who aspired to attend college.
- California's college- and school-age population was relatively homogeneous at the beginning, with the vast majority of students being native English-language speakers;
- The Community College mission was relatively narrow, with a strong emphasis on offering the lower division courses necessary for either transfer to a university or an associate degree.
- Annually, the legislature and governor appropriated adequate state resources to fund enrollment growth at the UC, CSU, and the Community Colleges, with the strong political commitment to keep student fees low at the public universities and nonexistent at the community colleges.

Clearly, California higher education is operating in a very different world now than existed in the 1960s. None of the four factors mentioned in the previous paragraph are true today. The environmental conditions that framed the Master Plan in the 1960s no longer exist. Efforts to maintain the status quo of existing policies and practices are likely to result in continued and growing restrictions on student access, particularly for Latino and African American students. The trends point to declining affordability for students at all three public systems of higher education, with mandatory student fees increasing more rapidly than funding for need-based financial aid. Inadequate support will bring continued deterioration of quality in the academic and research programs offered by the public community colleges and universities and therefore in the skills of the graduates of these programs. The conditions exist for continued poor production of baccalaureate recipients, further weakening California's economic competitiveness with other states and countries. It is imperative that thoughtful policy proposals, based upon data-driven policy research, be considered by California's policy makers nd that leadership be exerted to make the appropriate (but extremely difficult) policy changes as soon as possible. Among the large-scale policy issues that need to be considered immediately are the following:

*The Higher Education Master Plan eligibility guidelines should be reviewed and revised to recognize the realities of the 21st century.* The Master Plan guidelines (directing that the public universities serve the top one-third of high school graduates and the community colleges serve the remaining two-thirds) were developed when California's economy was dominated by manufacturing industries. As we enter the 21st century, California is operating in an international economy that is increasingly driven by information- and technology-based industries. The current competitive economic environment is increasingly dependent upon employees with baccalaureate and graduate degrees, particularly in science, engineering, and information technology. California's Silicon Valley has found it necessary to obtain special federal immigration legislation to permit hiring of large numbers of technical workers from other countries. Millions of Latino immigrants in the state, on the other hand, can find only low-skill, low-pay, no-benefits work.

Given this development, as well as California's need to be competitive with the other countries, should a larger share (more than 33 percent) of the high-achieving high school graduates be admitted into the universities directly from high school? Currently, high school graduates who are not in the top 33 percent of their class can only access public universities through the transfer process from the community colleges after two years of lower division coursework. As indicated previously, many of these students, particularly Latino and African American students, are currently lost in the transfer shuffle.

The structure of California higher education requires an effective student transfer process. More than two-thirds of the students in public postsecondary education begin their education at a community college and then have the opportunity to transfer to a university. Policy options need to be considered that will strengthen the student transfer process and facilitate the effective movement of students from the community colleges to the universities. Research by Stephen Handel and his colleagues (chapter 8 of this volume) indicates that a formal Dual Admissions Program will increase access to the public universities, especially for students from educationally disadvantaged backgrounds, if the program attends to the lessons learned during the pilot. These programs provide participating students a guarantee of admission to a specific UC or CSU campus contingent upon the completion of specific coursework at a community college. Their research indicates that DAP efforts will be successful if four conditions are meet: universities provide a full-range of enrollment options, including access to the most selective universities; universities and colleges provide ongoing transfer advising and guidance to the participating students; colleges and universities work together regionally in the coordination of institutional missions; The campuses are funded at a level that allows them to be fully implemented.

During the 2003–2004 California legislative session, Senate Bill 1785 (Scott) was enacted to mandate a "dual admission" type program, directing the community colleges and the California State University campuses to work together in defining a clear road map to the baccalaureate degree for all community college transfer students interested in transferring to the CSU. If there were successful implementation of this new law it could begin the process to improve the transfer function in California higher education.

*The community college finance mechanism is broken – a new finance policy is needed.* The California Community College (CCC) system is the foundation of California higher education, serving more than 1.6 million students annually. While the community colleges enroll the largest number of students in California higher education, the program-based funding approach for the CCC is a K-12 rather than a postsecondary model. As a result, according to a recent report for the California Assembly Higher Education Committee, the major weaknesses of the current approach are: (a) funds are not generated with sufficient sensitivity to the real costs of providing instructional services, (b) extensive bureaucratic restrictions are placed on the expenditure of funds; (c) unjustifiable differences exist in revenues among the districts; (d) local districts have limited flexibility to raise additional revenue; (e) while the student fee revenue is kept by each of the community college districts, this revenue serves as an offset to General Fund apportionment funding rather than as an enhancement; and (f) the state-level statutory mission of the community colleges is so broad that the institutions, by necessity, are under-funded (California Assembly Committee on Higher Education, 2003, p. 2–3).

California needs to implement a new community college funding mechanism that will treat the community colleges as an equal partner with the California State University (CSU) and the University of California (UC) in California's system of higher education. The National Center for Public Policy and Higher Education has reached a similar conclusion, arguing that the existing community college funding mechanism "rewards access but not success, and it is insufficiently responsive to regional differences, particularly regional variations in growth rates of populations to be served" (National Center for Public Policy and Higher Education, 2004, p. 20). Current California law provides many objectives but no clear priorities for California's community colleges. The statutory missions of the community colleges are lower division academic and vocational instruction, remedial education, teaching English to adults, adult noncredit education, community services courses and programs; job training; and research on student learning and retention.

The limitations on the availability of state funding for community colleges make it impossible to fully fund all of the courses and programs consistent with these several missions. Action is needed to identify the highest two or three statewide priorities and specify that limited state funds will be used to address these priorities first, before directing state funds to other priorities on this list. While legislative leadership will be needed to accomplish this change in statute, leadership within the community college system will also be needed to develop a consensus on this important and complicated issue.

*California needs a higher education finance policy that focuses on performance and outcomes.* Historically, California's higher education finance policy has typically aimed to increase student demand or access. State funding for the University of California and the California State University has been provided to support enrollment growth, increasing costs from inflation and special initiatives, or new categorical programs. This approach, in good budget years, has provided UC and CSU adequate resources to enroll the increasing number of eligible students and establish the requested new program or student service. However, this funding approach is not linked with any performance outcomes beyond the number of students enrolled.

In a recent report, the National Governor's Association (NGA) Center for Best Practices concluded that "governors and state legislators have a power tool, state finance policy, to influence high school and postsecondary outcomes" (NGA, 2003). The center also concluded that "postsecondary institutions need clearer signals from the state that degree completion is as important as enrollment" (NGA, 2003). Thus far, California governors and the legislature have not used higher education finance policy to promote any objectives beyond enrollment. For example, in the current higher education compact agreement between Governor Schwarzenegger, the UC, and the CSU, the universities received minimum funding level commitments for the next six fiscal years, through 2010–2011. The UC and CSU also committed to maintain quality, improve student and institutional outcomes, and annually report information on these topics. However, there is no indication that either UC or CSU will lose resources if student outcomes deteriorate, or that the institutions will get more resources if the outcomes improve. In short, there is no link between funding and desired outcomes. This compact continues the funding approach that has been followed for California higher education for each of the past three decades.

To make better progress in this area, the National Governor's Association has recommended that states establish performance benchmarks for postsecondary attainment, emphasize degree completion rates and credentials, certificates, and degrees conferred above all other performance indicators, and consistently direct more funds for completion, rewarding good performance with additional funding. The California legislature and governor should implement a performance-based funding model that links approximately three percent of the institution's annual funding to performance outcomes like degree completion. Institutions respond to funding incentives, and the current incentives are linked to the numbers of students enrolling. Every student that graduates creates a new enrollment opportunity for another student, thereby expanding opportunities for access.

Annual changes in student fee levels should be directed by policy rather than by state budget needs. California higher education policy makers have long held the view that student fees (or tuition) should be low at the public universities and nonexistent at the public community colleges. The developments during the past three years clearly demonstrate that this view is no longer applicable. Students at the UC and CSU now pay annual fees (or tuition) at levels that are common in most other states. While California's community college students pay fees that are still the lowest in country (approximately 50 percent of the fee level charged in the next lowest state, New Mexico), California no longer adheres to the explicit policy statements in the 1960 Master Plan on this topic. Instead, revenue from increases in student fees is being used to backfill for reductions in state funding for student enrollments. The California legislature and governor, working with the institutional governing boards, should adopt and follow a long-term approach for annually raising the amount paid by students in the public colleges and universities, based upon a policy that assures gradual, moderate, and predictable student fee increases. This approach should replace the policy followed during the past decade, when the legislature, the governor, and the institutional governing boards reduced fee levels in good fiscal years and dramatically increased fee levels in bad fiscal years.

## CONCLUSION

The political and the educational leadership in California need to initiate a dramatic and comprehensive review and revision of the various polices that guide higher education in the state. The existing policies were developed more than 40 years ago, and California has changed greatly since the 1960s. While California continues to serve effectively the best-prepared high school graduates and has a high college participation rate, the state performs poorly in other respects. California's economy is dependent upon a large pool of knowledgeable workers. Unfortunately, California ranks in the bottom among the states in certificate and degree completion rates. Without changes in the state's higher education policies, California's economy will have increasing difficulty competing internationally. We know that higher education is the engine that drives the state's economy. We also know that existing state policies are not supportive of an expansive, effective higher education system. If the policies are not soon revised, the state's economy will not be competitive and its residents, increasingly racial and ethnic minorities, will be left behind in their quest for a better future.

## REFERENCES

Boyd, Donald J. (2002). *Stae spending for higher education in the coming decade.* National Center for Higher Education Management Systems, San Jose.

California Assembly Committee on Higher Education. (2003). *Community college funding: What revisions should be made in community college finance?*

California Postsecondary Education Commission (CPEC). (2004, June). *Student access, institutional capacity, and public higher education enrollment demand, 2003–2013.*

California Postsecondary Education Commission (CPEC). (2004). *University eligibility study for the class of 2003.*

National Center for Higher Education Management Systems (NCHEMS). (2005). Information Center for State Higher Education Policy Making and Analysis (http://www.highereredinfo.org/dbrowser/index.php).

National Center for Public Policy and Higher Education. (2004, May). *Ensuring access with quality to California's community colleges*, San Jose.

National Governor's Association Center for Best Practices. (2003). *Ready for tomorrow: Helping all students achieve secondary and postsecondary success.*

Shulock, N., & Moore, C. (2004). *Facing reality: California needs a statewide agenda to improve higher education outcomes.* San Jose: Institute for Higher Education Leadership and Policy.

Shulock, N., & Moore, C. (2005). *Variations on a theme: Higher education performance in California by region and race* (p. 17). Sacramento: California State University, Institute for Higher Education Leadership.

GARY ORFIELD
PATRICIA GÁNDARA

Chapter Twelve

# *Conclusion: Fateful Decisions*

The nation's institutions of higher education are a source of immense pride for our states and communities and central to the dreams of millions of young people and their families. In a society where knowledge and credentials are essential for success, higher education offers the best chance for a bright future. For students without powerful family resources, it is often the only chance to securely arrive in the middle class. In a very rapidly changing society with large and growing populations of non-White students, figuring out how higher education can serve a highly diverse and economically stratified society is an immense challenge. Very few institutions will have so large an impact on the future of our nation as our colleges and universities.

Great public universities, like the University of California, are tangible expressions of the commitment of the generations that created them in order to increase opportunity and build an economically strong society. That commitment lasted through wars and depressions and expressed the deeply shared ideas of progress and mobility within American society. Postwar California built its booming economy, in good part, on the remarkable creation of a system of world-class public research universities and a vast expansion of campuses to serve the state's youth.

When one looks at the present situation and compares what has been funded with what is truly needed, however, the picture is disconcerting. As the need escalates, the commitment wanes and the resources and policies fall short. In the economic booms of the 1980s and 1990s, we failed to make the bold commitments to expanding opportunities that past generations made under much less favorable conditions. We cut our taxes, failed to control costs in health care, criminal justice, and the military and reduced our investment in human capital. In national higher education policy, we shifted more subsidies from the poor to the middle class. Those most hurt by the failure to keep the promise of earlier generations are the surging numbers of low-income students and students of color who are the majority now in California and will soon become the majority nationally.

The studies reported in this book offered two fundamentally different diagnoses of where we are and what we need to do about access to higher education. One was the vision of those within the system of the nation's largest state, people who have invested their skills and intelligence in trying to make a system with some remarkable achievements work in hard times. Those chapters tended to recognize problems and propose adjustments—things that the authors believed are actually possible to achieve in a polarized political environment and in a public sector starved of resources and burdened by uncontrollable expenses. These are serious, practical, and very useful suggestions. Many of the changes they suggested can be done and should be done. But they are not enough.

On the other hand are researchers who looked at the entire system and saw massive failure to serve the state's rapidly growing and changing population, a failure that extends through all levels of public education. They concluded that there is fundamental injustice in the system and that sweeping changes would be needed at all levels of education if the state wishes to avert certain economic and social catastrophe. Their recommendations would obviously require much larger public resources to both give higher priority to higher education in general and to specific policies to increase equity. These analyses suggest that marginal changes simply cannot deal with problems of the scale that state higher education systems are now facing.

We believe that there are important things that can make a difference for many students now, some of which would merely involve reversing recent decisions that are making a bad situation even worse. Given all the obstacles to large policy changes in a conservative era with limited public resources, it is important to do as many of these things as possible and as quickly as we can. If we could eliminate obviously unfair advantages such as giving some students from affluent schools credit for taking courses that do not even exist in schools serving the most poor children, that would help a little. If we could automatically place students with little knowledge about high school courses into classes that could make college a viable option unless they opted out and signed a statement saying they did not want to go to college, it would be helpful. If the small pre-collegiate preparation programs that now provide skills training, campus experiences, and special supports of varying kinds for perhaps a tenth or a twentieth of eligible students were more available, they could raise college-going rates in high poverty areas. If the financial aid process could be streamlined and made more intelligible to people who do not themselves have college educations, more students could find the financial help they need. If we could more appropriately assess the talent and knowledge of children whose native language is not English, we could serve them better and provide real postsecondary opportunities for them. If we had more faculty who shared the experience and understood the cultures of non-White students, it would help those students and enrich the educational experience of their White peers. If we seriously pursued a multidimensional outreach and affirmative admissions program of the type approved by the Supreme Court in the 2003 University of Michigan cases, it would be possible to reverse the serious losses of minority students from what had been a very modest level of representation before California voters outlawed affirmative action. There are many more good and sensible suggestions requiring relatively modest expenditures that would be worth doing. In a time of shrinking opportunity, no possibility should be overlooked. We should not waste time debating whether or not small policy initiatives are enough, we should simply do them so long as there is evidence that they work.

At the same time, however, it is clear that none of these proposals would have the capability to produce more than modest improvements in the distribution of opportunities that will become continuously more scarce and contentious because of the systematic under-investment in higher education over the last quarter-century. In fact, in an increasingly constrained situation, it is doubtful many of the incremental steps will be delivered effectively. Each budget crisis will tend to reduce efforts not clearly tied to what policy makers see as core institutional necessities. When policy possibilities are trapped inside a box of declining public resources and conflicting commitments that are either unavoidable or have more support, the society is trapped on a down escalator.

One of the advantages of a period of reactionary politics, such as we find ourselves in now, is that energy that might have gone into advocating marginal changes that cannot now be enacted can instead be used to think about what really needs to be done and what large changes could make a substantial difference. We have a very rich country, which has for some time impoverished its public sector with excessive tax cuts and ill-advised expenditures that will no doubt provoke the need for even greater public investments in the future to maintain national security. But we have had experiences with widely differing policy frameworks in the past, and we know that it is possible to build a more equitable society.

It is critical that we recapture the kind of imagination and vision that powered the expansion of higher education in America, particularly during those periods when government made an explicit commitment to expanding opportunity. Each state has its own story, but the movement to create land-grant colleges that began during the Civil War, the wide expansion of college opportunity created by the GI Bill after World War II, and the bringing down of racial and gender barriers and the great expansion of college scholarship aid that came during the civil rights era were all hugely beneficial for the colleges, for the economy, and for creating real social mobility and highly skilled workers for the nation. Public opinion polls consistently show that the public is willing to pay higher taxes for better educational opportunity. What we are lacking is not the means to act on a different scale but the vision and the leadership to explain the things that are truly worth paying for, that will make us all better off if we invest in them.

The reality is that the bargain made in California nearly a half century ago (and that served as a model in a number of other states) to build a world-class higher education system with access points at every level is no longer adequate. Since then higher education has become far more decisive in shaping peoples' lives but the state's will to pay for higher education has become much less, even as California has been transformed from an overwhelmingly White state to a state with a shrinking White minority and a rising Latino community that is the future majority. In part because it has not been adjusted and implemented in light of these central trends, the Master Plan has failed in some critical respects and is obviously not capable of responding to the present and coming problems.

The compromise central to the 1960 California Master Plan was to offer everyone access to college but to offer costly research university opportunities only to a selective few. Access for the great majority of students, including the vast majority of poor, working-class, and minority students, was to be provided through comprehensive four-year colleges for the top third, and for all the rest through local community colleges, which were free until the state slashed taxes in the tax revolt of 1978. The Master Plan permitted heavy investments to create a system of world-class universities for a small minority of the students (the top 12.5 percent), a system of larger, somewhat selective teaching campuses, the California State Universities (for the top 30 percent), and a vast system of low-cost, open-access, two-year schools. There was a very clear vision for the research universities and it was realized with great success. The theory was that the creation of this elite system would be fair because anyone could go to community colleges, which would provide real preparation for the upper level institutions who would then accept them as transfer students. The idea was that these would be aligned institutions in the sense that they would have courses that offered the genuine equivalent of freshman and sophomore university classes.

The research university theory worked, but the community college transfer possibilities did not work on any significant scale and the record was worst for the community colleges serving the most disadvantaged and excluded communities. The tripartite system is tiered in more ways than one. In addition to being ranked according to selectivity, the institutions in the tripartite system are also ranked according to funding. The University of California receives by far the lion's share of the state funding for higher education on a per capita basis, with the California State University second in line, and the community colleges, serving, in large part, the state's low-income students and students of color a distant third in funding. In fact, it competes more with K-12 education for funds than it does with higher education, as it is viewed as an extension of the lower system rather than an integral part of the upper system. This means that the Latino and Black taxpayers whose children have almost no hope of accessing the four-year campuses are providing much higher subsidies to the privileged White and Asian students who dominate those campuses. This constitutes an unfair transfer of wealth—and opportunity—from the least advantaged to the most advantaged in society, and, if it becomes widely understood will doubtless eventually harm the legitimacy of the system.

## A PERSPECTIVE ON THE PROBLEM

Decisions about higher education are usually low visibility and conducted in a very specialized little corner of policy making. Often things happen out of public glare and are treated as temporary or technical expedients when they actually add up to large differences in the futures of many young people. Since the decisions are low visibility, it might be more informative to start with the results and think about what a system with such results means. Rather than starting from the institutional perspective, perhaps it would be beneficial to start from the way the loss of college opportunity affects those who lose it. Perhaps we should think about how it would be if the opportunities were translated into dollars worth of human capital, since markets play such an important role in contemporary policy metaphors.

Imagine how the public would feel if many of the people in their neighborhood were being robbed of many thousands of dollars every year throughout their working careers and they knew that public officials were committing these robberies. Imagine if in some communities—mostly populated by Blacks and Latinos—the resulting impoverishment affected the vast majority of the residents and was helping to produce severe social collapse, undermining families and increasing crime. In fact, the existing system produces such loses. The robbery of opportunity is vague and indirect from the perspective of faculty, administrators, the public, and even the existing students. But it is a clear robbery of opportunity from large numbers of students and families who could greatly benefit from higher education, students as well-qualified as many who succeeded in the past. The robbery is not of cash or goods. It is much worse—the robbery of basic human capital and the loss of hope of entire communities.

In today's economy, education is the only permanently fixed capital a person has and a basic source of family and community success and stability. People who have only a high school diploma earned, in 2002, an average of $27,000 compared to $51,000 for college graduates, a $24,000 a year difference. Projected very crudely over 40 years, that would be $960,000 in 2002 dollars. Students with higher degrees, made possible by the BA, earn much more. That annual difference is equivalent to the return on a $600,000 investment paying 4 percent interest. That is the kind of capital that is lost when an eligible student does not receive a college education, and the loss is much more than the net worth of the typical American family. There would be outrage and it would be impossible for the officials to survive for even a short time if robberies on this scale were happening. There would be firings, impeachments, indictments, convictions, and ruin for the responsible officials. The press would go wild. People would be shocked and things would change. However, this happens through a series of largely invisible policy decisions, incrementally, in a way that makes the entire process abstract and unaccountable. It is the responsibility of policy analysts and community advocates to make those consequences clear.


## THE POLICY VACUUM

If all this is happening, why is their so little visible public alarm, so little leadership, and such general passivity by the faculties and students? Why do the national organizations representing minority communities say so little? How can all these forces let our institutions be transformed in a way that changes the mission and effect of the higher education system and their own campuses in an elitist direction? What's wrong?

Part of the problem is that the system and the various policies that affect it are complex and that there are few data and limited discussion about their social consequences. Newspapers and TV tend to focus on K-12 public school problems because they are local and thought to have a broader constituency. Students and faculty members see and complain about what they do not have or what has been cut back but they tend to focus on individual and immediate issues, not systemic effects on groups of individuals who are invisible because of their absence from the campuses. The major changes most negatively affect groups that are neither organized nor powerful and who play little or no organized role in the political process. The civil rights and community groups that represent them focus the bulk of their attention on education on issues about the public schools, particularly in big cities, since those issues are most visible and immediate.

One of the questions that this book raises is why the people who are being treated so unfairly in their generation—the students—are passively accepting a much worse deal than a less affluent society offered their parents. Why do they accept policies that do nothing for those at or near the bottom? Is education being seen even by the young as a competitive and scarce individual resource rather than something that must be provided to all in the interest of the common good? Have they bought into the argument that only those who benefit directly from public programs should pay to support them? Is the next step in this logic the abandonment of public affordable colleges altogether because not everyone who pays taxes sends children to them?

Faculty members as a group seldom think about the social and economic role of the university although there are always a few with that concern. In research universities the pressures focus so strongly on battles over issues of prestige, selectivity, and consequent attractiveness to graduate students and funding agencies that little time or effort is left to ponder the moral dimensions of university policy. The system seems to have little self-curing capacity in the absence of an external movement or mandate.

## MOVE FROM APATHY TO ACTION

The passage of Proposition 209 and the demise of affirmative action in California brought forth a period of serious reflection on the part of the university and the legislature about how to address the growing disparities among racial and ethnic groups in access to higher education. Among the initiatives suggested were a shift to socioeconomic status (SES) as a basis for outreach activities and consideration for college and university admissions. SES was modeled in every way possible to determine if it could be effectively used to re-equalize opportunity. By and large the strategy came up short. Using SES as a proxy for the inequalities that exist among racial and ethnic groups did little to close those gaps. A second strategy was to intensify outreach efforts and to locate and attend to those least advantaged in the public schools with the idea that the least advantaged were also students of color. There has been some success with these efforts, but they too were not the panacea hoped for. Frequently organized from outside the schools and operating outside their domain, they promote and support college-going for students who might not otherwise think of attending. Such programs have proliferated over the last two decades and most secondary schools in the country host at least a modest version of one of these programs. In spite of the critique that students need to be thinking about college at younger ages, the majority of these programs exist in high schools, less frequently in middle schools, and seldom in elementary schools.

Research we have conducted over the last several years (Gándara & Bial, 2001; Gándara, 2003; Gándara, 2004) leads us to the conclusion that well-implemented intervention programs that include a number of key components, such as careful monitoring of students, providing rigorous college-preparatory curriculum, extending the program intervention over critical transitions in students' education and over significantly long periods of time, making available a supportive peer group, and providing assistance with financial aid, can increase the college-going of low-income and ethnic minority students. Well-implemented programs appear to be effective at raising the aspirations of students and moving them from one rung on the postsecondary ladder to the next. However, in the absence of major school reform, these interventions are not likely to change the academic profiles of students sufficiently to catapult many of them far beyond where they began. In other words, there is little evidence that such programs produce significant gains in grades or test scores. However, students who have not thought about going to college are more likely to choose to go to a two-year college, and those who planned to enter a two-year college are more likely to consider a four-year school. Students who have the grades to be competitive at selective institutions are more likely to apply to those institutions. These are important outcomes albeit more modest than some might hope for. But even these benefits accrue to only a small portion of the students who could benefit from such intervention. One study showed that only 8 to 9 percent of eligible students receive such intervention in California schools, and another national study estimated that only about 5 percent of students who could benefit from such programs are ever enrolled. Major cuts have been proposed for the federal programs. Because their effectiveness is so highly dependent on personal relationships, they are labor intensive, and relatively expensive. Whether public funds are best invested in such ancillary programs or in strengthening the capacity of the public schools to deliver the services that students need is a question that is not answered in the literature but is overdue for study.

One unfortunate aspect to the state's outreach effort was that policy makers expected they would solve the problem of under-representation overnight. The belief was that if enough money was thrown at the problem over a short period of time, it could be solved in short order. Unfortunately, as we have noted in this volume, the problems of under-representation by some groups in society are deep-seated and based in the structure of society. They do not respond rapidly to quick and superficial "fixes," especially when the interventions do not affect the institutions that so painfully withhold the supports that such students require. In yet another budget crisis, and without impressive and immediate results to show for the expenditures in outreach, massive cuts of these programs were exacted on them in the 2003 budget. Thus, in their intensive form, they represent a short-lived effort to remedy the assault on affirmative action.

A third initiative has been the expansion of the University of California to a 10th campus in the Central Valley. This campus has been seen as an important step in increasing equity as it would presumably attract an under-served population from that region—an area that is home to many low-income students and students of color who have traditionally not attended the university. This solution, too, is limited in scope and has been under intense scrutiny during the budget cutting exercises that have prevailed since 2002–2003. Almost 900 students were welcomed to the campus in the Fall of 2005. It is not yet known to what extent this small increased capacity will provide additional opportunities for Blacks and Latinos who would not otherwise have attended UC.

The first essential step in the process of truly equalizing opportunity must be to understand what is happening and why and what the consequences are for inequality in the society. This was a basic goal of this book and the conference on which the studies are based, but that is only a start. This information is not going to be provided in a clear form by the universities since they are working out arrangements to preserve what they see as their essential services and personnel at the price of quietly, greatly increasing the burden on their students and excluding many students whose families simply lack the assets to pay and who are strongly discouraged from applying to college by the increase in tuition to levels they cannot imagine paying (very few lower income families have any real understanding of the complex set of financial aid programs so they tend to judge by the tuition cost, which they actually often overestimate). Those who find their way through that maze then face the rising competition for scarce space and the shrinking outreach and, in California, the killing of affirmative action.

Very few researchers in the nation concentrate their attention consistently on these issues and those who do have, for years, been trying to get attention for the deepening crisis. They do not represent any major interest groups, however, and the major forces in the field are the universities and the banks that now have a vast business in financing college attendance for students. Higher education organizations, in fact, frequently publish reports indicating that student debt is not too serious and college is still affordable, ignoring the extraordinarily unrepresentative nature of their student bodies compared to the average income in their states. In fact, in many states and on many campuses much more attention has been given in recent years to trying to raise the prestige of the campus or the state system by increasing entrance requirements and shifting financial aid away from a focus on student need toward using it as a tool to compete for high scoring students who might otherwise go somewhere else. One of the problems is that the media, with few exceptions, does not treat this as a serious issue. There was a great deal of attention on the Supreme Court fight on affirmative action because of the massive forces mobilized in that contest and the sense that a negative decision would be the last nail in the coffin of civil rights law. But many major reports, such as those resulting from hearings across the nation by a coalition of education groups led by the College

Board, received almost no press attention. A serious local accident or storm gets far more coverage than a report indicating that millions of well-qualified lower income students are not going to college.

Normally researchers believe that when they have provided and organized and interpreted the data, their work is done. We believe that both the writers and the readers of studies such as those in this book, particularly those in universities, have a further obligation if they are convinced by the data. To understand that your institution and your profession are part of a system that perpetuates and even deepens inequalities, often with self-serving and misleading statements about "merit," is not enough. To passively accept this situation and even to live off the income that universities obtain from compromises that too often have the effect of writing off the hopes of the poor and the excluded in our societies is to be part of the problem.

We need a network of people who will work relentlessly on these issues. In situations where there is huge social damage from policy choices but the victims are powerless and disorganized, an essential part of the effort to create and implement needed reforms is to generate an organized and effective reform group that will try to change the outcomes by confronting the policy makers and the institutions, articulating the unspoken social consequences of their actions. Such information might eventually reach a much broader constituency including the political leaders of the Latino and Black communities that are so negatively affected, as well as business and political leaders concerned with economic health and vitality and who understand the damage if the higher education institutions are not effectively serving groups that make up ever larger shares of the future labor market. It is not difficult for leaders to make decisions to simply maintain the institutional status quo and not worry about impacts if no one strongly raises the facts. If they were forced to defend clearly predictable growth of inequality and some important constituencies were informed and activated, then it could become quite different.

Parts of this reform constituency already exist and other parts could be assembled. There are thousands of people working on college access, admissions, financial aid, and diversity efforts in parts of institutions across the United States. The federal TRIO programs, dating from the War on Poverty of the 1960s, have an organized group across the country. Many of these people have deep understanding of the dilemmas institutions are facing, the impact on students, and what would be needed to improve access. They have national organizations that lobby reasonably effectively to preserve small college access efforts that offer limited help to a small fraction of the students who need it. What their groups do not have is either an overall strategy or good research to show the efficacy of their own programs or convincing proof of what is really needed to change outcomes. The small cadre of researchers working seriously on these issues are mostly in a handful of university centers and such specialized centers as the Pell Institute and the Patterson Institute, as well as a loose dispersed network of individual scholars. There was an effective, organized, and well-connected network of scholars who worked on the issues relating to the Supreme Court's affirmative action program, but the current issues are far broader. What is needed is an ongoing national discussion and network that leads to a coherent reform policy with clear priorities. This needs to be organized both nationally and within the major states. Basic needs include clear sources of information and training and networks for continuing exchange of information, for publicity of findings, for the development of national comparisons, and work on developing and sustaining the research and careers of people working in the field. The pieces exist, but they need to be woven together and sustained.

Since most of the decisions of urgent importance are at the state level, the sustained attention of a small handful of people working on the issues is urgently needed. Our conference suggested a substantial interest in such an enterprise and a desire both in the research and policy worlds for more perspective on where we are going and what our options may be. The goal for racial and economic justice in higher education work must be discussed seriously. Martin Luther King wrote: "The arc of the moral universe is long, but it bends toward justice." One might say that the battle for equity in higher education is very long but it must turn toward equality. The goal should be the goal that the federal Office for Civil Rights set in the 1970s for the illegally segregated public universities of the South—fair representation in universities reflecting the population of high school graduates in the state. Given the tremendous social and economic inequality and the segregated and profoundly unequal public schools for minorities and Whites, we are a long way from having equally prepared groups of graduates, even though the graduates represent only the surviving half of the Black and Latino students who were there in the ninth grade. It is not enough, however, for public officials of state-supported colleges to say that other parts of the state educational system have failed to prepare students sufficiently. Each part has its own responsibility to move things toward equality. We believe that this should be a central part of the mission and the plan of every public college and university and every state government, and that there should be a full review of progress published each year and an assessment of the steps needed to improve the record in the following year. We note that the chapter by Bensimon and her colleagues begins to set out a blueprint for doing this. Institutions and their leaders should be held accountable by governing boards, state legislatures, governors, and, if necessary, by courts and federal civil rights agencies, if they fail to make real progress over time.

If there is one thing that is abundantly clear from the experience of civil rights enforcement and racial change in the United States, it is that the system of segregation and inequality is deeply embedded in many institutional practices and in the minds of people at all levels and that it will tend to perpetuate itself even if overt discrimination ends unless there is an organized and effective effort to change it. Unequal preparation, unequal understanding of the system, unequal networks of information, and many forms of unequal expectations tend to pass between generations. If this syndrome is to be broken there must be a plan to change it followed by concerted and effective action. This must be a basic responsibility of universities if the problem of access is to get sufficient attention at the many levels of decentralized decision making in academic institutions, and there should be rewards and punishments attached to it and technical training and support for responsible officials. If raising the challenge produces nothing more than pious promises, the crisis will deepen.

These changes should not be framed as decisions to take from one group and to give to another. They can be the opportunity to replace simplistic and mechanistic systems of selecting students with approaches measuring a broader and deeper range of talents and experiences and perspectives that students would bring with them to the classrooms and the campus community. This would, of course, produce better information about candidates of all races and would be more difficult to manipulate than, for example, changing scores on tests with SAT prep courses and multiple test-taking to get a higher score to send in.

Beyond that, it is now quite clear, as the Supreme Court recognized in the University of Michigan affirmative action decisions in 2003, that multiracial campuses and classes provide a richer educational experience and better preparation for living and working in a multiracial society than one-race classes. The diversity of perspectives, experiences, and ideology that is associated with diverse classes enriches discussion and thought, and well-managed diversity helps to eliminate stereotypes and teach skills in relating across profound and dangerous lines of social division. These are skills that are extremely valuable in many settings in the future of a highly diverse society. So the actions needed to create a deeper diversity on campus rather than conflicting with academic success can well enrich it. Similarly, in terms of research, increasing the diversity of faculty and students can well produce a situation in which a broader range of research questions are examined from a broader range of perspectives. If done and framed in the right way, the changes necessary for increasingly integrating the campus can further the university's mission in many dimensions.

Finally, we need to remember two basic things—that we made huge progress on issues of access during the past in very difficult times in a society not nearly so rich as we are today. We created the world's greatest system of public higher education, we trained a new generation of creative leaders from among the World War II veterans the country feared would not be able to find jobs after the war. A generation later, during the civil rights era, our colleges helped create a substantial middle class and a rapidly growing intelligencia in communities that had never had one and were widely believed by Whites in a racially stratified society to be incapable of generating one. When we consider the scale of the challenges we face today, we have to look not only at the modest gains that can be won by skillfully managing the status quo but also keep in mind the example of truly great breakthroughs in our past, things the country is justly proud of, things that should help us understand what we can do. Clearly we need to work toward change on that scale.

The dream of public higher education in America was to provide opportunity for many and to provide transformative help to American communities and the economy. It was a dream of strong, unpretentious education that reflected the needs of each state and furthered its development. After World War II the strongest public institutions moved to reconstruct themselves in the image and likeness of the great private research universities, and the focus on research within disciplines produced some major intellectual gains, but somehow we have lost touch with the founding visions of America's public colleges and universities. In that tradition and in the examples of those transformative successes, perhaps we can find the confidence and the inspiration for the next transformation that would put our universities in the center of a successful and a fair multiracial society.

We have the capacity to realize this goal. California, although it has some of the nation's finest public universities, has lost ground in recent years, ranking 39th in the nation in expenditures between 2002 and 2005 (*Chronicle of Higher Education*, 2004). Moreover, California taxes itself at a lower rate than most other states on a per capita basis to fund its education system (NEA, 2004). It is the largest state and among the wealthiest, and it is the sixth largest economy in the world. It can do better. California can once again provide the model for what higher education—at its best—can be. The destiny of that state, and the nation, rests on the courage of policy makers, both within the universities and within the government, to move aggressively to recapture what has been lost, to reclaim the hope of millions of students who can make enormous contributions to this society if only given the chance.

## REFERENCES

Gándara, P. (2003). High school Puente: What we have learned about preparing Latino youth for higher education. *Educational Policy, 16*, 474–495.

Gándara, P. (2004). Equitable access and academic preparation for higher education: Lessons learned from college access programs. In R. Zwick (Ed.), *Rethinking the SAT in University Admissions* (pp. 167–188). New York: Routledge Falmer Press.

Gándara, P., with Bial, D. (2001). *Paving the way to postsecondary education: K-12 intervention programs for underrepresented youth.* Washington, DC: National Center for Education Statistics.

Hebel, S. (2004). State spending on higher education up slightly, a reversal from previous year, *Chronicle of Higher Education*. Retrieved December 17, 2004, from http://chronicle.com/free/v51/i17/17a02701.htm?cct

National Education Association (NEA). (2004). Rankings of the states. Retrieved on December 14, 2004, from www.NEA.org

# About the Contributors

ESTELA MARA BENSIMON has been a professor of higher education at the USC Rossier School of Education since 1995. She earned her doctorate from Teachers College, Columbia University. Her current research interests include equity and minority students, the use of inquiry approaches as a strategy for institutional change, and social action research. Previously she has written on academic leadership, women in higher education, and minority faculty. She is the founding director of the Center for Urban Education and conducts action research projects that focus on institutional change to improve minority student success in higher education. She is the president-elect of the Association for the Study of Higher Education.

LETICIA TOMAS BUSTILLOS is James Irvine Foundation Fellow and PhD student in the Rossier School of Education at the University of Southern California with an emphasis in higher education policy and administration. As a research assistant with the Center for Urban Education, she works on the Equity Scorecard Project, funded by the James Irvine Foundation, and the Equity for All Project, funded by the Lumina Foundation for Education and the Chancellor's Office of the California Community Colleges. Her interests include researching issues of equity in remedial education in regard to African American and Latino students and their implications for law and policy in higher education. She previously worked in K-12 education as an elementary school teacher and technology coordinator. She received her AB from Columbia University in English.

JORGE CHAPA is Professor and founding Director of Latino Studies at Indiana University, Bloomington. From 1988 through 1999, Chapa was a faculty member of the LBJ School of Public Affairs at the University of Texas, Austin. He also served as Associate Dean of Graduate Studies at

UT Austin for four years. In the first three years of his appointment the proportion of Latinos entering graduate programs increased by 25 percent and the African American proportion increased 15 percent. He served as an advisor to the U.S. Bureau of the Census from 1994 though 2002. His education includes a BA with Honors from the University of Chicago and an MA and PhD in Sociology and a separate MA in Demography from UC Berkeley. He has scores of publications reflecting his research focus on the low rates of Latino educational, occupational, and economic mobility, and on the development of policies to improve these trends. His edited book, *Apple Pie and Enchiladas: Latino Newcomers in the Rural Midwest*, was published in 2004 by the University of Texas Press. He is eager to begin research on maximizing minority higher education participation in the post-*Grutter* world.

BRIAN K. FITZGERALD is Executive Director of the Business-Higher Education Partnership, a non-profit membership organization of leaders of American corporations, universities, museums, and foundations. The forum harnesses the talent and energy of its members to examine issues of national importance, develop recommendations, and advocate for implantation of these recommendations with federal and state officials, the corporate and academic communities, and the general public. The forum has initiated several major initiatives including math and science education, innovation, and global competitiveness. Prior to joining the forum, Brian directed a federal advisory committee that advised Congress on higher education and student financial assistance.

PATRICIA GÁNDARA received her PhD in Educational Psychology from the University of California, Los Angeles. Professor Gándara's research interests are in equity and access in K-12 and higher education, the education of English learners and ethnically diverse populations. Current research projects include a study of peer and family influences on the formation of postsecondary aspirations of ethnically diverse, urban, and rural youth; the effectiveness of college access and early intervention programs for underrepresented students; and strengthening the academic pipeline for Latino, African American, and Native American students. Additionally, she serves as Associate Director of the University of California Linguistic Minority Research Institute (LMRI). She also directs the LMRI Education Policy Center at UC Davis, which sponsors research and colloquia on policy issues in the education of English learners.

SAUL GEISER is a Senior Research Fellow at the Center for Studies in Higher Education at the University of California, Berkeley, and serves as research consultant to the Board of Admissions and Relations with Schools, the UC faculty committee charged with formulating admissions policy. Dr. Geiser received his PhD in sociology at UC Berkeley and was formerly Director of Admissions Research for the UC system. His research has contributed to the development of a number of UC admissions initiatives, including UC's policy on Eligibility in the Local Context, which makes eligible the top 4 percent of graduates from each high school in California. Dr. Geiser's research on the predictive validity of the SAT II achievement tests in college admissions was a significant factor in the College Board's recent decision to redesign the SAT I in favor of a more curriculum-based test. In addition to admissions research, Dr. Geiser has directed the statewide evaluation of UC's outreach programs to disadvantaged students and schools in California.

BRUCE D. HAMLETT is currently the chief consultant of the Assembly Higher Education Committee in Sacramento, California. From 1992 through 2002, he served as executive director of the New Mexico Commission on Higher Education. For eighteen years, he worked with the California Postsecondary Education Commission, and prior to that he was an assistant professor of Political Science at Santa Clara University. His doctorate in international relations is from Claremont Graduate University.

STEPHEN J. HANDEL is the Director of Community College Initiatives for The College Board, a national position designed to highlight the importance of community colleges in promoting educational excellence and diversity in American higher education. Prior to this position, Stephen was a member of the president's staff for the University of California and served as the Director of Community College Transfer Enrollment Planning and Undergraduate Outreach for the ten-campus UC system. Steve was responsible for student transfer, including the development of statewide outreach policies and programs designed to increase the number of students transferring to UC from a California Community College. At the president's office, Steve also held positions in the Office of Undergraduate Admissions and Outreach and the Office of Student Affairs and Services. Prior to his work at the UC president's office, Steve held positions at the University of California, Los Angeles, in the Division of Honors, the College of Letters and Science, and the Department of Psychology. Steve earned his PhD and MA degrees in Developmental Psychology from the University of California, Los Angeles, with emphases in cognitive and social development. He began his higher education career at Cosumnes River Community College in Sacramento, earning an AA degree, and transferred to California State University, Sacramento, where he earned BA degrees in communication studies and psychology.

LAN HAO is a PhD student in the division of Educational Policy and Administration and a research assistant in the Center for Urban Education in the

Rossier School of Education at the University of Southern California. Her research interests include higher education accountability and the implementation of equity-oriented models to bring about equitable educational outcomes for historically underrepresented students. She is currently working on her dissertation, *Assessing Equitable Postsecondary Educational Outcomes for Hispanics in California and Texas*, for which she was awarded the USC Urban Initiative Dissertation Fellowship in 2005. Before coming to the United States, she worked at Tsinghua University in Beijing for five years as a project coordinator for international cultural and academic exchange programs. She holds a BA in English from Tsinghua University and an MEd from the University of Southern California in Postsecondary Administration and Student Affairs.

MARGARET HEISEL is Associate to the University of California Vice President for Educational Outreach and Executive Director of Outreach, Admissions and Student Affairs at the University of California's Office of the President. In this position, she served as chief of staff for the Strategic Review Panel and the Outreach Task Force. Prior to these posts, she held a variety of positions in Student Academic Services at the University's Office of the President and at University of California, Davis. She holds a PhD in Spanish and Latin American Studies from the University of Kansas and has taught Spanish literature at the University of New Orleans, Middlebury College, and at the University of the Pacific.

BARBARA A. HOBLTIZELL is the director of Transfer Preparaton Policy and Programs at the University of California, Office of the President. She joined the University of California in 1993 after a successful career in the private sector, working for several years on the Berkeley campus before moving to the president's office.

CATHERINE L. HORN is an assistant professor at the University of Houston. Her work addresses issues related to high stakes testing, higher education access, affirmative action, and diversity. She has written on the effectiveness of alternative admissions policies in creating racially or ethnically diverse student bodies. Horn recently coedited (with P. Gándara and G. Orfield) a special volume of *Educational Policy* (2005), which analyze the educational access and equity crisis in California, and *Higher Education and the Color Line* (with G. Orfield and P. Marin, 2005), looking at the future of access and equity in U.S. higher education.

PATRICIA MARIN is a higher education research associate at The Civil Rights Project at Harvard University. Her work focuses on issues of inclusion and equity in higher education, with a particular emphasis on policy. She has collaborated with social scientists, higher education administrators, association representatives, researchers, policy experts, attorneys, and government officials. She is coeditor of *Higher Education and the Color Line: College Access, Racial Equity, and Social Change* (with G. Orfield and C. L. Horn, 2005).

JULIE A. MENDOZA is Co-Director of the California Opportunity Indicators Project for the University of California All Campus Consortium on Research for Diversity (UC/ACCORD) and concurrently holds a post-doctoral position at the UCLA Graduate School of Education and Information Studies. UC/ACCORD conducts research to promote equitable K-12 college preparation and increase student access, eligibility, and retention across California's diverse population. Her research agenda explores the relationship between education and social mobility by examining low-income and select minority communities—Latinos, African Americans, and Asians—and their experience in public education and government programs. Dr. Mendoza was a contributing author for the Harvard Civil Rights Study, "Confronting the Dropout Crisis in California." She is the lead researcher for the LAUSD Best Practices Study, an initiative in the district to increase student achievement. She is the author of the forthcoming report, "Dropouts in LAUSD: Keeping Track of the Leavers," which will delve further into the dropout and graduation rate crisis facing Los Angeles and the state. Dr. Mendoza earned a BA in Communications Studies an MA in Urban Planning from UCLA, and an EdM and EdD in Administration, Planning, and Social Policy from Harvard Graduate School of Education.

COLLEEN MOORE is the Research Specialist for the Institute for Higher Education Leadership & Policy at California State University, Sacramento. She designs and conducts policy-relevant research on higher education issues related to the Institute's agenda. She has over twelve years of experience conducting research for use by policy makers, most recently on topics related to community college transfer and higher education enrollment, finance, and accountability. Ms. Moore holds a bachelor's degree in psychology from University of the Pacific and a master's in Public Policy and Administration from California State University, Sacramento.

JEANNIE OAKES is Presidential Professor in Educational Equity and Director of UCLA's Institute for Democracy, Education & Access (IDEA) and the University of California's All Campus Consortium on Research for Diversity (UC ACCORD). IDEA addresses the relationship between educational access and the broader political economy in diverse Los Angeles through a program of multidisciplinary scholarship and activities. UC ACCORD is a multi-campus unit of the University of California that conducts research to inform more equitable K-12 college preparation and increased student access, eligibility, and retention across California's diverse population. Oakes's own research examines schooling inequalities and follows the progress of educators and activists seeking socially just schools. She is the author of 17 books and monographs and more than 100 published research reports, chapters, and articles. *Keeping Track: How Schools Structure Inequality* (Yale University Press, 1985) was named one of the top 60 books of the century by the Museum of Education at the University of South Carolina. Oakes's most recent book, *Becoming Good American Schools: The Struggle for Virtue in Education Reform* (Jossey-Bass, 2001) won the American Educational Research Association's Outstanding Book Award. She is also the recipient of the Southern Christian Leadership Conference's Ralph David Abernathy Award for Public Service and the Jose Vasconcelos World Award in Education.

GARY ORFIELD is a professor of education and social policy at the Harvard Graduate School of Education and director of The Civil Rights Project at Harvard University, which he cofounded. He is interested in civil rights, education policy, urban policy, and minority opportunity, and in the impact of policy on equal opportunity for success in America. His recent work includes studies of changing patterns of school desegregation and of the impact of diversity on the educational experiences of law students. Orfield has also been involved with development of government policy and has served as an expert witness in court cases related to his research. Among his numerous books, he has most recently published *Dropouts in America: Confronting the Graduation Rate Crisis* (2004).

CHARLES A. RATLIFF is currently serving as the state-appointed Special Trustee to Compton Community College and is charged with guiding the district back to full accreditation. Prior to accepting this position, Dr. Ratliff served as the Chief Deputy Director of the California Postsecondary Education Commission, which is charged with the coordination of all public and private colleges and universities in the state. He left that position to become a senior consultant to the California Legislature and played a key role in developing a new Master Plan for Education covering preschool to postsecondary education. He began his career in education more than 35 years ago as a counselor and administrator of Upward Bound programs and subsequently became involved in educational policy analysis.

MARIA VERONICA SANTELICES is a PhD candidate at the Gradute School of Education at the University of California (UC) at Berkeley. Her research interests include measurement and program evaluation, testing, and higher education policy. She has worked at the University of California Office of the President in the Research and Evaluation unit where, under the leadership of Saul Geiser, she analyzed admission and outreach policies. Previously she had worked at Policy Analysis for California Education (PACE) as part of a team that evaluated Child Care Providers Retention Incentive Programs in California. Mrs. Santelices also worked with the Early Academic Outreach Program at UC Berkeley designing and conducting formative and summative evaluations of some of their academic programs. She received her BA from Catholic University of Chile in 1997 and a master's in public policy from the Goldman School of Public Policy at UC Berkeley in 2001.

DAVID SILVER is an educational methodologist and project director with the UC ACCORD Opportunity Indicators Project. His substantive interests are in the areas of educational equity, access to postsecondary education, school dropout, and the social, psychological, and environmental factors through which educators can improve outcomes for those least well served by our public schools. His graduate work was in the area of education policy and planning at the Harvard Graduate School of Education and in the area of quantitative methods at UCLA's Graduate School of Education. His published papers and presentations have used structural equations and multilevel modeling to analyze data collected through original surveys and existing data sources. They include: "No Safe Haven II: The Effects of Violence Exposure on Urban Youth," in the *Journal of the American Academy of Child and Adolescent Psychiatry*; "Overcoming Social Challenges for Youth," a paper presented at the APA Institute on Psychiatric Services; and "A Multilevel Model of School Dropout," a paper presented at the American Education Research Association Annual Meeting.

NANCY SHULOCK is Director of the Institute for Higher Education Leadership & Policy at California State University, Sacramento (CSUS). The Institute conducts applied research and leadership activities to help policy makers and educators improve higher education in California. Principal areas of research and interest include accountability, community colleges, and higher education finance and governance. She is a professor of public policy and administration and teaches public management and public budgeting. She served as Associate Vice President for Academic Affairs at CSUS for 16 years. She began her state policy work with the California Legislative Analyst's office, where she worked on K-12 and higher education issues. She has a BA in history from Princeton University, a master's in public policy from UC Berkeley, and a PhD in political science from UC Davis.

# Index